Northumberland p128

Cumbria p42

North Yorkshire p173

Lancashire p104

W. Yorkshire p180

ENGLAND

Conwy p213

Cheshire p29

Derbyshire p57

Lincolnshire p110

Nottingham-shire p129

Gwynedd p216

Shropshire p144

Leicestershire p108

Rutland p142

Norfolk p114

Powys p223

Worcester-shire p168

Warwickshire p161

Northampton-shire p125

Cambridgeshire p28

Ceredigion p212

WALES

Herefordshire p87

Bedford-shire p15

Suffolk p154

Pembrokeshire p222

Carmarthenshire p211

Monmouth-shire p220

Gloucestershire p77

Buckingham-shire p25

Hertfordshire p95

Essex p75

Cardiff p210
Glamorgan p215

Oxfordshire p132

Bath & NE Somerset p13

Wiltshire p162

Berkshire p17

Surrey p156

Kent p101

Somerset p146

Hampshire p84

W. Sussex p159

E. Sussex p158

Devon p61

Dorset p71

Isle of Wight p97

Cornwall p30

Channel Islands p182

CONTENTS

Key to Symbols ....Inside flap

Introduction and The Condé Nast Johansens Promise ..1

25th Anniversary Listing 2

How to Use this Guide 4

Awards for Excellence 8

Recommendations in Great Britain & Ireland:

England 12

Channel Islands 181

Ireland 185

Scotland 189

Wales 209

Mini Listings

Hotels & Spas – Great Britain & Ireland 2007 224

Historic Houses, Castles & Gardens 2007 228

Hotels & Spas – Europe & The Mediterranean 2007 ..232

Hotels, Inns, Resorts & Spas –
The Americas, Atlantic, Caribbean & Pacific 2007 237

Indexes 253

Road Maps 260

Condé Nast Johansens Guide Order Form 271

Guest Survey Reports 272

INTRODUCTION

Andrew Warren, Managing Director, Condé Nast Johansens Ltd.

Today, more than ever, the discerning traveller searches out for accommodation that offers something more than just a place to sleep, which is why I am delighted to present you with our 2007 Recommendations. With the emphasis on personal service and comfort these small hotels, inns, restaurants and country houses offer an intimate and often very unique experience.

Within these pages you will find a breadth of variety, design and value which we hope will give you both inspiration and assistance, be it for an informal few days by the sea, an anniversary treat or simply a tranquil break.

2007 marks the 25th anniversary of our first publication, *Derek Johansen's Recommended Hotels in Great Britain*. Over 50 hotels and country houses recommended in the very first edition are with us today and these inaugural Recommendations are listed on page 2. Country houses that appeared in the first edition can be identified by our special 25 years symbol at the top edge of their entry page

We encourage your comments as they help us to compile a more useful Guide each year and also directly contribute to the nominations for our Annual Awards. You may wish to complete a "Guest Survey Report" printed at the back of this Guide.

Above all, please remember to mention 'Johansens' when you make an enquiry or reservation and again when you arrive. You will be made especially welcome.

THE CONDÉ NAST JOHANSENS PROMISE

Condé Nast Johansens is the most comprehensive illustrated reference to annually inspected, independently owned accommodation and meetings venues throughout Great Britain, Ireland, Continental Europe, the Mediterranean, the Americas, Atlantic, Caribbean and Pacific.

It is our objective to maintain the trust of Guide users by recommending, following annual inspection, a careful choice of accommodation offering quality, excellent service and value for money.

Our team of over 50 dedicated Regional Inspectors visit thousands of hotels, country houses, inns, resorts and spas throughout the world to select only the very best for recommendation in the 2007 editions of our Guides.

No property can appear unless it meets our exacting standards.

INAUGURAL RECOMMENDATIONS

Celebrating Our 25th Anniversary

The following hotels appeared in the very first (1983) edition of
Derek Johansen's Recommended Hotels – Great Britain
and we are pleased to continue to recommend them all today.

Eight of these inaugural Recommendations appear in this Guide and are, highlighted below with their page number. You can also identify them by the special 25 years symbol, which appears at the top of their page entry.

The other inaugural Recommendations listed appear in our Recommended Hotels & Spas 2007 Guide.

Ardanaiseig, Argyll & Bute, Scotland
Armathwaite Hall Hotel, Cumbria, England
The Arundell Arms, Devon, England
The Atlantic Hotel and Ocean Restaurant, Jersey,
    Channel Islands
Bailiffscourt Hotel & Health Spa, West Sussex, England
Ballathie House Hotel, Perth & Kinross, Scotland
The Bath Priory Hotel and Restaurant, Bath & North East
    Somerset, England
Bodysgallen Hall & Spa, Conwy, Wales
Buckland Manor, Worcestershire, England
Budock Vean - The Hotel on the River, Cornwall, England
Careys Manor Hotel & Senspa, Hampshire, England
Chewton Glen, Hampshire, England

▼
Conrah Country House Hotel, Ceredigion, Wales, *p212*
The Cottage in the Wood, Worcestershire, England
Cringletie House, Scottish Borders, Scotland
The Crown At Whitebrook, Monmouthshire, Wales, *p221*
Culloden House, Highland, Scotland
Dalhousie Castle and Spa, Midlothian, Scotland
The Devonshire Arms Country House Hotel & Spa,
    North Yorkshire, England
Dormy House, Worcestershire, England
The Evesham Hotel, Worcestershire, England
The Feversham Arms Hotel, North Yorkshire, England
The Four Seasons Hotel, Perth & Kinross, Scotland, *p205*
The Garrack Hotel & Restaurant, Cornwall, England
Gidleigh Park, Devon, England
Great Fosters, Surrey, England
Heddon's Gate Hotel, Devon, England, *p69*
Hob Green Hotel, Restaurant & Gardens, North Yorkshire,
    England
Hotel Maes-Y-Neuadd, Gwynedd, Wales, *p219*
Homewood Park, Bath & North East Somerset, England

Hotel Riviera, Devon, England
The Idle Rocks Hotel, Cornwall, England
The Izaak Walton Hotel, Derbyshire, England
Lainston House Hotel, Hampshire, England
The Lodore Falls Hotel, Cumbria, England
Lords of the Manor Hotel, Gloucestershire, England
Lower Slaughter Manor, Gloucestershire, England
The Lugger Hotel, Cornwall, England
Lythe Hill Hotel & Spa, Surrey, England
The Montagu Arms Hotel, Hampshire, England
The Nare Hotel, Cornwall, England
Northcote Manor Country House Hotel, Devon, England
Orestone Manor & The Restaurant at Orestone Manor, Devon,
    England
The Palace Hotel, Devon, England
Passford House Hotel, Hampshire, England
The Pheasant, Cumbria, England, *p44*
Plumber Manor, Dorset, England
Porth Tocyn Country House Hotel, Gwynedd, Wales, *p216*
Riber Hall, Derbyshire, England
Rothay Manor, Cumbria, England
St Michael's Hotel & Spa, Cornwall, England
Seckford Hall, Suffolk, England
The Spa , Kent, England
The Springs Hotel & Golf Club, Oxfordshire, England
The Swan Hotel At Bibury, Gloucestershire, England
Talland Bay Hotel, Cornwall, England
Warpool Court Hotel, Pembrokeshire, Wales
Whatley Manor, Wiltshire, England

▼
Yeoldon House Hotel, Devon, England, *p61*

HOW TO USE THIS GUIDE

To find a country house, small hotel, inn or restaurant by location:

· Use the **county maps** at the front of the Guide to identify the area of the country you wish to search.

· Turn to the relevant **county section** where the properties are featured alphabetically by location.

· Alternatively, use the **maps** on pages 260-270 at the rear of the Guide. These maps cover all regions of Great Britain & Ireland and each property is marked.

There are 37 properties which did not feature in our last (2006) edition and these are identified with a "NEW" symbol at the top of the page.

To find a Recommendation by its name or the name of its nearest town, look in the indexes on pages 253-256.

The indexes also list Recommendations by their amenities such as swimming pool, golf course on-site, etc.

If you cannot find a suitable hotel where you wish to stay, you may decide to choose one of **Condé Nast Johansens Recommended Hotels & Spas** as an alternative. These establishments are listed by place names on pages 224-226.

Once you have made your choice please contact the property directly. Rates are per room, including VAT and breakfast (unless stated otherwise) and are correct at the time of going to press but you should always check with the hotel before you make your reservation. When making a booking please mention that Condé Nast Johansens was your source of reference.

We occasionally receive letters from guests who have been charged for accommodation booked in advance but later cancelled. Readers should be aware that by making a reservation with a hotel, either by telephone, e-mail or in writing, they are entering into a legal contract. A hotelier under certain circumstances is entitled to make a charge for accommodation when guests fail to arrive, even if notice of the cancellation is given.

All Guides are obtainable from bookshops, by calling Freephone 0800 269397, by using the Guide Order Forms on page 271 or at our Bookshop at www.johansens.com

CONDÉ NAST JOHANSENS

Condé Nast Johansens Ltd, 6-8 Old Bond Street, London W1S 4PH
Tel: +44 (0)20 7499 9080 Fax: +44 (0)20 7152 3565
Find Condé Nast Johansens on the Internet at: **www.johansens.com**
E-mail: info@johansens.com

Publishing Director:	Patricia Greenwood
PA to Publishing Director:	Olivia Broughton
Hotel Inspectors:	Jean Branham
	Geraldine Bromley
	Robert Bromley
	Henrietta Fergusson
	Pat Gillson
	Marie Iversen
	Pauline Mason
	John O'Neill
	Mary O'Neill
	Fiona Patrick
	Liza Reeves
	Leonora Sandwell
	Nevill Swanson
	David Wilkinson
	Helen Wynn
Production Manager:	Kevin Bradbrook
Production Editor:	Laura Kerry
Senior Designer:	Michael Tompsett
Copywriters:	Stephanie Cook
	Sasha Creed
	Norman Flack
	Sarah Koya
	Debra O'Sullivan
	Rozanne Paragon
	Leonora Sandwell
Marketing & Sales Promotions Executive:	Charlie Bibby
Client Services Director:	Fiona Patrick
Managing Director:	Andrew Warren

Copyright © 2006 Condé Nast Johansens Ltd.

Condé Nast Johansens Ltd. is part of The Condé Nast Publications Ltd.

ISBN 1 903665 29 9

Printed in England by St Ives plc
Colour origination by Wyndeham Icon

Distributed in the UK and Europe by Portfolio, Greenford (bookstores). In North by Casemate Publishing, Havertown (bookstores.)

Message in a bottle.....
Hildon delivers to your door!

☎ 01794 302002 or www.hildon.com

2006 Awards For Excellence

The winners of the Condé Nast Johansens 2006 Awards for Excellence

The Condé Nast Johansens 2006 Awards for Excellence were presented at the Awards Luncheon held at Jumeirah Carlton Tower, London, on November 14th, 2005. Awards were received by properties from all over the world that represented the finest standards and best value for money in luxury independent travel. An important source of information for these awards was the feedback provided by guests who completed Condé Nast Johansens Guest Survey Reports. Guest Survey Reports can be found on page 272.

Most Excellent Country House Award
TAN-Y-FOEL COUNTRY HOUSE – Conwy, Wales, p213

"With spectacular views across to the peaks of Snowdonia this eclectic country house offers contemporary comfort and tranquillity whilst the exceptional culinary skills of Janet Pitman ensures diner is nothing short of delicious."

Most Excellent Traditional Inn Award
THE INN AT WHITEWELL – Lancashire, England, p107

"Standing on the banks of the River Hodder this charming and quirky Inn offers genuine hospitality delivered with great passion."

Most Excellent Restaurant Award
THE LEATHERNE BOTTEL RIVERSIDE RESTAURANT
– Berkshire, England, p21

"You almost feel on holiday. Delicious seasonal menus taking influence from modern European and the vibrant Pacific Rim can be enjoyed in the bright restaurant or al fresco on a balmy summers day at a riverside table."

Most Excellent Coastal Award
ROMNEY BAY HOUSE HOTEL – Kent, England, p102

"Sitting proudly on an unspoiled stretch of coastline with spectacular far reaching views. An ideal spot to unwind and relax under the attentive care of the dedicated owners, Clinton and Lisa Lovell."

Most Excellent Service
TORAVAIG HOUSE – Isle of Skye, Scotland, p200

"Anne Gracie and Kenneth Gunn are passionate about the hotel and the recent refurbishment has created one of the island's most sort after retreats."

Champagne Taittinger Wine List of the Year Award (Country Houses Category)
KNOCKOMIE HOTEL – Moray, Scotland, p203

"Reaching their decision the judges commented on a well thought out wine list that leads the reader through an excellent choice of well-priced wines each with a friendly and educational description often endorsed by wine writers' quotes."

PENHALIGON'S
LONDON

Pacific Direct

Condé Nast Johansens preferred Toiletries partner for 8 years

Email: sales@pacificdirect.co.uk

Worldwide Sales Tel: +44 (0)1234 347 140   Fax: +44 (0)1234 346 480

www.pacificdirect.co.uk   Princeton Court, Pilgrim Centre, Brickhill Drive, Bedford MK41 7PZ, England, UK

The Perfect Gift...

Condé Nast Johansens Gift Vouchers

Condé Nast Johansens Gift Vouchers make a unique and much valued present for birthdays, weddings, anniversaries, special occasions or as a corporate incentive.

Vouchers are available in denominations of £100, £50, €140, €70, $150, $75 and may be used as payment or part payment for your stay or a meal at any Condé Nast Johansens 2007 Recommended property.

ENGLAND

Recommendations in England appear on pages 13-180

For further information on England, please contact:

Cumbria Tourist Board
Ashleigh, Holly Road, Windermere, Cumbria LA23 2AQ
Tel: +44 (0)15394 44444
Web: www.golakes.co.uk

East of England Tourist Board
Toppesfield Hall , Hadleigh, Suffolk IP7 5DN
Tel: +44 (0)1473 822922
Web: www.visiteastofengland.com

Heart of England Tourism
Larkhill Road, Worcester, Worcestershire WR5 2EZ
Tel: +44 (0)1905 761100
Web: www.visitheartofengland.com

Visit London
6th Floor, 2 More London Riverside, London SE1 2RR
Tel: 0870 156 6366
Web: www.visitlondon.com

One North East Tourism Team
Stelle House, Gold Crest Way, Newburn Riverside,
Newcastle-Upon-Tyne, N15 8NY
Tel: +44 (0)191 375 3000
Web: www.visitnorthumbria.com

North West Tourist Board
Swan House, Swan Meadow Road, Wigan, Lancashire WN3 5BB
Tel: +44 (0)1942 821 222
Web: www.visitnorthwest.com

Tourism South East
40 Chamberlayne Road, Eastleigh, Hampshire, SO50 5JH
Tel: +44 (0)23 8062 5400
Web: www.visistsoutheastengland.com

South West Tourism
Woodwater Park, Exeter, Devon EX2 5WT
Tel: +44 (0)1392 360 050
Web: www.visitsouthwest.co.uk

Yorkshire Tourist Board
312 Tadcaster Road, York, Yorkshire YO24 1GS
Tel: +44 (0)1904 707961
Web: www.ytb.org.uk
Yorkshire and North & North East Lincolnshire.

English Heritage
Customer Services Department , PO Box 569, Swindon SN2 2YP
Tel: +44 (0) 870 333 1181
Web: www.english-heritage.org.uk

Historic Houses Association
2 Chester Street, London SW1X 7BB
Tel: +44 (0)20 7259 5688
Web: www.hha.org.uk

The National Trust
Heelis, Kemble Drive, Swindon, SN2 2NA
Tel: 0870 242 6620
Web: www.nationaltrust.org.uk

or see **pages 228-230** for details of
local attractions to visit during your stay.

Images from www.britainonview.com

THE COUNTY HOTEL

18/19 PULTENEY ROAD, BATH, SOMERSET BA2 4EZ

The County Hotel, winner of the AA Guest Accommodation of the Year Award 2001, the Little Gem Award by the RAC 2000-2005 and the English Tourism Council's Gold Award, stands in the centre of Bath. It is an attractive stone-built building with a frontage enhanced by arched sash windows and twin balconies ornamented with open stone balustrades. Completely refurbished in 1999, décor and sympathetic modernisation have resulted in the creation of elegant, relaxing accommodation. The 22 exquisite en-suite bedrooms have every home comfort. Many have splendid views over the Cricket ground and Bath Abbey. Breakfast is served in an intimate dining room which opens onto a conservatory where morning coffee, afternoon tea and light lunches can be ordered. Dinner is not available but the hotel's owners will happily help select one of the many nearby restaurants for an evening out. Drinks can be enjoyed in the stylish bar or lounge. The hotel has a non-smoking policy apart from the bar area. Bath's attractions include the Roman Baths, pump room, Royal Crescent, the thriving theatres and fascinating museums. Ample parking is available.

Our inspector loved: Spotlessly clean and a super location in the centre of Bath with parking.

Directions: From the M4/jct 18 take the A46 and then the A4 towards Bath. Just before the city centre turn left onto the A36 ring road and follow signs for Exeter and Wells. The hotel is on the right after the Holburne Museum.

Web: www.johansens.com/countyhotelbath
E-mail: reservations@county-hotel.co.uk
Tel: 0870 381 8455
International: +44 (0)1225 425003
Fax: 01225 466493

Price Guide:
single £80
double £110–£190

THE RING O' ROSES

STRATTON ROAD, HOLCOMBE, NEAR BATH BA3 5EB

Directions: From Bath take the A367 towards Shepton Mallet. At Stratton-on-the-Fosse, turn left towards Holcombe. The hotel is on the left.

Web: www.johansens.com/ringoroses
E-mail: info@ringoroses.co.uk
Tel: 0870 381 9181
International: +44 (0)1761 232478
Fax: 01761 233737

Price Guide:
single £65-£75
double/four poster £85-£95

Situated in the old village of Holcombe, The Ring O' Roses country inn is a rural haven nestling high on the Mendip Hills yet is only a few miles from Bath, Wells and Bristol. The inn is steeped in history and is named after the well-known nursery rhyme reminiscent of the plague that devastated the village. An atmosphere of comfort and conviviality pervades the hotel, enhanced by oak panelling in the lounge, antiques and the rich textures and warm colours of the expertly chosen décor. Guests will love to read by the crackling log fire in winter or in the picturesque and sunny gardens that overlook Downside Abbey in warmer months. Elegant bedrooms are spacious and individually decorated in a traditional style. Sumptuous, freshly prepared dishes are created with imagination and flair, complemented by an extensive wine list. There is plenty to do for both history and nature lovers in the area. The ancient St Andrew's church retains impressive original features and has a beautifully tended churchyard surrounded by lovely woodland and hillside walks. Luccombe Pond, which was built by monks in medieval times still has plenty of fish and is a birdwatcher's paradise.

Our inspector loved: *The comfortable, friendly atmosphere, and lovely views of Downside Abbey.*

CORNFIELDS RESTAURANT & HOTEL

WILDEN ROAD, COLMWORTH, BEDFORDSHIRE MK44 2NJ

Nestling in the undulating Bedfordshire countryside, yet a mere 6 miles from Bedford, Cornfields Restaurant & Hotel is a haven for gastronomes in search of a peaceful retreat to unwind and indulge. The inn dates back to the 17th century and features an abundance of original beams and has an inglenook fireplace. Traditional comforts have been retained throughout, and king-size beds invite guests to retire in the spacious newly-opened bedrooms, all of which have been individually appointed. However, the property's true appeal lies in its cuisine and its owners' vision to create freshly cooked dishes using locally sourced produce. After a preprandial drink in the lounge, guests adjourn to the 2 candlelit rooms, the largest of which opens on to a private enclosed garden. Starters such as stilton, walnut and bacon fritters with a redcurrant and port sauce are delicious and main courses available include British classics such as pork with mild grain mustard and caramelised apples. The smaller of the 2 dining rooms can be hired for private use and is ideal for exclusive dining or business meetings. The university city of Cambridge, with its hallowed academic institutions and renowned museum, theatres, restaurants and river, beckons to be explored while Woburn and Huntingdon are also nearby.

Our inspector loved: The tempting comfort of the welcoming fire in the inglenook on a grey day.

Directions: From the A1 take the A421 in the direction of Bedford then take the second turn on the right (approximately 2 miles).

Web: www.johansens.com/cornfields
E-mail: reservations@cornfieldsrestaurant.co.uk
Tel: 0870 381 8340
International: +44 (0)1234 378990
Fax: 01234 376370

Price Guide:
single £70–£90
double £120
suite £150
four poster £160

MILL HOUSE HOTEL WITH RIVERSIDE RESTAURANT

MILL HOUSE, MILL ROAD, SHARNBROOK, BEDFORDSHIRE MK44 1NP

Directions: From Bedford take the A6 north. Sharnbrook is signed.

Web: www.johansens.com/millhousesharnbrook
E-mail: info@millhousehotelandrestaurant.co.uk
Tel: 0870 381 9189
International: +44 (0)1234 781678
Fax: 01234 783921

Price Guide:
single £75-£90
double/twin £95-£110
enquire about special breaks

Mill House Hotel with Riverside Restaurant stands in an idyllic riverside location with gardens sloping down to the meandering waters of the River Great Ouse where a mill pond and weir still exist to this day. Just 6 miles north of the market town of Bedford, which boasts a history with roots dating back to Viking times, and 15 minutes south of the growing commercial centre of Rushden, there are 10 en-suite bedrooms allowing for overnight guests, mini breaks and longer stays. The hotel is ideally suited for both holiday and business visitors alike. Vases of fresh flowers abound and in the cooler months an open fire welcomes guests to the entrance hall. Service is of the highest standard, individual and attentive. The restaurant offers a memorable dining experience at affordable prices and uses locally sourced seasonal vegetables, many of which are grown by the market gardener next door and are delivered daily. The wine list includes selections from Europe and the New World, both classic and younger, to suit all palates. Daily specials for food and wine are available with lunch starting at £5.95. Perfectly located between Oxford and Cambridge, with Grafham Water, Silverstone and Woburn all within easy reach of this little gem of a hotel.

Our inspector loved: *The cool elegance of the restaurant with its captivating view.*

THE COTTAGE INN

MAIDENS GREEN, WINKFIELD, BERKSHIRE SL4 4SW

Situated down a country lane, yet easily accessible, The Cottage Inn offers a welcoming feel as soon as you turn into its gravel drive. Red and white clothed tables shaded by umbrellas offer al fresco dining on a summer's day or evening, whilst the restaurant with its friendly bar is as conducive to a romantic twosome as it is to a larger party or business occasion. 2 private dining areas, one leading into a secluded garden, are available upon request and perfect for family and special occasions as well as small wedding parties. The menu is varied and delicious and comes in generous portions, along with a fantastic selection of wines and champagnes. The inn has been run by its owners, Bobby King and Jon Mee, for 18 years, and usually one or the other is on hand to ensure the very high standards for which it is renowned are maintained. Bedrooms are located in the garden area of the cottage with their own entrance. They are very comfortable, spacious and popular with corporate and leisure guests alike. Visitors can take advantage of nearby golf courses, as well as Windsor for its famous castle, excellent shopping and theatre, Legoland and Ascot.

Our inspector loved: *The friendly staff, cosy comfortable bedrooms and cottage gardens.*

Directions: Take J6 from the M4 and join the A330 towards Ascot. Just past the crossroads for the B3022 turn left into Maidens Green. The inn is 200 yards on the right.

Web: www.johansens.com/cottageinn
Tel: 0870 381 9234
International: +44 (0)1344 882242
Fax: 01344 890671

Price Guide:
(including continental breakfast)
weekdays £87.50
friday/saturday £65–£87.50
sunday £65

THE CHRISTOPHER HOTEL

HIGH STREET, ETON, WINDSOR, BERKSHIRE SL4 6AN

This former 17th-century coaching inn in the heart of historic Eton is the perfect base for those wishing to explore the many gems found in the region, including Ascot, Marlow, Oxford, Legoland, Windsor Castle, Eton College and Dorney Olympic Rowing Lake. It is also excellently placed for the enticing shopping town of Windsor, which is just a short walk over the bridge, and Windsor railway station is within easy reach for trips further afield to London. The hotel is a comfortable, contemporary, boutique style residence with neutral décor and teak furniture throughout all of the rooms and suites, located in the main house and courtyard buildings. Modern bathrooms are complete with slate floors, chrome and wooden fittings, ceramic walls and power showers. There is a relaxing coffee/wine bar – ideal as a meeting point for friends– which serves light meals and snacks - WiFi facilities available. Breakfast is served in the restaurant which is also available for private functions, smal wedding parties and informal meetings for up to 30. Nearby health, beauty and fitness facilities are available

Our inspector loved: *This contemporary, well located hotel.*

Directions: Exit M4 at Jct5; follow signs to Eton. The hotel is in Eton High Street with its own car park through the archway.

Web: www.johansens.com/christophereton
E-mail: sales@thechristopher.co.uk
Tel: 0870 381 8526
International: +44 (0)1753 852359
Fax: 01753 830914

Price Guide:
single £99–£110
double/twin £130–£145
superior double/twin £158–£175
junior suite £180–£200

THE INN ON THE GREEN, RESTAURANT WITH ROOMS

THE OLD CRICKET COMMON, COOKHAM DEAN, BERKSHIRE SL6 9NZ

With open views over the village green and beyond, The Inn on the Green is situated in the heart of the picturesque village of Cookham Dean near Maidenhead. A heartfelt welcome is warmly offered in this sophisticated restaurant and hotel, which is furnished to an extremely high standard, with attractive colour schemes, imaginative décor and comfortable furniture. A cosy bar is the perfect place to relax and the adjoining dining room opens onto a spacious terrace in the summer, a sunny spot for early evening dining. The inn is as ideal for a special stay or dinner with friends as it is for weddings, corporate meetings and exclusive use. Individually decorated bedrooms are beautifully appointed and benefit from all modern conveniences such as DVD players and surround sound, some with a marvellous four-poster bed. Guests can explore the local woods, which provide many excellent walks and the Thames, which is only 2 kilometres away, winds through the beautiful Thames Valley; an enchanting day out. Local attractions include Windsor Castle, the second home of the Royal family, Legoland and the pretty riverside town of Marlow, which has numerous unique shops and restaurants. The inn is also within easy reach of London. Oxford, Eton, Henley and Heathrow.

Our inspector loved: The cosy bar and restaurant and the stunning bedrooms.

Directions: From the M4 take junction 8/9 towards Marlow. Follow the signs to Cookham Dean and turn right by the war memorial on the Old Cricket Common. Bear left and look for black and white building. car park is to the rear.

Web: www.johansens.com/innonthegreen
E-mail: reception@theinnonthegreen.com
Tel: 0870 381 8639
International: +44 (0)1628 482638
Fax: 01628 487474

Price Guide:
£90–£160

THE ROYAL OAK RESTAURANT

PALEY STREET, MAIDENHEAD, BERKSHIRE SL6 3JN

Directions: Exit M4 at junction 8/9. Follow A330 (signposted Ascot) through Holyport and then take the B3024 to and through Paley Street. The Royal Oak is on the left.

Web: www.johansens.com/royaloakpaley
E-mail: landlord@theroyaloakpaleystreet.com
Tel: 0870 381 8396
International: +44 (0)1628 620541

Price Guide:
starters from £3.75
mains from £9.50

Jointly owned by Nick Parkinson and his father Michael, the television chat show host and journalist, the AA Rosette-awarded Royal Oak has been described as a "pub/restaurant worth going out of your way for, or visiting for a special family, friends or business lunchtime or evening occasion". It is certainly an attractive roadside hostelry in the little village of Paley Street, just outside Maidenhead, which is even more pleasing on entry. The well-stocked bar, much frequented by locals, is welcoming, friendly and cosy with well maintained Fullers beer. It is a room of character where one can completely relax in the comfort of soft easy chairs, large sofas and barstools. Leading off from the bar is the intimate bistro style restaurant, where Nick has stamped his international hotel experience with first class service and where diners can enjoy a delicious choice of modern British cuisine. Local produce is used whenever possible with the emphasis on tasty fish, meat and vegetarian dishes. Menus are complemented by a good selection of wines, digestives and vintage port. The Royal Oak also hosts a number of jazz music nights throughout the year featuring artists such as Daniel Bedingfield, Keisha White and Jamie Callum. Within easy reach are Windsor, Henley, Ascot and Marlow as are London and Reading.

Our inspector loved: The ambience, atmosphere, convivial surroundings and interesting memorabilia.

 # THE LEATHERNE BOTTEL RIVERSIDE RESTAURANT

THE BRIDLEWAY, GORING-ON-THAMES, BERKSHIRE RG8 0HS

Uniquely situated on the banks of the Thames, surrounded by water meadows and rolling hills, yet easily accessible from London, The Leatherne Bottel offers peace and tranquillity with no distractions except for ducks and swans and the occasional rowing 8. Guests can enjoy the cosy and sunny restaurant or dine al fresco on the Mediterranean terrace river deck. Chef, Julia Storey, who has been at The Leatherne Bottel for 10 years, lovingly and passionately prepares meals from the finest of fresh ingredients, whilst guests unwind completely! Herbs and salad leaves are grown in the garden to create unusual salads which may include mustard, orach, mibuna, lemon basil and pineapple sage. There is also an abundance of fish, shellfish and caviar in the summer and game in the winter. Much thought and time has been taken in the choosing of the wine list which includes hidden treasures and wonderful armagnacs and cognacs. The Leatherne Bottel is as ideal for a get together with friends for lunch or dinner as it is for impressing corporate guests and overseas visitors. The set dinner menu and lighter lunch menu are available from Monday to Thursday. A full à la carte menu is on offer every day and the restaurant is open for Sunday lunch. For a special occasion or treat The "Leatherne Bottel" launch for a river journey for up to 8 is available.

Our inspector loved: The magic of this very special riverside restaurant

Directions: Signed off the B4009 Goring–Wallingford road. Down track to river. From the M4, junction12: 20 minutes. From the M40, junction 6: 25 minutes. Oxford is 30 minutes drive and London is 60 minutes.

Web: www.johansens.com/leathernebottel
E-mail: leathernebottel@aol.com
Tel: 0870 381 8685
International: +44 (0)1491 872667
Fax: 01491 875308

Price Guide: (monday – thursday)
set dinner menu from £24.50
light lunch menu from £8.95

NEW

L'ORTOLAN RESTAURANT

CHURCH LANE, SHINFIELD, READING, BERKSHIRE RG2 9BY

L'Ortolan could be called the fulfillment of chef patron Alan Murchison's vision to create a restaurant where guests can find perfection in cuisine, comfort and service. He and his talented team guarantee a unique culinary experience at this delightfully situated, Michelin-starred establishment surrounded by beautiful grounds. Within easy reach of Reading, Oxford, and London, it is regarded as not only one of the finest restaurants in the area, but also a welcoming venue that can accommodate a variety of occasions, from family parties and themed events to corporate dining and business meetings. Lunches and dinners are exceptional and excellent value for money. There is an imaginative variety of menus that include á la carte, lunchtime du jour, vegetarian, working lunches and "menu surprise". Classic French cuisine with a modern twist is presented to an impeccable standard and complemented by a magnificent wine list. A particular choice "house speciality" which never fails to impress is the "Chef's Table" in the kitchen where diners can watch the chefs at work while enjoying the fruits of their labour. 3 stunning private rooms in addition to an elegant restaurant and conservatory are also available. Closed Sunday and Monday.

Directions: Exit M4 at junction 11 and take A33 towards Basingstoke. At first roundabout turn left. Go through Three Mile Cross and turn left at mini roundabout after garage. After approximately 1 mile turn right at The Hungry Horse pub. L'Ortolan is on the left.

Web: www.johansens.com/lortolan
E-mail: info@lortolan.com
Tel: 0870 381 8349
International: +44 (0)1189 888 500
Fax: 01189 889 338

Reading
Windsor
Newbury

Price Guide:
menu du jour lunch 3 course £21
menu gourmand £55 (lunch/dinner)

Our inspector loved: *The many dining and culinary experiences available.*

STIRRUPS COUNTRY HOUSE HOTEL

MAIDENS GREEN, WINDSOR, BERKSHIRE RG42 6LD

Set back from the road, this family-owned and run hotel sits amidst 10 acres of pretty grounds, which extend to the rear and sides. Its comfortable walk through bar is popular with guests and locals alike, and serves excellent bar meals in an informal atmosphere. Alternatively the contemporary award-winning restaurant offers an á la carte menu and an extensive wine list. Most of the well-sized bedrooms, each with its distinctive freshness, style and charm, have views over the gardens, and provide all the facilities one would expect; they range from standard rooms to junior suites, several of which are suitable for families. The hotel is as ideal a location for a relaxed weekend break as it is for business and corporate events and meetings. There are 3 bright and pleasant air conditioned conference rooms, a newly refurbished function room and 2 syndicate rooms, catering for 2 to 100 delegates. Stirrups is also a popular choice for weddings, from a small intimate gathering to a full blown party! Its convenient location means it is within easy reach of Windsor, Legoland, Royal Ascot and London. Weekend breaks and Legoland packages are available

Our inspector loved: *The glorious grounds and comfortable country house feel.*

Directions: From the M4 take J8/9, and join the A330 towards Ascot. Turn right onto the B3022 and the hotel is 200 yards on the left. From the M3 take J3 onto the A332.

Web: www.johansens.com/stirrups
E-mail: reception@stirrupshotel.co.uk
Tel: 0870 381 9238
International: +44 (0)1344 882284
Fax: 01344 882300

Price Guide:
single from £105
double/twin from £110
suite from £140

CANTLEY HOUSE

MILTON ROAD, WOKINGHAM, BERKSHIRE RG40 5QG

This fine Victorian building is reached from an impressive driveway and is surrounded by fields and open countryside. A traditional hotel with many homely and comfortable features as well as beautifully presented bedrooms and bathrooms, it also offers some extremely modern elements such as high-speed broadband Internet access in most bedrooms. Rooms in the Clocktower Wing are large, bright and sunny, and most have access to their own patio leading onto the glorious landscaped grounds which include a sunken garden, lavender walk and peaceful ponds. The hotel is an excellent venue for a leisure stay as it is for relaxed meetings and conferences as well as private occasions, and its flexible facilities include The Briar, a 17th-century barn that seats up to 100 people. Miltons is the hotel's atmospheric restaurant, which is situated around its own courtyard and serves tasty and imaginative modern cooking for dinner and lunch. In winter an open fire adds to its cosiness. Another welcome feature is the beauty and pampering zone, which offers an array of tempting treatments. Windsor, Royal Ascot, Legoland and Oxford are all easily accessible from the hotel. Weekend packages are available.

Directions: Follow the A329 into Wokingham. Keep in right hand lane through the town centre into Broad Street and take the right hand filter into Rectory Road. At traffic lights turn left into Glebelands Road, then bear right into Milton Road. The hotel is on the right after a mini-roundabout.

Web: www.johansens.com/cantley
E-mail: reservations@cantleyhotel.co.uk
Tel: 0870 381 9233
International: +44 (0)118 978 9912
Fax: 0118 977 4294

Price Guide:
single from £100
double/twin from £120

Our inspector loved: The dedication of the owners to continuous improvement of this unique hotel.

THE DINTON HERMIT

WATER LANE, FORD, AYLESBURY, BUCKINGHAMSHIRE HP17 8XH

This interesting inn takes its name from the reputed executioner of Charles I, who after performing the deed, allegedly hid himself in a cave nearby. The names of the bedrooms and décor in the main building reflect this period in history. 400 years old and Grade II listed, The Dinton Hermit has been beautifully restored by owners Debbie and John Colinswood. The attractive buildings do not disappoint upon entry with a cosy bar and open log fire leading through to a welcoming restaurant that serves tasty, modern British cuisine. Each double bedroom is en-suite and fully equipped; period rooms have been embellished with open wood beams and four-poster beds and have adjoining bathrooms; the contemporary rooms in the converted barn are refreshing and cosy. The property is surrounded by farmland and an expanse of fields gives visitors open views. Being easily accessible from major motorway networks and the towns of Aylesbury and High Wycombe make the Dinton Hermit an ideal stopover for a weekend walking break, a corporate stay, wedding party or an evening of dining with friends and relaxation. Golf and shooting weekend breaks are available

Our inspector loved: *The friendly staff and very attractively furnished bedrooms.*

Directions: Ford is between Aylesbury and Thame, off the A418. ` 15minutes from the M40.

Web: www.johansens.com/dintonhermit
E-mail: dintonhermit@btconnect.com
Tel: 0870 381 9295
International: +44 (0)1296 747473
Fax: 01296 748819

Price Guide:
double £80–£100
four-poster £125

THE IVY HOUSE

LONDON ROAD, CHALFONT-ST-GILES, BUCKINGHAMSHIRE HP8 4RS

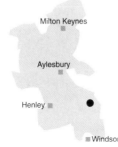

Directions: The Ivy House is located between Amersham and Chalfont St Giles on the A413 (London Road). It is easily accessible from the M40, A40 and M25.

Web: www.johansens.com/ivyhousebucks
E-mail: anthony@theivyhouse-bucks.co.uk
Tel: 0870 381 9236
International: +44 (0)1494 872184
Fax: 01494 872870

Price Guide: (weekend rates available)
single £75
double/twin £95

This lovely 200-year-old brick and flint Grade II listed building certainly makes an interesting and inviting first impression. It is set just off the road, but as soon as you step inside, peace descends and traditional English hospitality takes over. Upon encountering the friendly owners and staff it comes as no surprise that The Ivy House is the recipient of many local and national awards. In the bar, comfortable old armchairs surround open fireplaces, and below its wooden beams guests can enjoy wines from an extensive international wine list, a wide range of malt whiskies, a well-stocked bar and varied beer selection to make the most hardened of real ale enthusiasts proud. The Ivy House serves a menu that covers all tastes and requirements, from traditional English cuisine to more intricate dishes and specials and its' fun children's menu comes complete with quizzes and puzzles. Set in the beautiful Chiltern countryside offering stunning views, the freehouse continuously improves offerings which last year included the addition of 5 individually furnished bedrooms, an extended bar and al fresco patio area. The Ivy House is as suitable for an evening with friends, family gatherings, a private event, a comfortable business stay, a walking weekend or special occasion.

Our inspector loved: *The traditional bar, informal restaurant and themed bedrooms.*

BULL & BUTCHER

TURVILLE, BUCKINGHAMSHIRE RG9 6QU

A quintessential English pub, The Bull & Butcher is nestled between the Chiltern Hills and the chocolate box village of Turville whose history dates back to 796 AD. Proud if its traditional pub food, real ales and local chat, it provides the perfect venue for Sunday and mid week lunch, a meeting place with friends, or a relaxed corporate venue. Fresh, home cooked dishes include slow roasted lamb shank and grilled sea bass, served either in the intimate non-smoking Windmill Lounge or the Well Bar with its 50 foot well, large open fireplace, original 16th century floor tiles and natural wooden beams. Throughout the year there are numerous themed occasions such as "Salsa Night", "The Fish Market" week and "Sushi Night" as well as music from local acoustic artists. Turville is also renowned as the inspiration for the Vicar of Dibley TV show; Midsomer Murders is also filmed here, and on top of the steep ridge overlooking the village is the windmill featured in the film Chitty Chitty Bang Bang. Other local attractions include the many excellent walks, the pretty towns of Marlow and Henley, and although the pub itself has no bedrooms, staff are happy to recommend nearby Bed & Breakfasts and Hotels. The latest addition of a self-contained converted barn provides flexible space and facilities for meetings and private functions.

Our inspector loved: The village pub atmosphere and delicious food.

Directions: From the M40 take junction 5 towards and through Ibstone. At the bottom of the hill turn right at the T-junction towards Turville. The Bull & Butcher is in the centre of the village.

Web: www.johansens.com/bullandbutcher
E-mail: info@thebullandbutcher.com
Tel: 0870 381 8451
International: +44 (0)1491 638283

Price Guide:
midweek lunches from £
evening meals from £
Sunday lunch menu from £

27

NEW

THE TICKELL ARMS, RESTAURANT

1 NORTH ROAD, WHITTLESFORD, CAMBRIDGESHIRE CB2 4NZ

Directions: Take the M11, junction 10 and take the A505 (east). The village is signed within a mile.

Web: www.johansens.com/tickellarms
Tel: 0870 381 8634
International: +44 (0)1223 833128
Fax: 01223 835907

Price Guide:
starters from £3.75
mains from £9.50

Peterborough

Ely

Huntingdon

● Cambridge

The Georgian Grade II listed Tickle Arms is stylish and just that little bit different. Quirky touches and antique furnishings include a long bar for visitors to lean on, whilst the main dining area is elegant and decorated in a traditional style with dark polished tables and candlesticks, and classical music adds to the ambience. The conservatory boasts a stunning show of Bougainvillea in the summer and leads onto the patio and award-winning garden. Here, the large pool is full of huge, glistening koi carp and oriental ducks add further colour and entertainment. Two menus are available combining the best local produce sourced daily and are complemented by an excellent wine list with selections from over 100 bins. The à la carte menu includes dishes such as sauté of foie gras, hand-dived Scottish sea scallops, pan fried sea bass with palourdes clams, Barbary duck breast and tarte tatin with caramel sauce and bourbon vanilla ice cream. The al fresco menu features lighter dishes such as salads and omelettes. Guests are requested not to smoke or use mobile telephones throughout the property, however, smoking is permitted at the bar and on the Terrace. The Imperial War Museum at Duxford is just a couple of minutes' drive away and the university city of Cambridge and horse racing at Newmarket are within easy reach. Closed on Mondays.

Our inspector loved: The carved King and Queen chairs in the bar.

 [70]

BROXTON HALL

WHITCHURCH ROAD, BROXTON, CHESTER, CHESHIRE CH3 9JS

Built in 1671 by a local landowner, Broxton Hall is a black and white half-timbered building set in 5 acres of grounds and extensive gardens amid the rolling Cheshire countryside. The mediaeval city of Chester is eight miles away. The hotel provides every modern comfort while retaining the ambience of a bygone age. The reception area reflects the character of the entire hotel, with its magnificent Jacobean fireplace, plush furnishings, oak panelled walls and carved mahogany staircase. On cool evenings log fires are lit. The small but well-appointed bedrooms are furnished with antiques and have en-suite bathrooms as well as every modern comfort. Overlooking the gardens, the restaurant receives constant praise including 2 RAC Dining Awards and RAC Rosette. French and English cuisine is served, using local game in season and freshly caught fish. There is an extensive wine list. Breakfast may be taken in the sunny conservatory overlooking the lawned gardens. The hotel is an ideal venue for business meetings and conferences. Broxton Hall is the perfect base from which to visit the North Wales coast and Snowdonia. There are a number of excellent golf courses nearby and racecourses at Chester and Bangor-on-Dee. Special breaks available. The restaurant and library are open all day for non residents.

Our inspector loved: *The cosy antique filled rooms and pretty landscaped garden.*

Directions: Broxton Hall is on the A41 Whitchurch – Chester road, eight miles between Whitchurch and Chester.

Web: www.johansens.com/broxtonhall
E-mail: reservation@broxtonhall.co.uk
Tel: 0870 381 8387
International: +44 (0)1829 782321
Fax: 01829 782330

Price Guide:
single £75
double/twin £85–£140

TREHELLAS HOUSE HOTEL & RESTAURANT

WASHAWAY, BODMIN, CORNWALL PL30 3AD

Directions: Washaway is located on the A389 half-way between the towns of Bodmin and Wadebridge. Approaching from Bodmin, Trehellas House is situated to the right, set back from the main road and accessed by a slip road.

Web: www.johansens.com/trehellas
E-mail: enquiries@trehellashouse.co.uk
Tel: 0870 381 8953
International: +44 (0)1208 72700
Fax: 01208 73336

Newquay   Bodmin

Penzance   Falmouth

Isles of Scilly

Price Guide:
single £65–£95
double £80–£120
suite from £165

This early 18th-century Grade II listed Cornish courthouse, steeped in history, is surrounded by 2 acres of grounds. Inside, its traditional features combine with attractive and comfortable modern furnishings. The beamed atmospheric restaurant, with its beautifully preserved Delabole slate floor and elegant décor, serves the best locally sourced fish, meat, poultry, vegetables and cheeses to create delicious English and European dishes. An extensive wine list includes selections from the local Camel Valley vineyard. Following a recent refurbishment the 11 bedrooms are all en suite and comfortably furnished with patchwork quilts and iron bedsteads. The chandelier-lit Courtroom Suite still retains the magistrates' dais and moulded cornice providing elegant and spacious accommodation. Outside, guests may wish to stroll in the pleasant gardens or enjoy the heated swimming pool (May - September) and for the more energetic there are many walks along the Camel trail. The village of Rock is a popular base for sailing and fishing and at nearby Daymer Bay is the little church where poet John Betjeman is buried. The Eden Project is just 12 miles away, tickets are available from the hotel.

Our inspector loved: *The warm welcome, relaxed atmosphere and the tasteful locally sourced menus.*

TRELAWNE HOTEL – THE HUTCHES RESTAURANT

MAWNAN SMITH, NEAR FALMOUTH, CORNWALL TR11 5HT

A very friendly welcome awaits guests, who will be enchanted by the beautiful location of Trelawne Hotel, on the coast between the Rivers Fal and Helford. Large picture windows in the public rooms, including the totally refurbished spacious lounge/bar, ensure that guests take full advantage of the panoramic vistas of the ever-changing coastline. The bedrooms are charming, many with views of the sea. The soft colours of the décor, the discreet lighting and attention to detail provide a restful atmosphere, in harmony with the Wedgwood, fresh flowers and sparkling crystal in The Hutches Restaurant, which has been awarded an AA Rosette. The menu changes daily and offers a variety of inspired dishes, including local seafood, game and fresh vegetables. Ideally located for coastal walks along Rosemullion Head and the picturesque Helford Estuary. There are also a wealth of famous gardens within the area. "Slip Away Anyday" spring, autumn and winter breaks. The Royal Duchy of Cornwall is an area of outstanding beauty, with many National Trust and English Heritage properties to visit and a range of leisure pursuits to enjoy. The hotel is closed during January.

Our inspector loved: The location, welcome, and superb cuisine.

Directions: From Truro follow the A39 towards Falmouth and turn right at the Hillhead roundabout. Take the exit signposted Maenporth and travel for 3 miles. Trelawne Hotel is at the top overlooking Falmouth Bay.

Web: www.johansens.com/trelawne
E-mail: info@trelawnehotel.co.uk
Tel: 0870 381 8954
International: +44 (0)1326 250226
Fax: 01326 250909

Price Guide:
single £69–£89
double £95–£170

CHANDLERS WATERSIDE APARTMENT

30A PASSAGE STREET, FOWEY, CORNWALL PL23 1DE

Directions: From Exeter take the A30 towards Bodmin and then the B3269 to Fowey.

Web: www.johansens.com/chandlersfowey
E-mail: info@wisterialodgehotel.co.uk
Tel: 0870 381 9204
International: +44 (0)1726 810800
Fax: 01726 6616213

Price Guide: (minimum 2-night stay)
2-night stay from £300

With its network of climbing narrow streets, bustling harbour and ancient buildings, Fowey is one of the most picturesque coastal towns in Britain and has the added attraction of beautiful National Trust countryside surrounds and superb scenic walks. This luxury, 1-bedroom marina apartment, 1 of 3 apartments owned by Sally and James Wilkins, is situated in a prime waterfront position in the heart of the town, just a short stroll from the intriguing variety of shops and excellent restaurants. Chandlers is like an elegant boutique hotel with the privacy of its own front door, has every comfort and amenity for the discerning visitor who seeks a relaxing break away from the stress of 21st-century living. This includes a mooring, which can accommodate a 13-foot yacht. A delightfully decorated and furnished lounge has a balcony with fabulous panoramic views over the harbour towards the house of author Daphne du Maurier in Bodinnick. The views are equally superb from the well-equipped kitchen/dining area and the en-suite master bedroom has a king-size bed and every home comfort. Chocolates and fresh fruit welcome guests upon arrival and the tariff includes daily housekeeping services and breakfast – ready to be cooked. Private dining and spa treatments can be arranged. Outdoor pursuits include boat trips and water sports.

Our inspector loved: The view of the ever-changing estuary.

TREVALSA COURT COUNTRY HOUSE HOTEL & RESTAURANT

SCHOOL HILL, MEVAGISSEY, ST AUSTELL, CORNWALL PL26 6TH

Built overlooking the sea in the 1930s the Trevalsa was discovered by owners Klaus Wagner and Matthias Mainka in 1999, who lovingly set to work to restore the casual but elegant atmosphere of a country house. Blending traditional and modern styles, its oak-panelled hall and dining room, beautiful lounge and mullioned windows recall the ambience of a bygone age, whilst the newly refurbished en-suite bedrooms are simply and classically furnished. All principal bedrooms have splendid sea views even the ground floor rooms. The hotel's beautiful gardens are above the sheltered Polstreath Beach and access to its sloping sands and coves for swimming and fishing is directly available from the garden. A footpath also leads to the harbour and typically Cornish streets of Mevagissey, and St Austell, with its 18-hole golf course and modern sports centre, is just 5 miles away. Trevalsa Court's location makes it an excellent base for touring all parts of Cornwall. The award-winning Lost Gardens of Heligan and the Eden Project, fast becoming a top visitor destination for the 21st century, are nearby.

Our inspector loved: *The beautiful new suites and the welcome – so genuine.*

Directions: On approaching Mevagissey on the B3273 from St Austell go through Pentewan, climb the hill and turn left at the crossroads at the top. Trevalsa Court Hotel is ½ mile on the left.

Web: www.johansens.com/trevalsa
E-mail: stay@trevalsa-hotel.co.uk
Tel: 0870 381 8955
International: +44 (0)1726 842468
Fax: 01726 844482

Price Guide:
single £65–£108
double/twin £98–£160
suite £150–£200

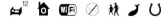

LOWER BARN

BOSUE, ST EWE, CORNWALL PL26 6ET

Directions: From St Austel roundabout turn left onto the B3273 signposted Mevagissey. Pass Pentewan Beach and at the crossroads turn right then follow signs for Lower Barn.

Web: www.johansens.com/lowerbarn
E-mail: janie@bosue.co.uk
Tel: 0870 381 8565
International: +44 (0)1726 844881

Price Guide:
single from £80
double £100-£120
suite from £120

Nestled in the heart of Cornish countryside, on the beautiful Roseland Peninsula, near St Austell, the award-winning Lower Barn delightfully stands within almost 2 acres of rural gardens at the end of a meandering country lane. Awarded the AA's Best Guest House 2005-6, this is a haven of peace and tranquillity, and a unique romantic hideaway run by resident owners Mike and Janie Cooksley who provide more than just a first-class bed and breakfast. Emphasis has been placed on quality, attention to detail, rest, relaxation, and thoughtful touches such as fresh flowers and luxury linen. Excellent candle-lit dinners can be arranged; imaginative and extensive menus feature the finest local produce and the freshest of fish from nearby Mevagissey. The house has no alcohol licence but visitors are welcome to bring their own; there is no corkage charge. Individually designed bedrooms are decorated and furnished to the highest standard and have extensive facilities from stylish contemporary bathrooms to living rooms, exposed beams, DVD players and fridges. A fully-equipped spa features a garden hot tub and a large Native American tepee where many of the treatments are performed. The Lost Gardens of Heligan and the Eden Project are within easy reach.

Our inspector loved: The peace and tranquillity at this beautiful, tucked away haven.

THE OLD COASTGUARD HOTEL

MOUSEHOLE, PENZANCE, CORNWALL TR19 6PR

The Old Coastguard Hotel is beautifully situated above the charming fishing village of Mousehole, a quaint hideaway nestled between the rolling headlands of West Cornwall. Lush sub-tropical gardens lead down to the sea, beach and rock pools, part of a truly breathtaking coastline. The friendly, helpful staff make guests' stay an unforgettable experience, and the contemporary interior creates a superb relaxing ambience. Rooms are comfortable and elegantly appointed, and stunning panoramic views of little fishing boats and yachts can be enjoyed from one of the many bedroom balconies. Daily changing, delectable meals are served in the highly acclaimed restaurant where innovative menus feature locally sourced dishes and fresh fish from nearby Newlyn fish market. There are miles of Cornish coastal paths and bridleways nearby and Mousehole Harbour is a few minutes' walk away; a wonderful place to sit and reflect upon a perfect sojourn, described by Dylan Thomas as "the most beautiful village in England". It has a sandy beach for children, good local quays and boats. There is always the opportunity to explore the winding country lanes that lead to tucked away coves and villages.

Our inspector loved: *The magnificent location, the welcome, and the feeling of not wanting to leave.*

Directions: Follow the A30 to Penzance, then signs to Mousehole. The hotel is on the left upon entering the village.

Web: www.johansens.com/oldcoastguard
E-mail: bookings@oldcoastguardhotel.co.uk
Tel: 0870 381 8522
International: +44 (0)1736 731222
Fax: 01736 731720

Newquay
Bodmin

Penzance
Falmouth

Isles of Scilly

Price Guide:
single £40–£100
double £80–£140
premium plus £110–£160

PRIMROSE VALLEY HOTEL

PRIMROSE VALLEY, PORTHMINSTER BEACH, ST IVES, CORNWALL TR26 2ED

Directions: Contact the hotel for detailed directions or visit the website.

Web: www.johansens.com/primrose
E-mail: info@primroseonline.co.uk
Tel: 0870 381 9377
International: +44 (0)1736 794939
Fax: 01736 794939

Price Guide: (There is an additional £1 per room per night, which is donated to the Marine Conservation Society. This can be removed at guest's request.)
double £95-130
suite £150–£210

This charming, modern small hotel is a short stroll from the historic St Ives harbour and the picturesque town centre streets that characterise this renowned artists' colony. It also enjoys direct access to the 1km-long Blue Flag Porthminster Beach. This Edwardian seaside, villa-style house is family-friendly, and welcoming owners Andrew, Sue and Rose have extensively refurbished since purchasing the property in 2001. Their efforts to make the hotel one of distinction have been rewarded with a Silver in the Cornwall Tourism Awards - Hotel of the Year and the first hotel in Cornwall to win full green accreditation with an award from the Green Tourism Business Scheme in recognition of its innovative moves towards sustainability. Individual bedrooms have hardwood or restored original floors, comfortable beds, luxurious duck-down duvets and sumptuous pillows; 4 overlook the harbour. The new suite comprises a king-size bed, walnut furniture, silk curtains and under-floor heating in the en suite with a slipper bath and separate Philippe Starck deluge shower. The suite lounge has a 26" flat-screen TV and DVD player, integrated stereo system, red leather sofa, and walnut flooring. Atlantic Ocean views are enjoyed from the terrace where drinks, including an extensive wine list, can be savoured. Snacks are available in the licensed café bar and early suppers from June to September.

Our inspector loved: The new beautiful and unique suite - absolute luxury.

NEW

ROSE-IN-VALE COUNTRY HOUSE HOTEL

MITHIAN, ST AGNES, CORNWALL TR5 0QD

Steeped in 18th-century history, this Georgian manor house, tucked away in a Cornish wooded valley, is a stone's throw from Mithian village offering a calming retreat from the stresses of daily life. The stunning North Cornish coast provides the perfect backdrop for this 18-bedroom country house hotel, which is elegantly appointed with comfortable furnishings, cosy fireplaces and plush fabrics. The bedrooms and suites have en-suite bathrooms whilst The Rose Suite, with queen-size four-poster bed, spa bath and sitting room, is a favourite for honeymooners and romantics. During the day, guests can browse the books in the library, unwind in the drawing room, take a dip in the heated swimming pool, hot tub or take to the gardens and enjoy a hearty Cornish cream tea. For further gastronomic indulgence, a dinner at the Valley Restaurant is a must. Start with pancetta salad with croutons and sweet Dijon dressing followed by supreme of wild trout with peas and almond butter. Rose-in-Vale is a haven for wildlife: the valley is home to badgers, foxes, rabbits, woodpeckers, owls and buzzards. The National Maritime Museum and The Eden Project provide fine day-trip options.

Our inspector loved: *The tranquil, relaxing atmosphere in this tucked away little gem.*

Directions: From the major A30 roundabout just north west of Truro, take the B3277 signed for St Agnes. After 500 metres pick up the brown signs for Rose-in-Vale Hotel.

Web: www.johansens.com/roseinvalecountryhouse
E-mail: reception@rose-in-vale-hotel.co.uk
Tel: 0870 381 8537
International: +44 (0)1872 552202
Fax: 01872 552700

Price Guide:
single from £70
double/twin £140–£190
suite from £180

HIGHLAND COURT LODGE

BISCOVEY ROAD, BISCOVEY, NEAR ST AUSTELL, CORNWALL PL24 2HW

Directions: From the A30 take the A391 to St Austell then turn left onto the A390 through St Blazey Gate. Turn right into Biscovey Road and the hotel is approximately 300 yards on the right.

Web: www.johansens.com/highlandcourt
E-mail: enquiries@highlandcourt.co.uk
Tel: 0870 381 9290
International: +44 (0)1726 813320
Fax: 01726 813320

Price Guide:
single from £95
double £130–£220

Tucked away within 2 acres of secluded, picturesque grounds, this idyllic award-winning Cornish retreat is the perfect place for relaxation where guests can forget the stresses of everyday life and enjoy a range of in-house holistic therapies designed to soothe the body and soul. Sumptuous and tasteful décor is used throughout and a cosy winter fire in the lounge enhances the delightful ambience for savouring an evening drink, good book or chat amongst friends. Fresh flowers adorn beautifully presented bedrooms, all designed with luxurious fabrics and Egyptian cotton sheets to ensure the utmost in comfort. Resplendent views of St Austell Bay and Carlyon Bay Golf Course can be appreciated from each of the private patios that adjoin the rooms. Start the day with an invigorating shower and end with an indulgent soak amidst sensual aromatherapy candles. Local catch has a strong influence on the skilfully prepared menu complemented by fresh, organic produce and finished with wonderful desserts. This superb cuisine may be taken in the charming dining room or al fresco on the balcony on warm summer evenings. Nearby St Austell and Fowey are part of the Cornish Riviera with its magnificent coastal path and intimate coves to explore. A local beach is close by and the Eden Project can be reached on foot (just 1 mile). Alternatively, the hotel offers supervised tree climbing.

Our inspector loved: This delightful little gem that sparkles throughout.

WISTERIA LODGE & APARTMENTS

BOSCUNDLE, TREGREHAN, ST AUSTELL, CORNWALL PL25 3RJ

Wisteria Lodge & Apartments is peacefully tucked away on the outskirts of St Austell, within walking distance of Carlyon Bay in the heart of Cornwall. Idyllically located, the Lodge offers the best of British hospitality and has gained a reputation for hosting fantastic parties. Emphasis on comfort and relaxation alongside first-class interior design have been used within the spacious surroundings to provide an elegant respite from the stresses of day-to-day life, which is enhanced by the extremely friendly, personalised service. Luxurious, individual bedrooms have every amenity and wonderful features such as four-poster beds, whirlpool baths and balconies. The ground floor suite has large French doors leading to a well-tended garden whilst fresh fruit and flowers, fluffy bathrobes and bathsheets add to guests' sense of well-being. Evening meals are available Wednesdays to Saturdays in the AA 3 Star-awarded restaurant where Head Chef Bob Whitley serves a daily changing menu created from the finest local produce in a candle-lit, romantic setting. Each dish is personally prepared from guests' selection on the day. Treatments at Wisteria's Health & Beauty Salon, which specialises in pure chocolate therapy, include Reiki healing and Lastone therapy. Enjoy Cornwall's dramatic coastline, the Eden Project, which is 1 mile away, and the Lost Gardens of Heligan, 5 minutes by car.

Our inspector loved: This luxurious hotel offering just about everything.

Directions: On approaching St Austell on the A390 turn left opposite the garden centre, signposted to Tregrehan. Go left at Boscundle Close (the first turning to the left) and bear right.

Web: www.johansens.com/wisteria
E-mail: info@wisterialodgehotel.co.uk
Tel: 0870 381 9183
International: +44 (0)1726 810800
Fax: 0871 6616213

Price Guide:
double/twin £125-£190

THE HUNDRED HOUSE HOTEL & FISH IN THE FOUNTAIN RESTAURANT

RUAN HIGHLANES, NEAR TRURO, CORNWALL TR2 5JR

The Roseland Peninsula's wide vistas of sparkling blue sea, variable landscape, sub-tropical flowers, attractive little fishing villages and yachting resorts are as inviting as any to be found on the Italian Riviera. At its heart is this charming non-smoking hotel, which offers all the comfort and friendliness of an Georgian country home. Surrounded by 3 acres of beautiful gardens it extends peace, tranquillity and magnificent countryside views. The beach is approximately 1 mile away, and nearby, on the edge of Fal Estuary, is the fashionable sailing resort of St Mawes, with its dominant hillside castle built by Henry VIII as part of his coastal defences against possible French invaders. All the hotel's bedrooms are en-suite, delightfully decorated, well furnished and have every facility and little extras to make guests feel at home, including a hot water bottle. In the spacious and sunny dining room, with its tasteful décor and garden views, guests enjoy delicious cuisine complemented by a reasonably priced wine list that has something for all tastes. After dinner, coffee and homemade fudge may be enjoyed in the relaxed atmosphere of the sitting room, by the open log fire. For walking enthusiasts, the magnificent coastal footpath provides access to quiet coves and tidal creeks.

Directions: Take the A390 from St Austell towards Truro. Turn left on the B3278 to Tregony and pass through the village and turn left onto the A3078 towards St Mawes. The hotel is approximately 4 miles on the right .

Web: www.johansens.com/hundredhouse
E-mail: enquiries@hundredhousehotel.co.uk
Tel: 0870 381 9205
International: +44 (0)1872 501336
Fax: 01872 501151

Price Guide: (including dinner)
single from £85
double from £170

Our inspector loved: The friendly welcome, good service and relaxing atmosphere.

TREDETHY HOUSE

HELLAND BRIDGE, WADEBRIDGE, CORNWALL PL30 4QS

Set amidst 7 acres of grounds with views of the surrounding countryside, this elegant manor house is the perfect place to get away from the stresses of daily life. The property was formerly the home of Prince Chula of Thailand, the legal guardian of Prince Bira, famous motor-racing champion of the 1930s and 40s, and the house retains some memorabilia. Many original features have been maintained, such as granite fireplaces, beautiful plasterwork and Victorian tiled floors. The owners and their small team of dedicated staff ensure that every guest has a truly enjoyable stay. Each of the 10 individually decorated en-suite bedrooms is furnished to a high standard; some have views of the surrounding countryside whilst others look out to the inner courtyards. A hearty Cornish breakfast is served in the conservatory and dinner is available by prior arrangement. Alternatively, Tredethy House will be delighted to make reservations for guests at any one of the many first-class inns and restaurants nearby. The gardens provide ample opportunity for a relaxing stroll, and the secluded outdoor heated pool is perfect for a leisurely swim on a warm day. The house is ideally located for touring Cornwall; Padstow, the Eden Project and the Lost Gardens of Heligan are all within a 20-minute drive.

Our inspector loved: The location, peace and tranquility.

Directions: From the A30, turn right signed Helland (approximately 4 miles before Bodmin). Follow the signs to Helland, pass through the village and over Helland Bridge. Tredethy is on the right just before brow of hill.

Web: www.johansens.com/tredethyhouse
E-mail: enquiries@tredethyhouse.co.uk
Tel: 0870 381 9142
International: +44 (0)1208 841262
Fax: 01208 841707

Price Guide:
single from £87.50
double from £112
suite from £155

Nent Hall Country House Hotel

ALSTON, CUMBRIA CA9 3LQ

Directions: From A1 junction 58 onto the A68 then onto the A689. Nent Hall is on the left.

Web: www.johansens.com/nenthall
E-mail: info@nenthall.com
Tel: 0870 381 9210
International: +44 (0)1434 381584
Fax: 01434 382668

Price Guide:
single £50–£125
double/twin £79–£149
suite £169

Nent Hall Country House Hotel nestles within the Nent Valley just over a mile east of Alston, the highest market town in England. Originally built in 1738 by a local mine owner, Nent Hall has recently undergone major refurbishment to restore the large country house to its former glory. The hotel has a variety of en-suite bedrooms including feature rooms and suites. All rooms are luxuriously decorated and furnished with either traditional four-poster or brass beds. The opulent 5-room tower suite is also available for special occasions. The East Wing offers family, twin and wheelchair accessible accommodation. All rooms are non-smoking and enjoy TV and DVD facilities (complimentary DVDs may be borrowed from the extensive library). Meals may be taken in the relaxed Coach House Bar or in the more formal surroundings of the Valley View restaurant. Both have excellent menus and incorporate local fare complimented by an extensive wine list. The hotel also has a marquee available for weddings and corporate events and a bespoke planning service can be provided. Horse riding, shooting and guided walks can all be arranged. Nearby places of interest include Hadrian's Wall, the Lakes, Hexham and the Nenthead mines.

Our inspector loved: The rural location near England's highest market town.

LAKE HOUSE HOTEL

LAKE ROAD, WATERHEAD BAY, AMBLESIDE, CIMBRIA LA22 0HD

This luxury hotel combines a country house atmosphere with stylish décor and modern touches, and comes complete with spectacular views across Waterhead Bay, Windermere, Loughrigg Fell and the Langdale Pikes. Its relaxed and informal atmosphere lends itself to making the place one's own, and there are numerous areas to escape to, such as the lovely reading landings or indeed the sophisticated yet understated bedrooms. King size, twin or family, they are all en-suite and have TV, DVD and CD players as well as coffee and tea making facilities and fluffy bathrobes. Guests can come together in the lounge or dining area where a traditional Lakeland breakfast is served, and dinner can be enjoyed at the sister hotel, The Regent, just 400 yards away. Corporate guests are more than adequately catered for, with all conference, outdoor and entertainment requirements arranged upon request, and those looking to take full advantage of Lake House's grand yet intimate surroundings can book the entire hotel for private events such as birthdays, reunions, anniversaries and seasonal celebrations. Packages are tailor-made and include two hosts for the duration of your stay, a private chef, a celebration dinner and a cruise on Lake Windermere.

Our inspector loved: The contemporary and modern feel to this lake land hotel.

Directions: Junction 36 M6 - A591 past Windermere to Amleside. through the traffic lights at Waterhead. Lake House Hotel is 25 yards on the right.

Web: www.johansens.com/lakehousehotel
E-mail: info@lakehousehotel.co.uk
Tel: 0870 381 8492
International: +44 (0)15394 32360
Fax: 015394 31474

Price Guide:
single £75
double/twin £120–£140

43

THE PHEASANT

BASSENTHWAITE LAKE, NR COCKERMOUTH, CUMBRIA CA13 9YE

Directions: Just off the A66, The Pheasant is 6 miles east of Cockermouth and 8 miles north-west of Keswick. Signposted from A66

Web: www.johansens.com/pheasantcumbria
E-mail: info@the-pheasant.co.uk
Tel: 0870 381 9227
International: +44 (0)17687 76234
Fax: 017687 76002

Price Guide:
single £74–£90
double/twin £134–£186

Set in the staggering, unspoilt northern part of the Lake District only a few yards from Bassenthwaite Lake and surrounded by beautiful gardens and woodlands, this famous 17th-century coaching inn is renowned for its friendly hospitality and excellent service. It is an intimate venue with only 13 de luxe bedrooms furnished to an extremely high standard with stunning fabrics, antiques and subtle colour schemes to create a light and airy atmosphere. Relaxing coffees over the morning newspaper or a mouth-watering afternoon tea Cumbria style with homemade specialities such as scones and brandy butter are served in the hotel's 3 quiet and comfortable lounges. The wood-panelled bar with polished walls and oak settles is a wonderful setting for pre-dinner drinks with its traditional and convivial atmosphere. Delicious traditional Cumbrian specialities to suit all tastes are served in the popular beamed dining room, which features a daily changing menu and a wide selection of fine wines. Guests can enjoy the peaceful solitude of the hotel's own gardens and woodlands whilst bird watching, fishing or walking, or explore the day trips around the magnificent Lake District. There are various sporting expeditions offered by the hotel.

Our inspector loved: The comfort and Olde World ambience and charm of this traditional inn.

UNDERWOOD

THE HILL, MILLOM, CUMBRIA LA18 5EZ

Andrew and Wendy Miller personally run this delightful non-smoking country house which was once a Victorian vicarage. Beautifully restored, it stands within 8 acres of landscaped gardens, meadows and paddocks, between the picturesque Whicham Valley and Duddon Estuary. The tranquil and elegant surroundings include 2 relaxing lounges, as well as an indoor heated swimming pool with steam room and a tennis court. Each of the 5 fully equipped bedrooms is en suite and individually furnished. Hosts Andrew and Wendy pride themselves on offering guests the utmost in comfort and hospitality, and every evening prepare and serve a 4-course dinner which combines the best in local ingredients, along with a carefully selected wine list. A hearty breakfast provides the perfect start for those wishing to explore the surrounding area. Lakes Coniston, Windermere and Wastwater are within easy reach, and there is plenty of opportunity to enjoy the attractions of Cumbria by car or on foot. The less adventurous can unwind with a relaxing swim, a stroll around the grounds or a game of croquet.

Our inspector loved: Wendy's hospitality and Andrew's cuisine using mainly local and home-grown produce.

Directions: Leave the M6 at junction 36 and follow the A590 towards Barrow-in-Furness. At Greenodd turn right onto the A5092 towards Millom until reaching the A5093. Turn left and go through "The Green" and "The Hill". After ½ mile Underwood is on the right.

Web: www.johansens.com/underwood
E-mail: enquiries@underwoodhouse.co.uk
Tel: 0870 381 8959
International: +44 (0)1229 771116
Fax: 01229 719900

Price Guide:
single £40
double £80–£120

45

CROSBY LODGE COUNTRY HOUSE HOTEL

HIGH CROSBY, CROSBY-ON-EDEN, CARLISLE, CUMBRIA CA6 4QZ

Directions: From M6 junction 44 take A689 Brampton road for 3 miles; turn right through Low Crosby. Crosby Lodge is on the right at High Crosby.

Web: www.johansens.com/crosbylodge
E-mail: info@crosbylodge.co.uk
Tel: 0870 381 8461
International: +44 (0)1228 573618
Fax: 01228 573428

Price Guide:
single £90–£100
double £140–£190

Crosby Lodge is a romantic country mansion that has been converted into a quiet, efficient hotel without spoiling any of its original charm. Grade II listed, it stands amid pastoral countryside close to the Scottish Lowlands and the Lake District. Spacious interiors are elegantly furnished and appointed to provide the maximum of comfort. The personal attention of Michael and Patricia Sedgwick ensures that a high standard of service is maintained. All of the bedrooms are beautifully equipped, most with antique beds and half-testers. 2 bedrooms are situated in the converted courtyard stables overlooking the walled garden and in these rooms guests are welcome to bring their pet dogs. In The Lodge restaurant, extensive menus offer a wide and varied choice of dishes. Traditional English recipes are prepared by Roger Herring and his team, along with continental cuisine complemented by an extensive international wine list. Tables are set with cut glass and gleaming silver cutlery and in keeping with the gracious surroundings. Crosby Lodge, with its spacious grounds, is a superb setting for weddings, parties, business and social events. The 84 mile Hadrian's Wall walk passes by the hotel's woodland estate. Closed 24 December to 16 January. Special breaks available.

Our inspector loved: *Philippa Sedgwick's wine warehouse in the courtyard, selling quality wines and home-made produce.*

THE QUEEN'S HEAD HOTEL

MAIN STREET, HAWKSHEAD, CUMBRIA LA22 0NS

Situated on the edge of Estwaite Water overlooked by Grizedale Forest, Hawkshead is a charming village in the centre of the Lake District with narrow cobbled streets and half-timbered cottages. The 16th-century Queen's Head Hotel is located in the centre of the village and boasts many period features such as low oak-beamed ceilings, panelled walls and large open fireplaces. A warm ambience is created in the cosy lounge bar, which serves hand-pumped ales and displays the famous Girt Clog, measuring a full 20 inches in length, which was worn by John Waterson. Extremely comfortable non-smoking bedrooms, some with four-poster beds, have en-suite bathrooms and lovely décor; 2 family rooms are available. Mouth-watering English cuisine, including Herdwick lamb, local venison, pheasant and mallard as well as delicious seafood specialities is accompanied by an extensive international wine list. 3 award-winning self-catering cottages with all modern conveniences are situated at the rear of the hotel and are ideal for longer stays. Guests can visit the Beatrix Potter Museum, Village Heritage Centre and Parish Church or explore the lush fells and Tarn Hows, the jewel of the Lakes.

Our inspector loved: *The welcoming and friendly atmosphere of this traditional Lakeland village inn.*

Directions: Leave the M6, junction 36. Take the A590 to Newby Bridge then the second right and follow the road for 8 miles into Hawkshead. Drive through the village car park and turn right up the main street. The hotel is on the right.

Carlisle

Penrith

Windermere

Kendal

Web: www.johansens.com/queenshead
E-mail: enquiries@queensheadhotel.co.uk
Tel: 0870 381 8844
International: +44 (0)15394 36271
Fax: 015394 36722

Price Guide:
single £50–£65
double/twin £75–£114

WEST VALE COUNTRY HOUSE & RESTAURANT

FAR SAWREY, HAWKSHEAD, AMBLESIDE, CUMBRIA LA22 0LQ

Built from local stone in the 1890s, this former Victorian gentleman's residence nestles deep in the heart of the Lake District National Park on the edge of a delightfully quaint and tranquil village famed for its association with Beatrix Potter. She wrote her much loved books at "Hilltop," just a few minutes' walk away. It is a quintessential English rural location with captivating views overlooking Grizedale Forest and The Old Man of Coniston. Renovated and refurbished in traditional style, West Vale combines the grace of a bygone age with modern day comforts and refinements such as a complimentary decanter of sherry awaiting guests in their bedrooms. All bedrooms are en-suite, individually furnished, decorated to a high standard and have a wide range of facilities. Fresh fruit and complimentary slippers are provided in the de luxe rooms and the suite affords an adjoining lounge. Excellent classical cuisine is served in the elegant 2 AA Rosette-awarded restaurant. Local fresh produce is used whenever possible and the menu changes daily. Lake excursions can be enjoyed on Windermere; Ambleside and Coniston are a short drive away and Langdale and the Grizedale Forest are amongst many nearby natural attractions. Private fishing can be arranged. Closed in January. Special breaks available.

Directions: Take the M6/jct 36 then the A5074. Pass Windermere and take the A593 towards Coniston then the B5286 to Hawkshead. Take the B5285 towards Ferry and the hotel is on the right upon entering the Far Sawrey.

Web: www.johansens.com/westvale
E-mail: enquiries@westvalecountryhouse.co.uk
Tel: 0870 381 9378
International: +44 (0)1539 442 817
Fax: 01539 445 302

Price Guide:
single £78-£88
double £100-£140
suite £148-£158

Carlisle

Penrith

Windermere

Kendal

Our inspector loved: The delicious dinner cooked and prepared by Glynn, the owner.

THE WHEATSHEAF @ BRIGSTEER

BRIGSTEER, KENDAL, CUMBRIA LA8 8AN

A totally non-smoking inn with 3 excellent double en-suite rooms available to guests, the raison d'être of the Wheatsheaf is great food expertly prepared. Its renowned restaurant offers a seasonal à la carte menu, which is truly impressive, with an emphasis placed on locally sourced produce, games and meats, including rare breeds, fresh fish and seafood, which is delivered daily. Tucked away in the tranquil and picturesque Lakeland village of Brigsteer, situated just 3 miles from the medieval market town of Kendal, this really is the gateway to the Lakes. At the foot of Scout Scar, with its stunning panoramic views, and on the edge of a damson-growing region of Lyth Valley, Morecombe Bay is located to one side and the Old Man of Conniston to the other. Parts of the inn date back to 1762; it began life as 3 cottages plus a "shoe-ing" room for horses then became an alehouse and was licensed in the early 1800s. The décor is handsome and tasteful.

Our inspector loved: This delightful village inn, specialising in fine dining.

Directions: Take the M6, junction 36 then the A591 towards Kendal for 3 miles then turn left signposted Brigsteer. Turn left at the T-junction and The Wheatsheaf is 1 mile in the village of Brigsteer.

Carlisle

Penrith

Windermere

Kendal

Web: www.johansens.com/brigsteer
E-mail: wheatsheaf@brigsteer.gb.com
Tel: 0870 381 8495
International: +44 (0)15395 68254
Fax: 015395 68948

Price Guide:
single £65
double £65–£75

THE LEATHES HEAD

BORROWDALE, KESWICK, CUMBRIA CA12 5UY

Directions: From M6 Jct40 take A66 to Keswick, then B5289 to Borrowdale. The hotel is on the left, 3½ miles from Keswick. From the south, approach Keswick on A591.

Web: www.johansens.com/leatheshead
E-mail: enq@leatheshead.co.uk
Tel: 0870 381 8686
International: +44 (0)17687 77247
Fax: 017687 77363

Price Guide: (including dinner)
single £74–£90
double/twin £128–£180

Carlisle

● Penrith

Windermere

Kendal

The Leathes Head is an Edwardian country house set in a lovely location within the Borrowdale Valley. Log fires burn in the sitting room in winter and a delightful conservatory overlooks the Fells, affording guests the full benefit of the hotel's elevated position. Recently refurbished by owners Roy and Janice Smith it combines the charm and elegance of a bygone age with up-to-date standards of comfort. All bedrooms are en-suite with a wide range of facilities, and 2 superior double aspect rooms boast magnificent views stretching across to Catbells and Maiden Moor. Downstairs there are rooms suitable for the less mobile. Food is excellent, and award-winning chef David Jackson has built a well-deserved reputation for his daily changing menus and dishes which, where possible, include locally sourced ingredients. This high standard is also reflected in the extensive wine list. Guests can choose from a varied collection of books and board games, enjoy a leisurely walk or cycle ride, or simply relax with a drink in the bar. This is a non smoking house. Special breaks available.

Our inspector loved: *While enjoying breakfast watching the Woodpeckers and Red Squirrels eating the bird nuts outside.*

DALE HEAD HALL LAKESIDE HOTEL

THIRLMERE, KESWICK, CUMBRIA CA12 4TN

The key handed to guests upon arrival is more than just the key to the bedroom… it's the key to tranquility and total relaxation. This is the proud boast of the Hill family, caring owners of Dead Head Hall, situated in acres of mature gardens and woodlands in the heart of the Lake District. Red squirrels are often seen playing in the garden. Standing alone, on the shores of Lake Thirlmere, this historic hotel of distinction sits at the foot of majestic Helvellyn. It is a glorious 16th-century house of charm, character and luxury in what must be one of the most spectacular of settings. A bird watchers paradise. accommodation is exceptional, décor and furnishings are superb. The spacious bedrooms are welcoming, warm and sumptuous with those little extras that help make a visit memorable. Some of the rooms are in the Elizabethan house, whilst others are in the Victorian extension; all have stunning lake and mountain views as do both lounges. Diners can enjoy superb and imaginative cuisine created from the finest and freshest seasonal local produce, complemented by an extensive international wine list in the elegant oak-panelled 2AA Rosette-awarded restaurant. Special breaks are available. Closed 3rd -26th January.

Our inspector loved: The feeling of total peace and quiet - the only house on Lake Thirlmere.

Directions: On the A591, halfway between Keswick and Grasmere the hotel is situated along a private driveway overlooking Lake Thirlmere.

Web: www.johansens.com/daleheadhall
E-mail: onthelakeside@daleheadhall.co.uk
Tel: 0870 381 8470
International: +44 (0)17687 72478
Fax: 017687 71070

Price Guide: (including dinner)
single £120–£135
double £180–£260

HIPPING HALL

COWAN BRIDGE, KIRKBY LONSDALE, CUMBRIA LA6 2JJ

Directions: Hipping Hall lies on the A65, 2 miles east of Kirkby Lonsdale towards Settle and Skipton, 8 miles from the M6, junction 36.

Web: www.johansens.com/hippinghall
E-mail: info@hippinghall.com
Tel: 0870 381 8632
International: +44 (0)15242 71187
Fax: 015242 72452

Price Guide:
single from £90
double £140–£220

Hipping Hall was taken into new ownership in 2005, and an extensive restoration and sensitive refurbishment has brought it to life, whilst retaining its 300 years of history and ambience of old English charm. The use of bold fabrics and striking colours create vibrant interiors with an atmosphere of stylish elegance and comfort. Dinner is served in the magnificent 15th-century banqueting hall, complete with oak beams where guests can experience the unique modern cuisine of Head Chef, Jason Birkbeck. The Hall is keen to build on its excellent reputation for food and sources the finest local ingredients from local producers in their seasonal menu. Innovative menus include dishes such as roast breast of quail, ballotine of reared Lincolnshire rabbit, roast short loin of Kittridding Farm lamb and fillet of line caught Sea Bass. Visitors are encouraged to stay in one of the beautifully designed bedrooms, which in contrast to the richness of the downstairs public spaces are light and airy. All have handmade beds, exposed beams and some have baths and others have large walk-in showers; many overlook the pretty gardens. The hotel is located 2 miles from the beautiful market town of Kirkby Lonsdale at the heart of the Lune Valley and is nestled between the Lake District and Yorkshire Dales.

Our inspector loved: The delicious dinner in the 15th-century banqueting hall.

TEMPLE SOWERBY HOUSE HOTEL AND RESTAURANT

TEMPLE SOWERBY, PENRITH, CUMBRIA CA10 1RZ

Set in a lovely old walled garden, this delightful country hotel provides a welcoming and relaxing stay and is an ideal base from which to explore this area of outstanding natural beauty. Situated in the lush Eden Valley, between the Lake District and the Pennines, the house is a few minutes from Ullswater, perhaps the "most beautiful of English lakes." Resident owners Paul and Julie Evans can suggest a number of ideas for fascinating days out and places to visit whether walking or touring. The hotel is also well located for an overnight stay en-route to and from Scotland. Individually-styled bedrooms offer a choice of accommodations: The de luxe rooms featuring aqua-spa baths. 2 ground floor rooms are available in the Coach House, 20 yards from the main building. Dinner is served in the new Conservatory Restaurant, overlooking the walled garden. Awarded 2 AA Rosettes, the seasonally inspired à la carte menus blend contemporary and traditional British styles, prepared from the best of local and garden-grown produce. On fine days, enjoy drinks on the Terrace with views across the garden or, on cold winter evenings, in a cosy spot by a blazing fire in one of the elegant reception rooms. Special feature breaks include Wine Weekends, Activity Breaks, Easter and New Year.

Our inspector loved: Dining in the new garden restaurant overlooking the secluded walled garden.

Directions: On the A66, 7 miles from exit 40 off the M6, between Penrith and Appleby.

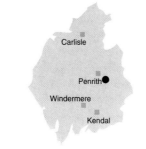

Web: www.johansens.com/templesowerby
E-mail: stay@templesowerby.com
Tel: 0870 381 8942
International: +44 (0)17683 61578
Fax: 017683 61958

Price Guide:
single £85–£105
double £115–£160

53

FAYRER GARDEN HOUSE HOTEL

LYTH VALLEY ROAD, BOWNESS-ON-WINDERMERE, CUMBRIA LA23 3JP

Awarded The Cumbrian Tourist Board Hotel of the Year 2002, this lovely Victorian house overlooks Lake Windermere in spacious gardens and grounds. This very comfortable hotel, where guests can enjoy the spectacular views over the water, offers a real welcome and marvellous value for money. The delightful lounges and bar and the superb air-conditioned restaurant all enjoy lake views. There is an excellent table d'hôte menu in the award-winning restaurant, which changes daily and uses local produce such as fish, game and poultry whenever possible. The wine list is excellent and very reasonably priced. Many of the attractive bedrooms face the lake, some have four-poster beds and whirlpool baths en suite. There are also ground floor rooms suitable for the elderly or infirm. The nearby Parklands Leisure Complex has a an indoor pool, sauna, steam room, badminton, snooker and squash complimentary to hotel residents. Special breaks are available. The Windermere Steamboat Museum, boating from Bowness Pier and golf at Windermere Golf Club and The Beatrix Potter Attraction are all close by.

Directions: Take junction 36 off the M6 then the A590 past Kendal. Take the B5284 at the next roundabout and turn left at the end. The hotel is 350 yards on the right.

Web: www.johansens.com/fayrergarden
E-mail: lakescene@fayrergarden.com
Tel: 0870 381 8517
International: +44 (0)15394 88195
Fax: 015394 45986

Price Guide: (including 5-course dinner)
single £79–£130
double £122–£280

Our inspector loved: The new, redesigned bedrooms with views over the gardens and lake.

LINTHWAITE HOUSE HOTEL

CROOK ROAD, BOWNESS-ON-WINDERMERE, CUMBRIA LA23 3JA

Situated in 14 acres of gardens and woods in the heart of the Lake District, Linthwaite House overlooks Lake Windermere and Belle Isle, with Claife Heights and Coniston Old Man beyond. Here, guests will find themselves amid spectacular scenery, yet only a short drive from the motorway network. The hotel combines stylish originality with the best of traditional English hospitality. Superbly decorated en-suite bedrooms, most of which have lake or garden views. The comfortable lounge is the perfect place to unwind and there is a fire on winter evenings. In the restaurant excellent cuisine features the best of fresh, local produce, accompanied by a fine selection of wines. Within the hotel grounds, there is a 9-hole putting green and a par-3 practice hole. Fly fishermen can fish for brown trout in the hotel tarn. Guests have complimentary use of a private swimming pool and leisure club nearby, while fell walks begin at the hotel's front door. The area around Linthwaite abounds with places of interest: this is Beatrix Potter and Wordsworth country, and there is much to interest the visitor.

Our inspector loved: *Walking through the landscaped gardens up to the tarn with its spectacular views of Lake Windermere.*

Directions: From the M6, junction 36 follow Kendal by-pass for 8 miles. Take the B5284, Crook Road, for 6 miles. 1 mile beyond Windermere Golf Club, Linthwaite House is signposted on the left.

Web: www.johansens.com/linthwaitehouse
E-mail: admin@linthwaite.com
Tel: 0870 381 8694
International: +44 (0)15394 88600
Fax: 015394 88601

Price Guide:
single £120–£150
double/twin £145–£300
suite £280–£320

BROADOAKS COUNTRY HOUSE

BRIDGE LANE, TROUTBECK, WINDERMERE, CUMBRIA LA23 1LA

Directions: M6 junction 36, A590/591 to Windermere. Go over small roundabout towards Ambleside, then right into Bridge Lane. Broadoaks is ½ mile on right.

Web: www.johansens.com/broadoaks
E-mail: trev@broadoaksf9.co.uk
Tel: 0870 381 8380
International: +44 (0)1539 445566
Fax: 01539 488766

Price Guide:
single £70–£160
double £90–£210

Carlisle

Penrith

Windermere ●

Kendal

Tucked away in Troutbeck, one of the prettiest areas of the Lake District, Broadoaks is a wonderful retreat from which to explore this beautiful part of England. Views from the first floor are truly breathtaking, reaching over Lake Windermere and the Troutbeck Valley into the 10 acres of private grounds that belong to the hotel. Designed to be relaxing and luxurious, yet mindful of the graceful building's Victorian past, all bedrooms are furnished with four-poster or antique brass bedsteads, and are fully equipped with the latest Jacuzzi, spa whirlpool and sunken bath. Rich oak panelling runs from the entrance hall into the cosy music room with Bechstein piano and open fire, where guests can enjoy pre-dinner drinks or after-dinner coffee. Rich red damask complements the Victorian dining-room and is a splendid setting for the award-winning restaurant, which has a wide reputation and a choice of á la carte and house menus. All guests have complimentary use of a local private leisure club or can relax in the grounds trying their hand at pitch and put. Golf, fishing, croquet and clay pigeon shooting can also be arranged.

Our inspector loved: *The relaxed and friendly atmosphere of this informal hotel with beautiful views over Troutbeck Valley.*

DANNAH FARM COUNTRY HOUSE

BOWMAN'S LANE, SHOTTLE, NEAR BELPER, DERBYSHIRE DE56 2DR

Set amidst an area of rural, unspoilt countryside high above the Ecclesbourne Valley on the edge of the Peak District, Dannah Farm Country House is a 5-star guest accommodation rated property. An exceptional 18th-century Georgian farmhouse conversion on the Chatsworth Estate, this is the only accommodation in the county to have been awarded both 5 stars from the AA and a Little Gem award from the RAC. Offering a unique service and a working farm within a tranquil and relaxed environment, Dannah Farm is located in the centre of England, easily accessed from the M1 and ideal for leisure, business travellers and now weddings requiring a serene ambience. The soothing bedrooms overlook rolling pastures and large, pretty gardens and are beautifully furnished with antiques and old pine; some have four-poster beds, private sitting rooms, Japanese-style tubs, hot tubs and whirlpool baths. Aromas of freshly baked bread escaping from the kitchen whet the appetite and for breakfast there are free-range eggs and locally supplied sausages. Dinner is by prior arrangement. Situated only 10 minutes from the World Heritage sites of Belper and Cromford, the countryside is criss-crossed with footpaths in all directions, whilst places nearby include Chatsworth, Haddon Hall, Dovedale and water sports at Carsington.

Our inspector loved: Its personality, a real gem that has a very special variety of rooms; a place to wind down.

Directions: From Derby take A6 Matlock road. At Duffield turn left onto B5023 towards Wirksworth. At traffic lights at Cowers Lane turn right onto A517 towards Belper, then 1st left to Shottle. Bowman's Lane is 100 yds past crossroads in the village.

Web: www.johansens.com/dannah
E-mail: slack@dannah.co.uk
Tel: 0870 381 8476
International: +44 (0)1773 550273/550630
Fax: 01773 550590

Price Guide:
single from £65
double/twin from £100

THE CHEQUERS INN

FROGGATT EDGE, HOPE VALLEY, DERBYSHIRE S32 3ZJ

Directions: The inn is situated on the A625, which links Bakewell and Sheffield, 6 miles from Bakewell on Froggatt Edge.

Web: www.johansens.com/chequerscalver
E-mail: info@chequers-froggatt.com
Tel: 0870 381 8422
International: +44 (0)1433 630231
Fax: 01433 631072

Price Guide:
double/twin £70–£90
four poster £75–£95

Since February 2002, Jonathan and Joanne Tindall have worked hard to instil their pleasant personalities into this popular country inn. Its tradition for hospitality dates back to the 16th century when it was built on the old pack horse road. A Grade II listed building, the inn was originally 4 houses and has been extensively refurbished yet retains many charming period features including a horse mounting block and old stables. Each of the bedrooms has its own personality and is cosy with comfortable, characteristic furnishings with private bathroom and individually controlled heating. Boasting a Rosette, The Chequers is proud of its cuisine and Chef Marcus Jefford creates a wide variety of European and British dishes from fresh ingredients, including local game in season. Meals are available all day at the weekends and Bank Holidays. On cooler evenings guests can relax by crackling open fires in the bar, recipient of Derbyshire Pub of the Year by Derbyshire Food and Drinks Awards, or enjoy breathtaking views from the elevated secret woodland garden. The surrounding Peak District is ideal walking country and perfectly situated for exploring along the Derwent River or Peak trails. Nearby is the historic castle and caverns of Castleton, Haddon Hall, Chatsworth House and the lively market town of Bakewell, famous for its puddings. Smoking is not permitted throughout the inn.

Our inspector loved: *The winter welcome and cosy atmosphere.*

THE WIND IN THE WILLOWS

DERBYSHIRE LEVEL, GLOSSOP, DERBYSHIRE SK13 7PT

Situated 12 miles from the centre of Manchester, with good road and rail links, this family-owned early Victorian country house has retained its original charm such as oak-panelling, traditional furnishings and open log fires. Set within 5 acres of land with unspoilt views of the Peak District National Park and surrounded by the heather-clad hills of The Pennines, the setting provides an escape from the pressures of modern-day life and the elegant surroundings of a bygone era. The dining room serves traditional English cuisine created from ingredients sourced from a range of local farms and farmers' markets. The bedrooms, with their splendid views, are decorated with antique furniture and numerous personal touches. The small conference suite has a private entrance and caters for prestigious corporate meetings in a peaceful atmosphere. Adjoining the grounds is a splendid 9-hole golf course, where guests can play within the beautiful scenery of the local countryside. Many activities can be arranged locally, including sailing, horse riding, hang gliding, fly fishing and pot holing. Places of interest nearby include Chatsworth, the industrial heritage of Glossop, Haddon Hall, Castleton, Bakewell, Holmfirth, Hayfield, Kinder Scout and the Lowry Centre in Manchester. Smoking is prohibited throughout the property.

Directions: 1 mile east of Glossop on the A57 then a further 400 yards down the road opposite the Royal Oak.

Web: www.johansens.com/windinthewillows
E-mail: info@windinthewillows.co.uk
Tel: 0870 381 9001
International: +44 (0)1457 868001
Fax: 01457 853354

Price Guide:
single from £75
double from £125

Our inspector loved: This peaceful early Victorian house.

THE PLOUGH INN

LEADMILL BRIDGE, HATHERSAGE, DERBYSHIRE S30 1BA

Directions: From M1 exit 29 take A617 west, then via A619 and A623 shortly after north onto B6001 towards Hathersage. The inn is within proximity of Sheffield, Manchester and East Midland Airports.

Web: www.johansens.com/ploughinnhathersage
E-mail: sales@theploughinn-hathersage.co.uk
Tel: 0870 381 8827
International: +44 (0)1433 650319
Fax: 01433 651049

Price Guide:
single £59.50–£89.50
double £79.50–£120

Nominated for the Condé Nast Johansens Most Excellent Traditional Inn 2006 Award, this delightful 16th-century inn is set amidst 9 acres of land, surrounded by idyllic countryside on the banks of the River Derwent. Two generations of the Emery family, Bob and Cynthia and their son Elliott, ensure a warm welcome and a very comfortable stay. All bedrooms are en-suite, have been tastefully decorated and are furnished to provide every modern comfort; guests may choose to stay in one of the three rooms housed in the main building or in the two luxury bedrooms located across the cobbled courtyard in September Cottage. A wide range of ales, whiskies, brandies and liquors as well as fine wines from around the world are served in the cosy bar complete with real log fire, and the intimate restaurant is the perfect place to enjoy a sumptuous meal in informal surroundings. The bar and à la carte menus offer an eclectic mix of traditional and modern European dishes prepared from the freshest seafood and best locally sourced produce chosen by Bob, a former butcher. Situated in the Peak National Park, the inn is an ideal base from which to explore the countryside and visit numerous attractions nearby such as Chatsworth House, Haddon Hall, Bakewell, Buxton, Castleton with its many caves and caverns, the famous Blue John Mine and the industrial heritage of Sheffield.

Our inspector loved: The newly created heated courtyard.

YEOLDON HOUSE HOTEL

DURRANT LANE, NORTHAM, NR BIDEFORD EX39 2RL

This glorious Victorian residence is set in 2 acres of beautiful gardens on the banks of the River Torridge, ideal for those who wish to unwind and enjoy the serenity of the surrounding countryside. It has recently been refurbished to create a comfortable, well-maintained oasis complemented by welcoming staff, who provide excellent service. The interior is warm and cosy and the comfortable lounge features historical stained-glass windows and interesting works of art. En-suite bedrooms are well equipped and individually decorated; one has a four-poster bed and some have balconies with river views. Garden rooms overlook the grounds, whose gently sloping lawns provide delightful areas to enjoy a pot of tea or glass of wine. Imaginative meals are painstakingly prepared using only fresh local ingredients and are served alongside a wide choice of fine wines in the elegant Soyer Restaurant, appropriately named after the greatest chef of the 19th century: Alexis Soyer. The ideal base for exploring the picturesque Devon countryside, the hotel is situated on the North Devon Way so is perfect for hikers. Exmoor and Braunton Burrows are only a short drive away and are havens for bird enthusiasts and walkers. There is a wealth of romantic castles and gardens to discover and the stunning coastline with rugged cliffs and coves is nearby. 3-day breaks are available throughout the year.

Directions: Leave M5 at Jct27 and join A361 towards Barnstaple. At Torridge Bridge roundabout follow signs for Northam towards Bideford.

Web: www.johansens.com/Yeoldon
E-mail: yeoldonhouse@aol.com
Tel: 0870 381 9019
International: +44 (0)1237 474400
Fax: 01237 476618

Price Guide:
single £65–£75
double/twin £105–£120

Our inspector loved: The newly refurbished top-floor bedrooms.

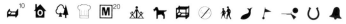

MILL END

DARTMOOR NATIONAL PARK, CHAGFORD, DEVON TQ13 8JN

Directions: From the M5 exit at junction 31 towards Okehampton. Take the A382 at Merrymount roundabout towards Moretonhampstead. Mill End is on the right.

Web: www.johansens.com/millend
E-mail: info@millendhotel.com
Tel: 0870 381 8734
International: +44 (0)1647 432282
Fax: 01647 433106

Price Guide:
single £80–£120
double/twin £120–£170
suite £170–£210

Gleaming white under slate grey roof tiles and with windows and doors opening onto a beautiful English country garden, Mill End, within top 200 AA Hotels, is an idyllic hideaway in Dartmoor's National Park. The lawned garden with its wide, deeply shrubbed and colourful borders runs down to the languid waters of the River Teign, a water wheel slowly turns in the courtyard to the enjoyment of guests and diners. Built in the mid 1700s the hotel was a former flour mill, and inside there are numerous little corner nooks, paintings and old photographs that imbue a feeling of seclusion, enhanced by the smell of wood smoke and polished wood. The delightful en-suite bedrooms have undergone major refurbishment incorporating excellent décor, lovely fabrics and attractive local hand-crafted furniture. Plus, of course, every facility one would expect. The elegance of the dining room is matched by the delicious award-winning cuisine of Master Chef of Great Britain, Barnaby Mason. His menus are full and varied; one shouldn't miss, for example, lobster ravioli with seared scallops and lemon grass broth followed by grilled turbot with aubergine caviar and a dark chocolate tort with burnt orange sauce and rosewater ice cream. An 18-hole golf course is nearby and pony trekking and shooting can be arranged.

Our inspector loved: *All the on going upgrades both within and without.*

THE NEW INN

COLEFORD, NEAR CREDITON, DEVON EX17 5BZ

Those wishing to escape the hectic pace of everyday life will be delighted with this lovely 13th-century thatched inn, located in a truly secluded valley beside a babbling brook featuring newly designed gardens which are a delight. The New Inn, a Grade II listed building of cob, has been tastefully renovated and refurbished over the years. Today it retains the character and ambience of a past era. A warm welcome is extended to guests from owners Melissa and Simon Renshaw and their talkative parrot, Captain! The AA 4 Diamond rated accommodation is excellent, with spacious and individually appointed bedrooms offering every comfort. In the winter months, the lounge is the place to sit and enjoy the cosy warmth of a log fire. 3 full-time chefs create memorable dishes, using the best and freshest local ingredients. The delightful menu includes, Tunis lamb - spicy lamb in a honey and citrus sauce served with caraway cous cous or salmon escalope with brandy sultanas and fish valoute, seasonal vegetables and potatoes. There is also a good selection of speciality dishes, grills and puddings. An extensive choice of drinks, including traditional ales, is served in the bars. The wine list has been awarded many accolades for its selection. The cathedral city of Exeter, Dartmoor and Exmoor are all close by.

Our inspector loved: The location, superb menus, and welcome from the owners.

Directions: Take the A377 Exeter-Barnstable Road. Coleford is signed 2 miles from Crediton.

Web: www.johansens.com/newinncoleford
E-mail: enquiries@thenewinncoleford.co.uk
Tel: 0870 381 8757
International: +44 (0)1363 84242
Fax: 01363 85044

Price Guide:
single £60–£70
double £75–£85

COMBE HOUSE HOTEL & RESTAURANT

GITTISHAM, HONITON, NEAR EXETER, DEVON EX14 3AD

Awarded Taste of the West - South West Restaurant of the Year 2005, Combe House is a wildly romantic, Grade 1 Elizabethan Manor, hidden in 3,500 acres of private Devon estate, yet close to the World Heritage coastline. Arabian horses and pheasants roam freely beside the mile of winding drive leading from the pretty thatched village of Gittisham. The alluring combination of heritage and a welcoming lived-in feel make this a special place for an indulgent mix of eating, drinking and relaxing in the country. Log fires, treasured antiques and fresh flowers abound and 15 bedrooms and suites, many with breathtaking views, exude style and individuality. In the Restaurant, guests are treated to innovative contemporary cuisine created by 2 Master Chefs of Great Britain, who draw extensively on the West Country's bounteous larder and Combe's own kitchen garden to weave their culinary magic. Add this to interesting wines from the ancient cellars, including a specialist Chablis collection.

***Our inspector loved:** The beautifully presented new Linen Suite, quite unique.*

Directions: M5 exit 28 to Honiton and Sidmouth or exit 29 to Honiton. Follow signs to Fenny Bridges and Gittisham (20 mins). A303/A30 exit Honiton, 5 mins.

Web: www.johansens.com/combehousegittisham
E-mail: stay@thishotel.com
Tel: 0870 381 8440
International: +44 (0)1404 540400
Fax: 01404 46004

Price Guide:
single £134
double/twin £164–£178
suite £308–£388

Barnstaple

Exeter
Sidmouth

Plymouth

HOME FARM HOTEL
WILMINGTON, NR HONITON, DEVON EX14 9JR

A gleaming white exterior, traditional thatched roof and 4 acres of grounds teeming with shrubs and colourful flower borders help make this former 16th-century farmhouse a charming and romantic retreat that eases away the stresses of modern living. Situated 3 miles from Honiton, gateway to the West Country, the hotel has been tastefully restored, renovated and refurbished to include 21st-century facilities alongside the character, ambience and enchanting features of a past era. A warm welcome is extended from the new owner Steve Lundy, who has strikingly upgraded the lounge, restaurant and bedrooms. There are spacious and individually appointed bedrooms in the main building and across a cobbled courtyard, with every comfort from widescreen TV and complimentary wireless Internet to sumptuous bathrooms and luxury toiletries. The Chesterfield-filled lounge bar is the place to relax over a good read or apéritif before enjoying Chef Lee Villiers' imaginative and beautifully presented cuisine in the stylish restaurant. Among his memorable creations are Devon ruby beef topped with local blue cheese butter and roasted duck breast served on bubble and squeak, accompanied by a vanilla and honey sauce. Within easy reach are National Trust properties such as Killerton and Knightshayes Court, wildlife parks, model villages and 6 golf courses.

Our inspector loved: *The lounge with sumptuous Chesterfields.*

Directions: Take the A303 to Honiton then join the A35 signposted to Axminster. Wilmington is 3 miles further on and Home Farm Hotel is set back off the main road on the right.

Web: www.johansens.com/homefarm
E-mail: info@thatchedhotel.co.uk
Tel: 0870 381 8604
International: +44 (0)1404 831278
Fax: 01404 831411

Price Guide:
single from £57
double £84–£110

ILSINGTON COUNTRY HOUSE HOTEL

ILSINGTON VILLAGE, NEAR NEWTON ABBOT, DEVON TQ13 9RR

The Ilsington Country House Hotel stands in 10 acres of beautiful private grounds within the Dartmoor National Park. Run by friendly proprietors, Tim and Maura Hassell, the delightful furnishings and ambience offer a most comfortable environment in which to relax. Stylish bedrooms all boast outstanding views across the rolling pastoral countryside and every comfort and convenience to make guests feel at home. The distinctive candle-lit dining room is perfect for savouring the superb cuisine, awarded 2 AA Rosettes, created by talented chefs from fresh local produce. The library is ideal for an intimate dining party or celebration whilst the conservatory or lounge is the place for morning coffee or a Devon cream tea. There is a fully-equipped, purpose-built gymnasium, heated indoor pool, sauna, steam room and spa. Some of England's most idyllic and unspoilt scenery surrounds Ilsington, with the picturesque villages of Lustleigh and Widecombe-in-the-Moor close by. Guests have easy access to the moors from the hotel. Riding, fishing and many other country pursuits can be arranged. Special breaks are available.

Directions: From the M5 join the A38 at Exeter following Plymouth signs. After approximately 12 miles, exit for Moretonhampstead and Newton Abbot. At the roundabout follow signs for Ilsington.

Web: www.johansens.com/ilsington
E-mail: hotel@ilsington.co.uk
Tel: 0870 381 8635
International: +44 (0)1364 661452
Fax: 01364 661307

Price Guide:
single £92–£98
double/twin £136–£164
suite £166–£174

Our inspector loved: *The beautiful new domed ceilinged restaurant with window wall overlooking the moor and views towards the magnificent Hay Tor.*

NEW

LYDFORD HOUSE
LYDFORD, NEAR OKEHAMPTON, DEVON EX20 4AU

Originally the home of celebrated Victorian artist William Widgery, idyllically located in Dartmoor National Park, this friendly family-run bed and breakfast is a wonderful place to unwind and relax. Large windows fill the rooms with light and look out to 8 acres of pretty, well-kept gardens and surrounding pastureland. The elegant lounge is cosy with its open log fire burning in the winter months, and spacious bedrooms are bright, airy and beautifully appointed with comfortable classical décor. For a particularly private stay, Widgery's Nest is a self-catering apartment nestled under the eaves of the hotel and boasts a spacious open-plan living area. During the summer a truly delicious home-cooked breakfast is eaten by the wide-open window, whilst traditional tearooms are licensed and serve tasty Devonshire cream teas and light lunches. The recently opened restaurant, La Cascata, (The Waterfall) serves Italian cuisine. The stables can accommodate guest horses, and with a full range of facilities and nearby stables, can provide horses for trekking and riding through the breathtaking Dartmoor landscape. Bicycles are available to hire and may be ridden along The Granite Way, a purpose-made cycle track, which runs past the hotel leading to historic Tavistock and Okehampton. The Lydford gorge and waterfall, run by the National Trust, is a short walk away.

Our inspector loved: The location, the grounds, and presentation.

Directions: From Exeter take the M5, junction 31 onto the A30. Take the exit after Okehampton onto the A386 towards Tavistock. The turning for Lydford House is approximately 6 miles further on.

Web: www.johansens.com/lydfordhouse
E-mail: info@lydfordhouse.com
Tel: 0870 381 8525
International: +44 (0)1822 820347
Fax: 01822 820539

Price Guide:
single from £40
double from £80

HEWITT'S - VILLA SPALDI

NORTH WALK, LYNTON, DEVON EX35 6HJ

Directions: Leave the M5 at junction 23, signposted Minehead, follow the A39 to Lynton.

Web: www.johansens.com/hewitts
E-mail: hewitts.hotel@talk21.com
Tel: 0870 381 8593
International: +44 (0)1598 752293
Fax: 01598 752489

Price Guide:
single £70–£95
double/twin £140–£240

This elegant, private 19th-century country house offers total peace and seclusion within 27 acres of gardens and woodlands. Once the home of the eminent Victorian, Sir Thomas Hewitt, it stands regally on high cliffs overlooking Lynmouth Bay and beyond, Wales. Approached by a meandering, residential driveway, the house sits just minutes from the centre of Lynton and is perfectly placed for walks along the Exmoor coastal path. The character of the house has been superbly retained with wonderful antiques, a sweeping oak staircase and beautiful stained glass windows by Burne-Jones. 2 self catering apartments are available all year round, and the warm, friendly "house party" ambience of Hewitt's means it lends itself perfectly to intimate gatherings. Exclusive use of the house is available on request. Dinner is available by prior arrangement and mouth-watering international dishes are created under the guidance of Italian chef and owner, Tito Spaldi. Local suppliers of venison, game, meats and cheeses are used to full advantage and the many fine wines on the accompanying list are truly first class. Guests can enjoy breakfast or a romantic dinner in the oak-panelled dining room, or in the summer, on the cliff terrace overlooking the bay.

Our inspector loved: *This little gem that offers total peace, tranquillity and privacy – a must.*

HEDDON'S GATE HOTEL

MARTINHOE, PARRACOMBE, BARNSTAPLE, DEVON EX31 4PZ

Hidden at the end of a quarter-mile private drive, this tranquil country house is superbly positioned on the slopes of the wooded Heddon Valley. With more than $2\frac{1}{2}$ acres of gardens and woodlands, it was built as a Swiss style lodge in 1890 and has enjoyed a lively history. Owners Anne and Eddie Eyles have a huge enthusiasm for Heddon's Gate, and offer a warm and friendly welcome to visitors. The décor of the hotel reflects its charming fusion of different ages and styles, and guest bedrooms range from Grandma's Room, in a Victorian style complete with four-poster bed, to the Indian Room, decorated and furnished with a colonial feel. The elegant dining room is ideal for enjoying a leisurely breakfast and sumptuous dinner, menus for which change daily. The proprietors source and prepare their ingredients with the utmost care, and they always aim to use the best fresh, local and seasonal produce. A complimentary traditional afternoon tea of homemade savouries, scones and cakes is also served. The natural beauty of Exmoor's coast, moorland, wooded combes and varied wildlife make it a walker's paradise, and there are many stately homes, gardens, museums and craft centres to explore. Breaks are available.

Our inspector loved: *This tucked away hidden haven. A walkers paradise offering total peace.*

Directions: From Blackmoor Gate (the junction of the A39 and A399) take the A39 towards Lynton. Pass Parracombe and Woody Bay Station on your left, then take next left at Martinhoe Cross.

Barnstaple
Exeter
Sidmouth
Plymouth

Web: www.johansens.com/heddonsgate
E-mail: hotel@heddonsgate.co.uk
Tel: 0870 381 8549
International: +44 (0)1598 763481

Price Guide: (including dinner)
single from £82
double/twin £156–£172

KINGSTON HOUSE

STAVERTON, NEAR TOTNES, DEVON TQ9 6AR

Directions: Take the A38 from Exeter or Plymouth. At Buckfastleigh take the A384 Totnes Road for 2 miles then turn left to Staverton. At Sea Trout Inn take the left fork to Kingston and follow signs.

Web: www.johansens.com/kingstonhouse
E-mail: info@kingston-estate.co.uk
Tel: 0870 381 8655
International: +44 (0)1803 762 235
Fax: 01803 762 444

Price Guide:
single £100–£110
double £160
suite £170–£180

The Kingston Estate nestles amongst the rolling hills and valleys of the South Hams region of Devon, bounded by Dartmoor and the sea, with the historic Kingston House at its heart, surrounded by beautiful, tranquil countryside. The mansion and its superb cottages have been restored by the Corfields without losing the 18th-century charm, and now offers some of the highest standards of accommodation to be found in the South West featuring 3 period suites, reached by way of the finest example of a marquetry staircase in England. Dine by candlelight in the elegant dining room on delicious local produce at tables set with sparkling crystal, shining silver and starched linen. In winter log fires crackle in the hearths, whilst in the summer drinks may be taken on the terrace overlooking the gardens. Hospitality and comfort are assured in this magnificent setting, which is also an ideal location for a wedding, party or conference. Up to 42 guests may be seated in the Marble Hall, up to 100 in The Garden Suite overlooking the Baroque gardens and fountain and up to 130 with a marquee in the walled garden; all provide memorable venues for a variety of events. New for 2006 is the indoor exercise pool, spa, sauna, mini-gym and billiards room. There are many places of interest to visit nearby including Dartington Hall, Dartmouth, Totnes, Dartmoor and Devon's famous coastline.

Our inspector loved: This beautiful country house, perfect for a wedding.

THE BRIDGE HOUSE HOTEL

PROUT BRIDGE, BEAMINSTER, DORSET DT8 3AY

Nestled in the heart of West Dorset countryside, The Bridge House Hotel is a beautiful old retreat partly dating back to the 13th century whose staff provide discreet and attentive service for a truly memorable experience. Splendid refurbished bedrooms, some with stone fireplaces and garden views, are spacious and have delightful bath or shower rooms. The gardens are enclosed within an ancient stone wall, a romantic suntrap ideal for lunches and candle-lit dinners. A quiet bar is the oldest room in the hotel with a quaint, sophisticated atmosphere and an impressive range of drinks. Comfortable armchairs and a large inglenook fireplace in the lounge create the perfect environment to relax before dinner or enjoy afternoon tea and homemade biscuits. The seasonal table d'hôte menu and daily à la carte specials offer flavoursome and innovative, fresh organic cuisine such as the acclaimed medallions of pork served with fresh figs and stilton sauce. The healthy breakfast is delicious and served in the conservatory overlooking the delightful gardens that are floodlit at night. The hotel is a 15-minute drive from the Jurassic Coast, a World Heritage Site with fossils, coastal scenery and extraordinary geology. There is also a wealth of historic houses, museums and places of interest to visit in the area.

Our inspector loved: The stunning interiors complemented by the use of local art, and the excellent cuisine making this a landmark destination.

Directions: From the M3 take the A303 Crewkerne exit then the A356 through Crewkerne. Take the A3066 to Beaminster and the hotel is 100 yards from the town centre car park on the left.

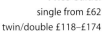

Web: www.johansens.com/bridgehousebeam
E-mail: enquiries@bridge-house.co.uk
Tel: 0870 381 8379
International: +44 (0)1308 862200
Fax: 01308 863700

Price Guide:
single from £62
twin/double £118–£174

YALBURY COTTAGE

LOWER BOCKHAMPTON, DORCHESTER, DORSET DT2 8PZ

Yalbury Cottage is a lovely thatched property dating back about 300 years. It offers guests a warm welcome and friendly, personal service in a pleasing Dorset hamlet close to Thomas Hardy's home. The 8 non-smoking en-suite bedrooms, in the modern part of the building, have been restyled in fresh pastel shades by Laura Ashley. The comfortable lounge, complete with large Inglenook fireplace and low beamed ceiling, is the perfect place to relax or enjoy a drink before dinner. The hotel prides itself on the high standard of cuisine served in the attractive dining room. Chef Ben Streak has a variety of imaginative dishes available, for example, warm red mullet salad with a West Country crab dressing; slow-roasted Dorset Horn lamb with steamed aubergine purée, gratin potatoes and lightly truffled lamb jus; raspberry-ripple cheesecake with a dark chocolate sorbet. Places of interest nearby include Athelhampton House, Abbotsbury Swannery, Corfe Castle and Sherborne Castle. Yalbury Cottage, only 8 miles from the magnificent Heritage Coast, is an excellent base from which to explore Dorset.

Directions: Lower Bockhampton is a mile south of A35 between Puddletown and Dorchester.

Web: www.johansens.com/yalburycottage
E-mail: yalburyEmails@aol.com
Tel: 0870 381 9015
International: +44 (0)1305 262382
Fax: 01305 266412

Price Guide:
single from £70
double from £112

Our inspector loved: The immaculate presentation and a real sense of welcome are the keynotes here. Add in a lovely breakfast and delicious dinner for a stay to remember with pleasure.

LA FLEUR DE LYS

BLEKE STREET, SHAFTESBURY, DORSET SP7 8AW

La Fleur de Lys restaurant was established in Shaftesbury 15 years ago, and owners David, Mary and Marc have built up an enviable reputation for fine dining and excellent service in a warm and relaxing atmosphere. The restaurant is recommended in various nationally recognised Eating Out guides, and it has recently undergone a major refurbishment to improve the ground floor bar, lounge, dining and reception areas, as well as bedroom facilities and access for the less able. The 7 individually decorated bedrooms are en suite with either a shower or bath, and have luxury robes, towels and toiletries as well as internet access, coffee, tea and homemade biscuits. There are different styles of rooms including a family room that sleeps 3 and a four-poster room for romantic occasions. The restaurant has a conservatory style function room with picture windows that can accommodate up to 14 people, also small wedding and anniversary celebrations of up to 40 can be catered for. The hotel is located in the centre of the beautiful hilltop town of Shaftesbury with its wonderful views over The Blackmore Vale, and provides the ideal base from which to explore the surrounding area and places of interest, so vividly described in the novels of Thomas Hardy.

Our inspector loved: *David's absolute commitment to your culinary pleasure – dinner here in this delightful restaurant with rooms is to be savoured.*

Directions: On the roundabout of the A30 and A350. Follow the signs into the town centre. La Fleur de Lys is situated at the top end of the town.

Web: www.johansens.com/lafleurdelys
E-mail: info@lafleurdelys.co.uk
Tel: 0870 381 8454
International: +44 (0)1747 853717
Fax: 01747 853130

Price Guide:
double for single occupancy from £75
double from £95
family £145

THE GRANGE AT OBORNE

OBORNE, NR SHERBORNE, DORSET DT9 4LA

Directions: Oborne can be found just off the A30 in between Sherborne and Milborne Port.

Web: www.johansens.com/grangesherborne
E-mail: reception@thegrange.co.uk
Tel: 0870 381 9240
International: +44 (0)1935 813463
Fax: 01935 817464

Price Guide:
single from £85
double from £100

This 200-year-old house nestles peacefully in formal gardens, just 1½ miles from historic Sherborne. Guests are welcomed by owners Jennifer Mathews and Jon Fletcher, and can relax in each of the 18 well-appointed and spacious bedrooms, all with modern facilities. Dinner is served in a most pleasant ambience, overlooking the attractive floodlit gardens. As its RAC Three Dining Awards attests, the restaurant specialises in both international and traditional cuisine. For those planning an event or occasion the hotel can provide a service for up to 120 guests, and is also suited to conferences and business meetings. This quiet haven is a most ideal escape from city life, and visitors will be able to unwind with horse riding, fishing or simply taking in the local scenery. Air enthusiasts are not to be left out and will be pleased to hear that the Fleet Aviation Museum can be found at Yeovilton. Keen golfers may use the golf course in close proximity to the hotel. Popular daytime excursions include visits to the impressive 8th-century abbey at Sherborne, and 2 castles, one built by Sir Walter Raleigh. The lovely Dorset coast and many National Trust properties are within easy reach.

Our inspector loved: *Food, rooms, setting, style – all created for guests' delight. Newly refurbished bedrooms complement excellent traditional restuarant service. All set in lovely Dorset.*

     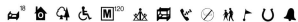

THE PUMP HOUSE APARTMENT

132 CHURCH STREET, GREAT BURSTEAD, ESSEX CM11 2TR

Situated in picturesque rural South East England, the Pump House Apartment is an immaculate 2-storey apartment in the village of Great Burstead. Spacious and fully equipped it is an extremely comfortable home from home. Part of a modern house, Pump House is set in its own secluded gardens, with an oriental pond and paddocks. Visitors can avail of an outdoor swimming pool heated to 80 degrees from May to September, and a full-sized hot tub/spa set in a glazed Canadian Redwood Gazebo, located in a suntrap walled courtyard with a decorative fountain. The house is very flexible and the air-conditioned Apartment can be let as a 1, 2 or 3-bedroom residence. 2-beautifully appointed lounges are available in addition to an elegant dining room and well designed kitchen with views over the pretty gardens. The village of Great Burstead is steeped in history, and its 14th-century church has links with the Pilgrim Fathers and early settlers of the USA. London is 30 minutes by train; Cambridge, Canterbury, Colchester and the Constable Country are within a 1-hour drive. Country walks are a pleasure, and golf, tennis and badminton are among the many sports available nearby.

Our inspector loved: The big hot tub in its gazebo in the suntrap walled garden.

Directions: Leave the M25 at junction 29 and join the A127. Travel in the direction of Southend then turn onto the A176 (Noak Hill Road) towards Billericay. Church Street is on the right and The Pump House Apartment is on the left before the church.

Colchester
Stansted Airport
Harlow   Chelmsford
Southend-on-Sea

Web: www.johansens.com/pumphouse
E-mail: johnwbayliss@btinternet.com
Tel: 0870 381 8842
International: +44 (0)1277 656579
Fax: 01277 631160

Price Guide:
£475–£1,050 per week
short breaks available

THE CROWN HOUSE

GREAT CHESTERFORD, SAFFRON WALDEN, ESSEX CB10 1NY

Directions: Situated on the B1383 off the M11 at either junction 9 or 10.

Web: www.johansens.com/crownhouse
E-mail: stayatthecrownhouse@onetel.net
Tel: 0870 381 8465
International: +44 (0)1799 530515 / 530257
Fax: 01799 530683

Price Guide:
single £65–£89.50
double/twin £84.50–£145

This Georgian hotel and award-winning restaurant, a restored coaching inn, is set within quiet, attractive gardens in the pretty village of Great Chesterford. The building is truly historic; the front is built on a 4th-century Roman wall and several priest holes have been preserved. Oak-panelled walls and flagstone floors enhance the warm and friendly atmosphere, and there is one of only two oriel windows in the area. Glowing fires add to the warmth in winter, whilst comfortable leather chairs in the lounge/bar create a welcoming ambience. The luxurious, individually designed bedrooms are all en-suite and provide all modern comforts. The restaurant serves exquisite, innovative dishes. Guests can enjoy the extensive menu, which is complemented by a carefully chosen wine list, in the intimate dining room or the vine-clad conservatory. The Crown House is an ideal venue for a romantic wedding. The historic market town of Saffron Walden with its antiques shops, museum and castle is worth a visit, as are nearby Cambridge, Newmarket racecourse, Audley End and Duxford Air Museum. Stansted Airport is within easy reach.

Our inspector loved: The double bath and big bathroom of The Crown Room.

BIBURY COURT

BIBURY COURT, BIBURY, GLOUCESTERSHIRE GL7 5NT

Past visitors to Bibury Court are reputed to have included Charles II and during the reign of George III, the Prince Regent. This gracious mansion dates from Tudor times, but the main part was built in 1633 by Sir Thomas Sackville, an illegitimate son of the 1st Earl of Dorset. After generations of illustrious owners, it became a hotel in 1968. The great house is set on the outskirts of Bibury, which William Morris called "the most beautiful village in England". As a hotel, it is run on country house lines with one of the main objectives being the provision of good food and wine in informal and pleasurable surroundings. Log fires during the cooler months add to the comfort of guests. There are some lovely panelled rooms in the house, many containing antique furniture. Many of the bedrooms have four-posters, all have private bathrooms and for those who like greater privacy there is the Sackville suite. Trout fishing is available in the Coln, which forms the southern boundary of the hotel's 6 acres of grounds, and there are golf courses at Burford and Cirencester. Water sports and riding are available nearby. Bibury Court is ideally placed for touring the Cotswolds, while Stratford, Oxford, Cheltenham and Bath are all within easy reach.

Our inspector loved: The beautiful, tranquil setting and pretty gardens..

Directions: Bibury is on the B4425, 7 miles from Burford and 7 miles from Cirencester.

Web: www.johansens.com/biburycourt
E-mail: info@biburycourt.com
Tel: 0870 381 8360
International: +44 (0)1285 740337
Fax: 01285 740660

Price Guide:
single from £125
double from £145
suite £230

NEW

LYPIATT HOUSE

LYPIATT ROAD, CHELTENHAM, GLOUCESTERSHIRE GL50 2QW

Directions: From M5. Leave at junction 11. Into Cheltenham on A40 apprx. 3 miles. Stay on A40 until Texaco Garage on middle roundabout. Turn right, then left into Andover road. Pass shops on right and through pedestrian lights, 100 yards sharp left into Lypiatt road and entrance is on the left.

Web: www.johansens.com/lypiatt
E-mail: stay@lypiatt.co.uk
Tel: 0870 381 8622
International: +44 (0)1242 224994
Fax: 01242 224996

Price Guide:
single £70–£90
double/twin £80–£110

Lypiatt House is located in Cheltenham's fashionable Montpellier district within convenient walking distance from the main shopping areas, theatres and places of interest. Gorgeous gardens, stunning contemporary décor and a homely atmosphere enhance the beautiful Victorian style and traditional features where privacy and comfort are of the utmost importance. The excellent staff ensures a warm welcome and a wonderful sense of ease and tranquillity whilst maintaining a high standard of attentive service. En-suite bedrooms have all modern amenities, are spacious and tastefully designed with a harmonious ambience, perfect for repose. The elegant drawing room is decorated in warm hues with an open fireplace, cosy furnishings and large windows that let in plenty of light; the perfect place to enjoy a favourite book. The honesty bar in the conservatory is ideal for a quick drink or socialising with friends. Lypiatt House serves a delicious breakfast and there are many restaurants within walking distance. There is ample parking available. Cheltenham is a charming town and has been described as one of the most beautiful in Europe by a leading architectural historian, and the hotel's great location makes it an ideal base for those wishing to explore the Cotswolds.

Our inspector loved: The comfort, immaculate standards and friendly staff in a great location for the centre of Cheltenham.

CHARLTON KINGS HOTEL

CHARLTON KINGS, CHELTENHAM, GLOUCESTERSHIRE GL52 6UU

Surrounded by the Cotswold Hills, on the outskirts of Cheltenham but just a few minutes by car to the heart of town, stands Charlton Kings Hotel. If you seek instant peace and solitude, follow the footpath running alongside the Hotel into the beautiful Cotswold countryside. The famous 'Cotswold Way' escarpment walk passes just ½ mile away. Quality, comfort and friendliness are the hallmarks of this lovely hotel. All of the rooms have been beautifully refurbished and most boast views of the Coltswold Hills and countryside. Standard rooms offer a high degree of comfort while superior rooms are much larger with many upgraded facilities ideal for a longer stay or that special occasion. The restaurant offers a variety of dishes to satisfy the most discerning of diners and requests from vegetarians or vegans can be readily accommodated. The enthusiastic and experienced staff have a great knowledge of the surrounding area which enables them to recommend and help plan guests' visits to places of interest, local events and entertainment. Cheltenham Spa is famous for its architecture, festivals and racing, there is also plenty on offer in the way of theatres, restaurants as well as a distinguished selection of shops. To the north, east and south lie numerous charming Cotswold villages and to the west the Forest of Dean, Wye Valley, Malvern Hills and much more.

Our inspector loved: An immaculate small hotel with a friendly welcome.

Directions: The Hotel is the first property on the left coming into Cheltenham from Oxford on the A40 (the 'Welcome to Cheltenham' Boundary Sign is located in the front garden!). M5 junction 11, 5 miles

Web: www.johansens.com/charltonkings
E-mail: enquiries@charltonkingshotel.co.uk
Tel: 0870 381 8416
International: +44 (0)1242 231061
Fax: 01242 241900

Price Guide:
single £65–£85
double £85–£125
family £120–£150

THE MALT HOUSE

BROAD CAMPDEN, GLOUCESTERSHIRE GL55 6UU

Directions: The Malt House is in the centre of the village of Broad Campden, which is just a mile from Chipping Campden.

Web: www.johansens.com/malthouse
E-mail: info@malt-house.co.uk
Tel: 0870 381 8714
International: +44 (0)1386 840295
Fax: 01386 841334

Price Guide:
single £85
double £125–£135
suite £145–£165

This beautiful 17th-century Cotswold home stands in the idyllic, quintessential English village of Broad Campden. Behind its modest golden stone roadside face The Malt House hides beautiful gardens, an orchard, stream, croquet lawn and brook. The house boasts many awards for its standard of accommodation and meals, and the rooms, including residents' sitting rooms, feature comfortable, cosy furnishings and antiques together with fresh flowers in abundance throughout the house. All bedrooms and suites are individually decorated and most overlook the wide lawns. From the quaint summer house terrace croquet and quoits may be watched whilst enjoying a leisurely drink before taking dinner in one of the many restaurants, bistros and public houses within walking distance. Dinner for parties of 12 or more can be prepared by arrangement only. The Cotswold English breakfasts include local brown eggs, soft fruits in season from the kitchen garden and home baked breads. Nearby places to visit include Hidcote Manor Gardens (NT), Chipping Campden Church, the Cotswolds, Cheltenham, Stratford-upon-Avon, Oxford and Bath, plus many markets, galleries, antique and gift shops.

Our inspector loved: That everything is as lovely as ever.

THE WILD DUCK INN

DRAKES ISLAND, EWEN, CIRENCESTER, GLOUCESTERSHIRE GL7 6BY

Here is a typical, lovely little picture postcard hotel; warm, welcoming and rich in history. Built of mellow Cotswold stone in the 15th century when Queen Elizabeth I was instigating a network of coaching inns throughout the country, The Wild Duck is as attractive inside as it is outside. Décor and furnishings are rich and elegant, fine old oil portraits adorn the walls, large open log fires enhance the welcoming ambience in winter, windows look out over a secluded garden that is perfect for al fresco dining in summer. Though old in years, the inn has all modern comforts and amenities. Each individually decorated bedroom is en-suite and has facilities to suit the most discerning visitor. Some of the rooms are on the ground floor, 2 have four-poster beds. Guests can enjoy a chat over drinks in a cosy bar or oak-panelled lounge before eating in style in the award-winning dining room. Traditional British and European menus offer superb seasonal dishes. In winter, specialities include game and fresh fish, which is delivered overnight from Brixham, Devon. All dishes are complemented by the extensive and excellent wine list. Within a mile of the inn is Cotswold Water Park with 80 lakes providing fishing and a range of water sports. Racing at Cheltenham and polo at Cirencester Park are nearby.

Our inspector loved: *Full of character with good food and a great atmosphere.*

Directions: Leave the M4 at junction 17 and follow Cirencester signs. Before the town turn right at Kemble and follow the signs to Ewen.

Web: www.johansens.com/wildduck
E-mail: wduckinn@aol.com
Tel: 0870 381 8997
International: +44 (0)1285 770310
Fax: 01285 770924

Price Guide:
single £70
double/twin £95
four poster £120
chinese suite £150

81

LOWER BROOK HOUSE

BLOCKLEY, NR MORETON-IN-MARSH, GLOUCESTERSHIRE GL56 9DS

Directions: Located in the village of Blockley just off the A44, between Moreton-in-Marsh and Broadway.

Web: www.johansens.com/lowerbrookhouse
E-mail: info@lowerbrookhouse.com
Tel: 0870 381 9297
International: +44 (0)1386 700286
Fax: 01386 701400

Price Guide:
single £80–£165
double £95–£165

This delightful stone 17th-century house stands serenely in the heart of a beautifully kept village that is one of the Cotswolds best kept secrets. Blockley is a conservation area within a designated Area of Outstanding Natural Beauty that maintains the peace and quiet of a bygone era with its wisteria covered cottages, dovecotes in picturesque gardens and babbling brook meandering down to the village and through the garden of Lower Brook House. The brook once provided power for 12 mills, 6 of which are the names of the hotel's guest rooms. The caring owners have done everything imaginable to make these rooms as comfortable as possible; all are en-suite, individually and tastefully furnished and offer every facility from television to fluffy bathrobes and homemade biscuits. 2 have four-poster beds and most have views over the village, with its 12th-century church, and onwards to the glorious countryside. A large, deep open fireplace is the centrepiece of the relaxing lounge, a favourite with guests who enjoy a social chat and apèritif before relishing the imaginative cuisine served in the highly acclaimed dining room. Local attractions include the Wildfowl Trust at Slimbridge and the Roman Villa at Chedworth. Blenheim, Warwick, Cheltenham and Bath are within easy reach.

Our inspector loved: The newly decorated bedrooms – all beautifully done.

THREE CHOIRS VINEYARDS ESTATE

NEWENT, GLOUCESTERSHIRE GL18 1LS

Three choirs is a 70-acre vineyard in the heart of the Gloucestershire countryside, and a rising star in English wine making. New this year are 8 beautifully appointed bedrooms in an idyllic location perched high on the vine terraces overlooking the estate below. Each has a private patio that catches the evening sun – a perfect spot to sip a chilled glass of wine chosen from the day's tasting. Comfortable beds and invigorating power showers will ensure a good night's sleep and refreshing start to the next day's lesson in vine cultivation! The emphasis at Three Choirs is on informality and the local staff offer the warmest of welcomes and cater for your every need during your stay. A wide-ranging menu of delicious and beautifully presented food accompanies the wines with tempting dishes like tartlet of avocado pear, tomato and cured ham with single Gloucester cheese and spiced fillets of black bream with marinated vegetables and coriander cream, and there is a good choice of vegetarian dishes. In addition to the wine tasting tour and exhibition on site, there is the Three Choirs Music Festival and Eastnor Castle to visit, and golf and riding can all be arranged nearby.

Our inspector loved: *The beautiful views of the rolling vineyards from both the bedrooms and restaurant .*

Directions: From the A40 take B4215 to Newent. Follow brown heritage signs to vineyard.

Web: www.johansens.com/threechoirs
E-mail: ts@threechoirs.com
Tel: 0870 381 8946
International: +44 (0)1531 890223
Fax: 01531 890877

Price Guide:
single £75
double £95–£105

THE MILL AT GORDLETON

SILVER STREET, HORDLE, NR LYMINGTON, NEW FOREST, HAMPSHIRE SO41 6DJ

Directions: M27, junction 1. A337 south for 11 miles near Lymington after the railway bridge and mini roundabout turn sharp right before Toll House Inn, head towards Hordle and inn is on right after about 1½ miles.

Web: www.johansens.com/gordletonmill
E-mail: info@themillatgordleton.co.uk
Tel: 0870 381 8558
International: +44 (0)1590 682219
Fax: 01590 683073

Price Guide:
single from £85
double/Twin £125
suite from £150

Basingstoke

Winchester

Southampton

New Forest

Portsmouth

Lymington

Tucked away in the verdant countryside between the New Forest National Park and the sea lies this idyllic ivy-clad 17th-century rural hideaway. Immaculately restored to its former glory, yet boasting every modern convenience, the Mill at Gordleton, winner of Condé Nast Johansens Most Excellent Value for Money Award 2005, must now be considered one of the most tasteful of Hampshire's many fine inns. The landscaped gardens epitomise rustic charm, and visitors weary of their hectic urban lifestyles will surely find peace in the garden and mill pond with its charming sluice gates. The inn is no less immaculate inside. The intimate restaurant, overlooking the river and serving succulent fare, is simply a delight. Bedrooms are being refurbished in a most stylish way with quite delightful bathrooms. The New Forest has a wealth of places to visit and things to do right at its very heart; history, architecture, castles, museums, gardens, walking, riding, wagon rides, fishing, boating and of course wonderful wildlife attractions.

Our inspector loved: *Liz Cottingham's continuing enthusiasm for her lovely hotel. Lots of ducklings this year!*

THE NURSE'S COTTAGE

STATION ROAD, SWAY, LYMINGTON, NEW FOREST, HAMPSHIRE SO41 6BA

This remarkable little house is centrally situated in a quiet village on the southern edge of the New Forest. For 70 years home to Sway's successive District Nurses, it is now a 5-bedroom hotel. The level of visitor provision cannot fail to impress, and Chef/Proprietor Tony Barnfield's dedication to guests' comfort and enjoyment of their stay ensures an exceptional level of repeat visits. A worthy winner of the Best Breakfast in Britain Award, the hotel guarantees a good start to the day. At dinner Tony and his young team offer "British Classic" and "House Speciality" menu choices served with style in the conservatory restaurant, overlooking the garden. The award-winning wine list with over 60 bins puts much larger hotels to shame and surprises with many in half bottles and no less than 13 by the glass. All bedrooms are on the ground floor and have refrigerators housing complimentary fruit juices, mineral water and fresh milk. Fruit, biscuits and chocolates add to the pampered feeling. The sparkling bright and warm bathrooms offer a generous array of toiletries. Non-smoking throughout. Places of interest nearby include the National Motor Museum at Beaulieu, Rothschild's Exbury Gardens and the yachting town of Lymington.

Our inspector loved: Tony Barnfield's never failing enthusiasm, and his innovative provision for guests' comfort and enjoyment.

Directions: From M27 Jct1 take A337 to Brockenhurst and then B3055 signed to New Milton. The Nurse's Cottage is in the centre of Sway village close to shops.

Web: www.johansens.com/nursescottage
E-mail: nurses.cottage@lineone.net
Tel: 0870 381 8774
International: +44 (0)1590 683402

Price Guide: (including dinner)
single £80
double/twin £150–£170

LANGRISH HOUSE

LANGRISH, NEAR PETERSFIELD, HAMPSHIRE GU32 1RN

Directions: Follow the A272 from the M3/A31 at Winchester (16 miles) or from the A3 at Petersfield (3 miles). Langrish House is signposted from the village on the road to East Meon.

Web: www.johansens.com/langrishhouse
E-mail: frontdesk@langrishhouse.co.uk
Tel: 0870 381 8679
International: +44 (0)1730 266941
Fax: 01730 260543

Price Guide:
single £72–£90
double £104–£128
suite £130.50–£145

Standing in 12 acres of beautiful mature grounds including a picturesque lake, Langrish House combines the welcoming ambience of a traditional country house with the facilities expected from a modern hotel. Extended by the present owners' forbears in 1842, it opened as a hotel in 1979 and remains very much a family home, expertly run by Nigel and Robina Talbot-Ponsonby, whose family portraits and heirlooms adorn the rooms. Each of the 13 individually decorated bedrooms overlooks the grounds, giving guests ample opportunity to savour Langrish's peace and tranquillity. All are fully equipped with en-suite bathrooms, direct-dial telephones, colour televisions and many thoughtful touches. Frederick's Restaurant affords glorious views of the lawns and surrounding countryside. Fresh regional produce features in the superb cuisine, which has won the house AA recognition for fine dining. Langrish House is an ideal venue for wedding receptions and business conferences and offers dining facilities for up to 100 people. This is an excellent base for touring the Hampshire countryside: Gilbert White's Selbourne, Jane Austen's Chawton, Goodwood and Cowdray Park are all close by.

Our inspector loved: *The comforts offered at this fine family home - a country house in the true tradition.*

THE SWAN AT HAY

CHURCH STREET, HAY-ON-WYE, HEREFORDSHIRE HR3 5DQ

Nestling in a river valley at the foothills of the majestic Black Mountains is Hay-on-Wye, a charming market town that is home to The Swan at Hay. This delightful Grade II listed hotel was built in 1823 and is wonderfully welcoming; its glowing interior creates a homely and peaceful ambience perfectly suited to unwinding amidst spectacular natural surroundings. Each guest room is individually decorated and has an en suite. Fine food is prepared with care in the elegant Cygnet restaurant or an informal quick snack can be enjoyed in the Bistro Bar, which is comfortable and has a relaxed atmosphere. There are many interesting attractions nearby in Hay where guests will relish the chance to explore the medieval maze of streets and alleys that hide dozens of antiquarian bookshops and a craft centre. There are also castles and ruined abbeys in the vicinity and Hereford Cathedral displaying The Mappa Mundi and maintaining England's largest chained library. The pretty riverbank, a mere stroll away, is a lovely place to admire the large groups of graceful swans or do some leisurely salmon fishing. The hotel has a licence to carry out weddings and has fantastic, spacious rooms that feature original timber beams.

Our inspector loved: *The new contemporary and informal Mallard Room.*

Directions: Hay on Wye stands on the England Wales border, 1 mile south of the A. 438 road and midway between Hereford and Brecon. The Swan at Hay is found on the west side of the town centre, fronting the main road to Brecon.

Leominster

Hereford

Ross-on-Wye

Web: www.johansens.com/swanathay
E-mail: info@theswanathay.co.uk
Tel: 0870 381 8628
International: +44 (0)1497 821188
Fax: 01497 821424

Price Guide:
single £67.50–£82.50
double/twin £95–£140

NEW

AYLESTONE COURT

AYLESTONE HILL, HEREFORD, HEREFORDSHIRE HR1 1HS

Directions: Follow signs for Hereford City Centre and then for the railway station. once on Commercial Street pass over the railway bridge and Aylestone Court is immediately on the right at the foot of Aylestone Hill

Web: www.johansens.com/aylestonecourt
E-mail: enquiries@aylestonecourt.com
Tel: 0870 381 8641
International: +44 (0)1432 341891
Fax: 01432 267691

Price Guide:
single from £75
double from £95
family from £120

Leominster

Hereford

Ross-on-Wye

Aylestone Court, an attractive Georgian town house, has been restored and extended to create an elegant and attractive environment, combining original features with modern comforts. There are 9 non-smoking en-suite rooms, each individually designed and furnished with colour televisions and tea and coffee making facilities. Dinner can be taken in AC's Restaurant, which also provides a cosy, relaxing bar. Breakfast meetings can be arranged upon request, and morning coffee and lunch are also served. 2 delightful rooms are licensed for civil weddings and can hold a maximum of 50-60 people for buffets, whilst the walled garden and patio areas provide the perfect backdrop for photographs and entertaining guests. There are 2 conference areas suitable for training events, meetings, interviews and client hospitality, and the hotel is happy to arrange different packages and facilities to meet specific requirements. Aylestone Court is conveniently located for Hereford's town centre as well as its train station, local businesses and shops. There are many historic houses and castles nearby and 2,000 miles of footpaths, unspoilt countryside, thriving market towns and black and white timber framed villages.

Our inspector loved: *This lovely Georgian house with a real home-from-home ambience.*

NEW

Seven Ledbury

11 THE HOMEND, LEDBURY, HEREFORDSHIRE HR8 1BN

This historic 16th-century inn has been subject to a modern refurbishment and is now a lively, atmospheric bar and restaurant with a terrace for al fresco dining. Extensive menus offer simple, wholesome food made to order such as risottos, homemade fishcakes and tapas. Fresh, mostly organic produce is sourced locally particular attention is paid to the use of traditional rare brred meats and seasonal produce, a healthy options menu is also available. The three guest rooms offer excellent value for money and are tastefully appointed with modern bathrooms. Although furnished in a contemporary style they feature the original sloping floors, and each room includes high-speed Internet access, televisions, DVD players and complimentary spa products. Seven Ledbury is located in the centre of the market town of Ledbury, with a good selection of shops, and within easy reach of Herefordshire's beautiful countryside.

Our inspector loved: The contemporary style of the bedrooms.

Directions: Junction 2 / M50, follow signs to Ledbury town centre. Seven is located in the centre of town.

Web: www.johansens.com/sevenledbury
E-mail: jasonkay@btconnect.com
Tel: 0870 381 8653
International: +44 (0)1531 631317
Fax: 01531 630168

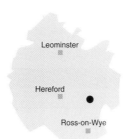

Price Guide:
single £65
double £85

THE VERZON

HEREFORD ROAD, TRUMPET, NR LEDBURY, HEREFORDSHIRE HR8 2PZ

Directions: 3 miles west of Ledbury on the A438.

Web: www.johansens.com/theverzon
E-mail: info@theverzon.co.uk
Tel: 0870 381 9348
International: +44 (0)1531 670381
Fax: 01531 670830

Price Guide:
single £70
double £80–£120
suite £120–£150

Leominster

Hereford

Ross-on-Wye

Conveniently located 3 miles west of the historic market town of Ledbury, this imposing Georgian country house dates back to 1790 and stands in over 4 acres of breathtaking rural countryside. New owners David and Gillian Pinchbeck took over the management in February 2004 and have since embarked on a programme of complete renovation with an emphasis on quality and comfort. The ambience is modern, yet welcoming and homely, and the friendly staff offer a personal, unobtrusive service. Guests can curl up with the paper on comfortable sofas in the lounge, which is warmed by an open fire on chilly days. The bedrooms, many of which have original fireplaces, have crisp white Egyptian percale sheets and luxurious goose down duvets and pamper guests with Molton Brown bath products. Guests can take a pre-dinner drink in the Mulberry Bar before sitting down to enjoy clean modern cuisine in the light and airy Terrace Brasserie. On sunny days the stunning new deck terrace with breathtaking views of the Malvern Hills provides the perfect setting for alfresco dining or a relaxing drink. The hotel is ideally located for exploring the cathedral cities of Hereford, Gloucester and Worcester, and is close to numerous areas of outstanding beauty. The Three Counties showground in Malvern is only a short drive away.

Our inspector loved: *The Kingston Black suite – stunning.*

FORD ABBEY

PUDLESTON, NR LEOMINSTER, HEREFORDSHIRE HR6 0RZ

Set deep in the Herefordshire countryside and surrounded by beautiful landscaped gardens, Ford Abbey stands in 320 acres of private, sheltered land. Modern luxury and comfort are combined with the traditional framework of this former Benedictine Abbey, which still maintains its original timber beams and weathered stone. Ford Abbey's 4 de luxe barn lodges are perfectly located for couples or families wishing to explore the surrounding countryside, which is the least developed in England, and the homely accommodation provides a welcoming base to return to. Each lodge has its own kitchen with every cooking and washing facility required together with cutlery, glass, tableware and linen. Alternatively, guests may stay in the main residence and enjoy bed and breakfast service. All bedrooms feature en-suite bathroom and the Abbott Suite has been specifically designed for guests with disabilities. Ford Abbey's restaurant serves fresh organic produce from Ford Abbey Farm and prides itself on the high standard of its food and fine collection of wines and malts on offer. The fitness room is situated opposite the lodges where a heated swimming pool enables guests to relax and unwind after a day's treck around the grounds or visit to one of the many nearby places of interest.

Our inspector loved: A stunning property in the most idyllic location – you will not want to leave.

Directions: Take the A49 towards Hereford then the A44 to Bromyard. Ford Abbey is signposted off to the left.

Web: www.johansens.com/fordabbey
E-mail: info@fordabbey.co.uk
Tel: 0870 381 9144
International: +44 (0)1568 760700
Fax: 01568 760264

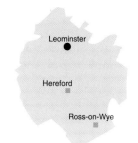

Price Guide:
double/twin £125–£180
suite from £180

91

MOCCAS COURT

MOCCAS, HEREFORDSHIRE HR2 9LH

Directions: Hereford Rail Station is approximately 10 miles away. Moccas Court is easily accessible from Birmingham, Cardiff and Bristol.

Web: www.johansens.com/moccas
E-mail: Bencmaster@btconnect.com
Tel: 0870 381 8406
International: +44 (0)1981 500 019
Fax: 01981 500 095

Price Guide:
double/twin £140-£195
dinner £35

This elegant Georgian Grade I listed building stands proudly amidst beautiful gardens, overlooking the River Wye. The house was built in 1780 by Sir George Cornewall and it has now passed to the current owners who have resided here for over 30 years. An ambience of intimacy and charm pervade the house. Each room displays family portraits and features magnificent furnishings in-keeping with the period of the house. Individually styled, the five en-suite bedrooms are spacious and offer views of the spectacular grounds. The Pleasure Ground Room, a popular choice with honeymooners, is the largest and looks out towards Moccas Deer Park and the river. Alternatively, there is the serenely decorated River Room overlooking the Wye, Brobury Scar and terraced gardens. Pre-dinner drinks may be taken in the library before adjourning to the extraordinarily beautiful Round Room for dinner; guests dine at a single table unless requested otherwise. Local lamb, beef and game can be sampled from the seasonal menu featuring impeccably cooked traditional, yet imaginative, cuisine. Moccas Court is the perfect backdrop for wedding receptions; up to 500 can be accommodated on the lawns. Please contact the hotel for a brochure.

Our inspector loved: *The beautiful rooms in this truly elegant, peaceful house. A real hidden gem - stunning!*

WILTON COURT HOTEL

WILTON, ROSS-ON-WYE, HEREFORDSHIRE HR9 6AQ

Offering abundant peace and tranquillity on the banks of the River Wye, this property is a true gem, surrounded by walled gardens with mature shrubs, sloping lawns and an enchanting river. Leaded windows and stone mullions are some of the many vestiges of the hotel's 15th-century origins. Affording a view of either the gardens or the river, the recently refurbished en-suite bedrooms are well-appointed, complete with hairdryer, alarm clock radio, tea and coffee making facilities, direct dial telephones and video teletext televisions. Guests may dine in the cosy bar, with its warm fire in winter, the light conservatory 2 rosette awarded Mulberry Restaurant with its view of the gardens or enjoy meals alfresco. The very best of fresh local produce is used wherever possible. Sports enthusiasts will be pleased with the local facilities which include canoeing, salmon fishing on the River Wye, horse riding, ballooning, tennis, cycling, bowling and golf. The hotel has ample car parking and is within walking distance from the bustling streets of Ross on Wye with its 16th-century market place. Tintern Abbey, The Malvern Hills, the Forest of Dean and The Cotswolds are some of the many areas that are worth exploring.

Our inspector loved: The beautifully decorated bedrooms and idyllic location overlooking the river.

Directions: From the M50, exit at junction 4 and turn into Ross at the junction of A40 and A49. Take the first right turning before the Wye River Bridge. The hotel is on the right facing the river.

Leominster

Hereford

Ross-on-Wye

Web: www.johansens.com/wiltoncourthotel
E-mail: info@wiltoncourthotel.com
Tel: 0870 381 9000
International: +44 (0)44 (0)1989 562569
Fax: +44 (0)1989 768460

Price Guide:
single £70–£110
double £90–£130
suite £120–£150

GLEWSTONE COURT

NEAR ROSS-ON-WYE, HEREFORDSHIRE HR9 6AW

Directions: From the M50, junction 4 follow the A40 signposted Monmouth. 1 mile past Wilton roundabout turn right to Glewstone. The Court is ½ mile on the left.

Web: www.johansens.com/glewstonecourt
E-mail: glewstone@aol.com
Tel: 0870 381 8556
International: +44 (0)1989 770367
Fax: 01989 770282

Price Guide: (closed for Christmas)
single £55-£75-£95
double £90-£110-£130

Glewstone Court is set in 3 acres of lawns and flower beds surrounded by orchards. Although secluded, this refreshing, unstuffy establishment is only 3 miles from Ross-on-Wye. Furnishings and the eclectic collection of antiques, bric-a-brac and works of art epitomise the relaxed, hospitable owners, Christine and Bill Reeve-Tucker. En-suite bedrooms are comfortable and individually decorated; each has a hospitality tray with delicious homemade biscuits, soft bathrobes, direct dial phone and colour television. A finalist for the Restaurant of the Year and Breakfast of the Year in the "Flavours of Herefordshire", Christine's food is innovative and prepared from good, fresh local ingredients; organic and free-range products are used whenever possible. Featuring modern and traditional British dishes, the cuisine is always created and served with care and attention to detail. Now, in their 21st year, accolades include an AA Rosette for cuisine and the AA Courtesy and Care Award. Herefordshire is marvellous walking country and there are many scenic routes to enjoy and explore by motor car. Alternatively, guests may relax by the log fires, or on fine days, recline in the garden. Places of interest nearby include Hay-on-Wye, the Welsh Marches, Hereford Cathedral, with the Mappa Mundi, and the Brecon Beacons. Bargain breaks are available all year except Bank Holidays and Cheltenham Gold Cup week.

Our inspector loved: *This place oozes character – relaxed and charming.*

REDCOATS FARMHOUSE HOTEL AND RESTAURANT

REDCOATS GREEN, NEAR HITCHIN, HERTFORDSHIRE SG4 7JR

Steeped in history dating back to 1450, Redcoats Farmhouse has retained its family ambience and offers warm and welcoming surrounds for guests in search of a traditional country house. The 12 individually-appointed bedrooms are bedecked with rich fabrics, chaise longues and chandeliers but those wishing to be pampered should opt for Bobbies Room, named after its former resident. The recently unveiled suite features a sitting room with all modern comforts and a sumptuous bathroom with walk-in shower and a Jacuzzi. Gastronomes will be delighted to discover the menus on offer in the dining rooms at Redcoats. The venue places a strong emphasis on its culinary offering and the à la carte menu features an array of seasonal choices including fresh native oysters, smoked haddock rarebit and rack of lamb. Brandy snaps, zabagliones and ice creams are all made at Redcoats but saving room for the cheeseboard is highly recommended. Conferences can be held on-site for up to 15 delegates whilst corporate awaydays with clay-pigeon shooting, archery and reverse steer driving can also be arranged. Hatfield House, Knebworth and Wimpole Hall are all nearby attractions worth exploring while the market town of Hitchin and the university appeal of Cambridge make ideal day trip options.

Our inspector loved: *Bobbies Room with its charming little story and the "wow" factor of the bathroom.*

Directions: Leave the A1(M) at junction 8 for Little Wymondley. At the mini-roundabout turn left. At the T-Junction turn right and the hotel is on the left.

Web: www.johansens.com/redcoatsfarmhouse
E-mail: sales@redcoats.co.uk
Tel: 0870 381 8851
International: +44 (0)1438 729500
Fax: 01438 723322

Stevenage   Stansted
Bishop's
Stortford
Hertford
St Albans

Price Guide: (weekend breaks available)
single £95–£115
double £111–£125
suite £145

THE WHITE HOUSE AND LION & LAMB BAR & RESTAURANT

SMITHS GREEN, DUNMOW ROAD, TAKELEY, BISHOP'S STORTFORD, HERTFORDSHIRE CM22 6NR

This delightful 15th-century Grade II listed country manor house is set amidst an acre of lovely gardens and offers first-class accommodation. Recently completely refurbished, all bedrooms have state-of-the-art bathrooms and double aspect windows adding a light and airy feeling to the very attractive and comfortable furnishings. A high-speed wireless Internet connection is available. First-class dining is available at The Lion & Lamb; free transport is offered for the 2-minute drive. Welcoming open fires in the traditional restaurant provide warmth on chilly days, whilst soft lighting and beautiful old blackened oak beams stretching across the ceiling create an intimate atmosphere. Service is professional but relaxed, with an emphasis on the high quality of the food, prepared with fresh ingredients and fish from Billingsgate, and accompanied by fine wines. There are numerous cosy eating areas and a most unusual country-style room with its own terrace and garden available for functions and meetings for up to 25 people. On sunny days the beer garden offers plenty of seating. The White House is conveniently close to Stansted Airport and within easy reach of East Anglia's many attractions. Cambridge and horse racing at Newmarket are also within easy driving distance.

Directions: Take the M11, junction 8 then the B1256 (originally the A120) in the direction of Takeley. The White House is about 1/4 mile beyond the traffic lights on the left-hand side.

Web: www.johansens.com/whitehousestansted
E-mail: info@whitehousestansted.co.uk
Tel: 0870 381 9334
International: +44 (0)1279 870257
Fax: 01279 870423

Price Guide:
single from £60
double from £75

Our inspector loved: The originality and ingenuity of the bathrooms.

NEW

WINTERBOURNE COUNTRY HOUSE

BONCHURCH VILLAGE ROAD, BONCHURCH, ISLE OF WIGHT PO38 1RQ

Winterbourne Country House has a historic literary claim to fame: Charles Dickens worked on his novel, "David Copperfield," whilst staying here in July 1849. It so impressed him that he wrote to his wife, "I have taken a most delightful and beautiful house – cool, airy, everything delicious – I think it is the prettiest place I ever saw in my life, at home or abroad." This sentiment is echoed by today's guests who find that although the house may have changed in usage and the accommodation and facilities improved over the years, it remains a place of great charm, character, elegance and style, with many of the original features that so entranced one of Britain's greatest writers. It is an ivy and rose-clad gem idyllically located in the most serene of settings close to one of the prettiest villages on the island. Enchanting lawned gardens ablaze with colour in season and contain a secluded swimming pool with sun terrace and a gently flowing stream, which lends to the tranquillity of those seeking nothing more than open-air relaxation. A private path from the garden leads to a shingle and sand beach. The 7 bedrooms, most with sea views, provide a high standard of comfort; there are 2 spacious lounges and the attractive dining room offers excellent cuisine.

Our inspector loved: The refinement and style. This new find will not disappoint.

Directions: From Newport take the A3020 to Shanklin via Rookley and Godshill. At Shanklin turn right at the first traffic lights towards Ventnor on the A3055. Bonchurch Village is signposted left immediately before Ventnor. Winterbourne Country House is on the right on this lane.

Web: www.johansens.com/winterbourne
E-mail: info@winterbournehouse.co.uk
Tel: 0870 381 8504
International: +44 (0)1983 852535

Price Guide:
single from £50
double/twin £90–£160

NEW

KOALA COTTAGE

CHURCH HOLLOW, GODSHILL, ISLE OF WIGHT PO38 3DR

Australian and English hosts Ric and Maggie Hilton provide a first-class service at this 5-star, award-winning hideaway. Guests staying 3 or more nights are presented with a complimentary gift pack of wine, roses and luxury chocolates. Each of the 3 de luxe suites has a private entrance, lounge and dining area and Victorian-style en-suite bathroom with cast iron roll-top bath and separate brass shower. The opulent décor in the bedrooms boasts king-size, superior half-tester beds dressed with plush damask drapes, French ornate furniture, chandeliers and provide fluffy robes, Sky TV, DVDs, CDs, books and games. Gourmet country breakfasts including free-range eggs, fresh baked crusty bread, locally produced preserves and old English kedgeree are served in the conservatory each morning. The spa and sauna villa offers a variety of health and beauty treatments ranging from Swedish body massage to luxury manicures and pedicures can be booked by prior arrangement. Situated in Godshill village, voted one of the prettiest villages in the UK, there are many scenic walks through breathtaking countryside and farms to visit, numerous tea gardens and gift shops, and the island's most historic church in its chocolate box surroundings. Exclusive personalised excursions such as champagne picnics can be arranged.

Directions: Take the ferry from Portsmouth, Lymington or Southampton to Fishbourne, Yarmouth, Ryde, East or West Cowes. Godshill is on the A3020 Newport to Shanklin Road. Church Hollow is opposite the Post Office.

Web: www.johansens.com/koalacottage
E-mail: info@koalacottage.co.uk
Tel: 0870 381 8503
International: +44 (0)1983 842031

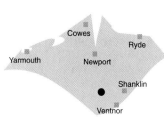

Price Guide:
double from £132
3/4 night breaks £199 per person

Our inspector loved: This unique find on the island. So dedicated to guests' comfort and enjoyment.

RYLSTONE MANOR

RYLSTONE GARDENS, SHANKLIN, ISLE OF WIGHT PO37 6RG

Carole and Michael Hailston are the new owners of this hidden gem uniquely located in 4½ acres of tranquil gardens on the fringe of Shanklin. Stunning views of Shanklin Bay are enjoyed from the manor gardens and a 2-minute walk through the gardens leads to the promenade and beach. An atmosphere of comfort and relaxation is engendered in the stylish day rooms where afternoon tea and a good book are just the thing on inclement days. The manor enjoys views of the lawns and well-tended flowerbeds and some rooms catch glimpses of the sea. Each bedroom is comfortably appointed and has en-suite facilities. The daily changing menu is served alongside a comprehensive wine list, which features worldwide and locally produced wine and after-dinner drinks may be taken in the bar lounge. Now open all year, this is a no-smoking hotel, no children under 16 are taken and dogs are not permitted. Rylstone Manor is a haven of peace in a delightfully protected environment. For the more active, water sports, fishing, riding and golf can all be arranged. In addition to being a walkers' paradise, the island has many other manor houses and gardens to visit. Nearby are the thatched cottages of Shanklin Old Village, Queen Victoria's Osborne House, Carisbrook Castle and Rylstone Gardens Countryside Centre.

Our inspector loved: *The new owners commitment to maintaining standards at this lovely house.*

Directions: Just off the A3055 Sandown to Ventnor road in Shanklin Old Village, follow signs directly into Rylstone Gardens.

Web: www.johansens.com/rylstonemanor
E-mail: mhailston@btinternet.com
Tel: 0870 381 8882
International: +44 (0)1983 862806
Fax: 01983 862806

Price Guide:
single from £52
double from £104
half board single from £69
double from £138

THE HAMBROUGH

HAMBROUGH ROAD, VENTNOR, ISLE OF WIGHT PO38 1SQ

Style is the hallmark of this delightful hotel situated high above the harbour, at the southern end of Ventnor Bay, with stunning views of the coastline, and at the rear, scenic views of St Boniface Down. Of the Hambrough's seven newly presented bedrooms with invitingly comfortable beds, two have splendid balconies upon which guests can relax and sip a cooling drink or evening aperitif whilst watching colourful yachts and the world drift by. The decor is minimalist throughout, the bedrooms and comfortable with flat screen TV's and DVD players - even an espresso machine. The bathrooms are a joy with underfloor heating and de luxe baths and showers. The relaxing bar is particularly welcoming for those who seek a morning coffee break, light lunch, afternoon tea, sundown cocktails or a nightcap after the superbly presented dinner. Executive Chef Craig Atchinson is a master of his craft, producing the most imaginative and inspired gourmet cuisine from the finest and freshest ingredients available from the market daily. Golf, sailing, riding and tennis can be arranged but for those preferring more sedate activities there are coastal and down walks or a peaceful, slow stroll through the calming Botanic Gardens to enjoy.

Directions: Take the ferry from Portsmouth, Lymington or Southampton to Fishbourne, Yarmouth, Ryde, East or West Cowes. Take A3054 to Newport then A3055 to Sandown, A5056 to Arreton/Sandown and B3327 to Ventnor. Hambrough Road overlooks the harbour at the southern end of the bay.

Web: www.johansens.com/thehambrough
E-mail: info@thehambrough.com
Tel: 0870 381 8658
International: +44 (0)1983 856333
Fax: 01983 857260

Price Guide:
single from £70
double £130–£200

Our inspector loved: The chic modern styling and stunning sea views.

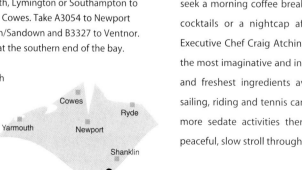

WALLETT'S COURT HOTEL & SPA

WEST CLIFFE, ST MARGARET'S-AT-CLIFFE, DOVER, KENT CT15 6EW

This listed Grade II house, recorded in The Domesday Book as "The Manor of Westcliffe", was transformed by the Oakley family, who discovered it in ruins in the late 70s. The result is a charming property, enveloped in a relaxing atmosphere and set in landscaped grounds near to The White Cliffs of Dover. The beautifully appointed bedrooms are comfortable and well-equipped with flat screen TV's and DVD's They are located in either the main house or barn conversions, the most recent of which also features an indoor swimming pool and leisure facilities. Fitness enthusiasts may use the steam room, sauna, spa pool, tennis courts and croquet lawn. The attractive restaurant, awarded 2 AA Rosettes, offers imaginative lunch and dinner menus. The dishes change every month to incorporate the fresh seasonal produce. Try the St Margaret's Bay lobster served with pilaff rice and roasted vegetables, Dover Sole Meuniere or Romney Marsh lamb. A proper spa, the hotel bottles its own water. Breakfast is another feast, with farm eggs, sausages made by the nearby butcher and homemade preserves.

Our inspector loved: This lovely old manor house set in beautiful Kentish countryside – an area of outstanding natural beauty – and a convenient drive to the port of Dover .

Directions: From A2 roundabout immediately north of Dover take A258 signposted Deal. After 1 mile turn right and the Court is on the right.

Web: www.johansens.com/wallettscourt
E-mail: wc@wallettscourt.com
Tel: 0870 381 8966
International: +44 (0)1304 852424
Fax: 01304 853430

Price Guide:
single from £109
double £129–£169

101

ROMNEY BAY HOUSE HOTEL

COAST ROAD, LITTLESTONE, NEW ROMNEY, KENT TN28 8QY

Winner of the Condé Nast Johansens Most Excellent Coastal Hotel in 2006, this spectacular house was built in the 1920s for the American actress and journalist, Hedda Hopper, by the distinguished architect, Sir Clough Williams-Ellis. The gracious drawing room overlooks the English Channel, panoramically surveyed through the telescope in the first-floor library. There is access to the beach, croquet lawn and golf course. A 5-minute drive to Lydd airport and you can fly to Le Touquet for lunch. Upstairs, designated non-smoking, the charming en-suite bedrooms are furnished with antiques. Wonderful cream teas can be enjoyed on the terrace in the sun-lit sea air. The chef-patron and his wife, both with London hotel/restaurant backgrounds, now offer an outstanding dining experience. There is so much history in Romney Marsh, renowned years ago for its smuggling. Caesar landed here in 55BC at Port Lympne and the famous Cinque Ports stretch along the coast. Canterbury Cathedral is within easy driving distance. Littlestone Golf Courses adjoin the hotel and windsurfing is popular. Less than 20 minutes' drive from the Channel Tunnel Terminal.

Directions: From New Romney head for the coast by Station Road leading to Littlestone Road – pass the miniature railway station – at the sea, turn left and follow signs for Romney Bay House for about a mile.

Web: www.johansens.com/romneybayhouse
Tel: 0870 381 8863
International: +44 (0)1797 364747
Fax: 01797 367156

Price Guide:
single from £60
double £85–£155

Our inspector loved: The welcoming and immaculate bedrooms together with the chef's excellent cooking. Golf and beach on the dooorstep.

LITTLE SILVER COUNTRY HOTEL

ASHFORD ROAD, ST MICHAELS, TENTERDEN, KENT TN30 6SP

Surrounded by mature gardens with raised rose beds, a pond and waterfall, this wood-framed, Tudor-style hotel is an unexpected find in the Weald of Kent. A combination of friendly, warm hospitality and service, traditional décor and a comfortable interior makes this an excellent choice for weekend or longer breaks and special occasions such as weddings and anniversaries. Peaceful conversation, social drinks or restful reading can be enjoyed in the beamed lounge where blazing log fires, at each end of the room, bring warmth and pleasure to a winter's day. Individually furnished guest rooms, some with fine views across the gardens, have every comfort. There are four-poster beds, Jacuzzi baths, a charming family room and a bridal suite. The Silver and Platinum suites offer extra luxury and feature a separate sitting room and Jacuzzi bathrooms. 2 guest rooms are particularly suitable for wheelchair users and boast mobility level 2. Sample succulent cuisine in the intimate restaurant and savour breakfast, morning coffee, lunch and afternoon tea in the Victorian conservatory. An especially attractive feature of the hotel is the octagonal hall with stained-glass windows, built to emulate a Kentish oast-house, which can accommodate up to 150 guests for a wedding or banquet. Nearby attractions include Leeds Castle, Canterbury and the medieval town of Rye.

Our inspector loved: The peaceful garden with its fish pool.

Directions: Exit the M20 at junction 9 and take the A28 to Tenterden.

Web: www.johansens.com/littlesilver
E-mail: enquiries@little-silver.co.uk
Tel: 0870 381 8424
International: +44 (0)1233 850321
Fax: 01233 850647

Price Guide:
single from £60
double/twin from £95
suites from £150

FERRARI'S RESTAURANT & HOTEL

THORNLEY, LONGRIDGE, PRESTON, LANCASHIRE PR3 2TB

Directions: Take the M6, junction 31a then the B6243 through Grimsargh to Longridge. Follow the signposts towards Chipping. Ferrari's is 100 yards past the Derby Arms on the left-hand side of the road.

Web: www.johansens.com/ferarris
E-mail: info@ferrariscountryhouse.co.uk
Tel: 0870 381 8459
International: +44 (0)1772 783148
Fax: 01772 786174

Price Guide:
single £45–£90
double/twin £60–£110

Set in 4½ acres of mature walled gardens, the impressive House as it was originally known was built by the Earl of Derby in 1830 as a shooting lodge, but today houses this family-owned and run Restaurant & Hotel. Susan and daughter Luisa oversee the kitchen and restaurant, which serves a combination of traditional English and Italian cooking, including such dishes as Insalata di Gamberi, Loin of Lamb Rosemary or Italian, Calamari Fritti and Sautéed pigs' Livers. Elsewhere members of the family are also very much in evidence, and the hotel and restaurant have been extensively refurbished. The comfortable bedrooms, standard through to de luxe, are individually styled, some have Jacuzzis and half-tester Tudor beds, and many feature antique furniture and garden views. As well as the main dining room there are 2 further function rooms, a fully licensed bar and resident's lounge, and while the Ferraris host numerous weddings each year they pride themselves on a personalised service, working together with each individual couple to provide the perfect day. Visitors to the area are spoilt for choice of places to visit, with the historic market town of Clitheroe and its famous Norman castle on the doorstep, as well as the natural beauty of rural Lancashire.

Our inspector loved: *The hospitality and friendliness at this family-run hotel.*

Springfield House Hotel

WHEEL LANE, PILLING, NEAR PRESTON PR3 6HL

Nestled in the glorious Fylde countryside this enchanting Georgian house is the perfect setting for relaxation. Resident owners Sara and Richard Coverley welcome guests into the warm, inviting ambience of their charming hotel, which was originally built as a family home for the young William Corless and his fiancé in 1840. Recent refurbishments have been sympathetic to the unique Georgian architecture, and is the ideal location for weddings, private functions and business meetings. Outside, 8 acres of grounds, encompassing meticulously manicured lawns and attractive walled gardens, provide a sensational backdrop for memorable photographs, while inside, 3 graciously furnished rooms seat 30, 100 or 150 buffet style. Each of the characteristic bedrooms has its own style, is embellished with fine linens and sumptuous fabrics and provides full private facilities for comfort and convenience. The restaurant menu is based on traditional British cuisine, prepared from the best local produce and served by hospitable, courteous staff. Visitors will find an abundance of activites in the area from exploring the old cobbled streets of Poulton-le-Fylde to Blackpool and its attractions which are 20 minutes away.

Directions: M6 junction 32. Onto the M55 junction 3 then on A585, then right onto A586 towards Fleetwood. Right on the A588 into Pilling the hotel is signposted on the left.

Web: www.johansens.com/springfieldhouse
E-mail: recep@springfieldhousehotel.co.uk
Tel: 0870 381 9213
International: +44 (0)1253 790301
Fax: 01253 790907

Price Guide:
single £55–£60
double £80–£90

Our inspector loved: This charming hotel in the Flyde countryside.

TREE TOPS COUNTRY HOUSE RESTAURANT & HOTEL

SOUTHPORT OLD ROAD, FORMBY, NR SOUTHPORT, MERSEYSIDE L37 0AB

Directions: From M6 take M57 to end of motorway follow signs for Bootle/Southport on A565. Bypass Formby on dual carriageway; as it changes to single carriageway, turn right at traffic lights to Tree Tops.

Web: www.johansens.com/treetopscountryhouse
E-mail: sales@treetopsformby.fsnet.co.uk
Tel: 0870 381 8950
International: +44 (0)1704 572430
Fax: 01704 573011

Price Guide:
single £63–£80
double £78–£110

The former Dower House of Formby Hall, Tree Tops, still retains the elegance of a bygone age, set in 5 acres of lawns and woods. Over the last 23 years, Lesley Winsland has restored the house to its true glory and has installed all the modern conveniences sought after by today's visitor. Spacious accommodation is available in well-appointed en-suite lodges with all the facilities a discerning guest would expect. An outdoor heated swimming pool has direct access to the sumptuously decorated Cocktail Lounge. Rich, dark leather seating, onyx-and-gilt tables and subtle lighting all contribute to the overall ambience, complemented by a truly welcoming and efficient staff. The restaurant and conservatory have been totally refurbished, cleverly incorporating some 21st-century ideas. A new menu offers a wonderful blend of traditional and modern, English and international cuisine. Table d'hôte, à la carte and lunchtime snacks are available, using only the freshest of local produce. Southport with its sweeping sands and famous Lord Street shopping centre is nearby. 10 golf courses including 6 championship courses are within a 5-mile radius.

Our inspector loved: *The light and airy restaurant with the modern international dining experience.*

THE INN AT WHITEWELL

FOREST OF BOWLAND, CLITHEROE, LANCASHIRE BB7 3AT

An art gallery and wine merchant all share the premises of this friendly, welcoming inn, the earliest parts of which date back to the 14th century. It was at one time inhabited by the Keeper of the "Forêt" – the Royal hunting ground, and nowadays it is not uncommon for shooting parties to stay or drop in for lunch. Set within grounds of 3 acres, the inn has a splendid outlook across the dramatically undulating Trough of Bowland. All bedrooms, including the luxury rooms in the coach house, have been attractively furnished with antiques and quality fabrics. All have hi-tech stereo systems with video or dvd players. The high-quality à la carte menu, created by head chef Jamie Cadman, features predominately English country recipes such as seasonal roast game, homemade puddings and farmhouse cheeses. Good bar meals and garden lunches are also offered. 8 miles of water is available to residents from the banks of the River Hodder, where brown trout, sea trout, salmon and grayling can be caught. Other sports can be arranged locally. Browsholme Hall and Clitheroe Castle are close by and across the river there are neolithic cave dwellings.

Our inspector loved: The new bar and terrace with spectacular views over the River Hodder.

Directions: From M6 take Jct32; follow A6 towards Garstang for 1/4 mile. Turn right at first traffic lights towards Longridge, then left at roundabout; follow signs to Whitewell and Trough of Bowland.

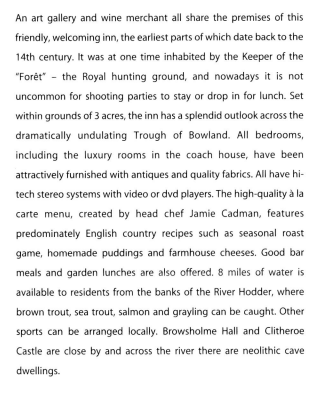

Web: www.johansens.com/innatwhitewell
E-mail: reception@innatwhitewell.com
Tel: 0870 381 8638
International: +44 (0)1200 448222
Fax: 01200 448298

Price Guide:
single £70–£94
double £96–£132
suite £118–£156

HORSE & TRUMPET

OLD GREEN, MEDBOURNE, NEAR MARKET HARBOROUGH, LEICESTERSHIRE LE16 8DX

Directions: Situated between Uppingham and Market Harborough.

Web: www.johansens.com/horseandtrumpet
E-mail: info@horseandtrumpet.com
Tel: 0870 381 9340
International: +44 (0)1858 565000
Fax: 01858 565551

Price Guide:
single £75
double £75

Set in the picturesque, traditional English village of Medbourne, fronting onto an immaculate bowling green, the Horse & Trumpet dates back to the 18th century. It has been lovingly restored and converted into a restaurant with rooms by Gill Pemberton and her team, and offers a relaxed atmosphere in peaceful surroundings. The Grade II listed main building has been built from local stone and the reconstructed roof is made from local straw thatch. In winter, guests can enjoy the blaze of an open fireplace in the main building. There are 4 superb en-suite bedrooms in the outbuildings, recycling many original features and materials such as an old saloon bar window that has been incorporated into the main door. An old iron bedstead forms part of the secluded rear courtyard's décor, which, on sunny days, provides the setting for alfresco dining. There are 3 attractive dining rooms. Chef Gary Magnani and his team create imaginative, modern British cuisine, which has been awarded 2 AA Rosettes, is the Highest Rated Restaurant in Leicestershire within the Good Food Guide 2005 and is the recipient of the special award for Best Newcomer. A multi-course tasting menu is available alongside the à la carte, complemented by individually matched wines. Private dining for parties of 8 - 32 can be accommodated.

Our inspector loved: *The huge mirror, complete with etched horse and trumpet in one of the dining rooms.*

SYSONBY KNOLL HOTEL

ASFORDBY ROAD, MELTON MOWBRAY, LEICESTERSHIRE LE13 0HP

Surrounded by 1.5 acres of Edwardian landscaped gardens overlooking the river Eye, on the edge of the attractive market town of Melton Mowbray, Sysonby Knoll has been owned and run by the same family since 1965. Originally a 6-bedroom house, it has been gradually transformed into the superb 30-bedroom hotel it is today. The original building houses the reception and lounge areas, decorated in period style, and forms part of a courtyard, with the bar, restaurant and conservatory overlooking the gardens and fields beyond. Furnished to a high standard, the bedrooms have en-suite facilities and all modern comforts; 9 are single, and the rest are either twin- or double-bedded. The 2 stunning four-poster rooms overlooking the gardens are ideal for a honeymoon or special break. A wide choice of menus is available in the restaurant, featuring excellent, freshly prepared food and fine wines from a comprehensive wine list. A 12-hole par 3 golf course is within 500m of the hotel, and Melton Mowbray has a golf club for those who prefer a more serious game. The hotel has a total of 5 acres of grounds with coarse fishing on the River Eye. Guests with pets are always welcome. Superb riding facilities are available nearby. The hotel is a 15-minute walk from the centre of Melton Mowbray with its 12th-century church and busy street markets on 3 days each week.

Our inspector loved: The warm welcome, and the imaginative menus.

Directions: From south: M1, jct 21a, follow A46, ignore A607. Turn off at Six Hills on A6006 (Melton). Or from A1 onto A606, go through Oakham and continue to Melton. From north: M1, jct 24, follow A6, turn onto A6006. Or from A1 take A607.

Burton-Upon-Trent

Melton Mowbray

Leicester

Hinckley

Web: www.johansens.com/sysonby
E-mail: reception@sysonby.com
Tel: 0870 381 9352
International: +44 (0)1664 563563
Fax: 01664 410364

Price Guide:
single from £64
double/twin from £77
four poster £110

BAILHOUSE HOTEL

34 BAILGATE, LINCOLN, LINCOLNSHIRE LN1 3AP

Directions: From the A1 take the A46 and follow signs to historic centre. At Bailgate go under the arch and the hotel is 200 yards on the right.

Web: www.johansens.com/bailhouse
E-mail: info@bailhouse.co.uk
Tel: 0870 381 9212
International: +44 (0)1522 520883
Fax: 01522 521829

Price Guide: (room only)
single £64.50-£125
double £79-£175
weekend breaks available

Scunthorpe
Louth
Lincoln
Grantham
Stamford

Dating from 1354 as a Baronial Hall, Bailhouse is a scheduled ancient monument that has evolved into a memorable hotel in Lincoln's Cathedral Quarter. Situated between the Norman Castle and second largest Cathedral in Britain, Bailhouse occupies a magnificent position in the heart of historic Lincoln. Surrounded by over 1,000 years of history, guests may stroll down Steep Hill to the modern and vibrant city centre. A thorough refurbishment has combined contemporary comfort with the charm and character of the building; well-worn flagstones in the entrance hall, beamed ceilings and an eclectic mix of antique and fine furnishings complement the magnificent architecture. The spacious, tranquil bedrooms enjoy views over the gardens, castle or Bailgate and are luxuriously decorated with opulent fabrics and four-poster or brass beds. Many rooms benefit from 42" plasma televisions and larger en-suite bathrooms with power showers. The attractive breakfast room doubles as a relaxed reading area. The many excellent restaurants on Bailgate are all within 2 minutes' walk. The secluded gardens feature a stone chapel and a number of self-catering cottages. This is an idyllic venue from which to explore Lincoln with the wolds, and horse racing at Market Rasen racecourse is a short drive away. A large secure car park is located within the gardens incorporating CCTV and electric gates.

Our inspector loved: *The wonderful surprises, and innovation.*

WASHINGBOROUGH HALL

CHURCH HILL, WASHINGBOROUGH, LINCOLN LN4 1BE

Washingborough Hall has been subject to an extensive refurbishment programme. With its solid stone walls, white framed windows and grand pillared entrance door, this listed Georgian manor house is one of the most attractive hotels in the county. Built circa 1700 as a private house, the first record of the owner here was that of George Fairfax, Rector of Washingborough, and his family. Secluded within 4 acres of wooded grounds and lawned gardens, 2 miles from the centre of historic Lincoln, this is an ideal retreat for those wishing to escape the bustle of everyday life. En-suite bedrooms are beautifully decorated and stylishly furnished; many offer superb views over the grounds. A spacious, delightfully decorated lounge is a comfortable and cool venue for summer guests seeking relaxation and, with its large York stone open fireplace, a warm, welcoming haven in winter for guests following a cheek-chilling walk. Mouth-watering cuisine is served in the superbly decorated dining room, which overlooks the gardens. Dishes are prepared from local produce by the talented Lincolnshire chef, Dan Wallis. Places of interest nearby include Lincoln's 11th-century cathedral and castle, the Aviation Heritage Centre, Lincolnshire Wolds and Horncastle, renowned for its selection of antique shops.

Our inspector loved: The peaceful and tranquil setting.

Directions: From Lincoln city centre drive down Broadgate and over Pelham Bridge. Take the B1188 towards Branston then left along the B1190 to Washingborough. In Washingborough turn right at the mini-roundabout along Church Hill. Washingborough Hall is on the left-hand side.

Web: www.johansens.com/washingboroughhall
E-mail: enquiries@washingboroughhall.com
Tel: 0870 381 8971
International: +44 (0)1522 790340
Fax: 01522 792936

Price Guide:
single from £70
double/twin from £95

THE CROWN HOTEL

ALL SAINTS PLACE, STAMFORD, LINCOLNSHIRE PE9 2AG

Directions: The town is signposted from the A1.

Web: www.johansens.com/crownstamford
E-mail: reservations@thecrownhotelstamford.co.uk
Tel: 0870 381 8464
International: +44 (0)1780 763136
Fax: 01780 756111

Price Guide:
single from £85
double from £100

Owned and managed by a lively and enthusiastic brother and sister team, The Crown Hotel has recently been transformed and upgraded. Situated in the heart of this attractive stone built town - a favourite with filmmakers searching for costume drama locations - all the traditional features, such as stone walls, beams and original floors, have been retained whilst the best of new technology is fitted throughout. Two new lounges are cosy and welcoming with extra comfortable seating and glowing open fires. Each of the airy bedrooms has been individually designed and features fresh, attractive fabrics; many afford charming views and original bathrooms. A Georgian townhouse is also available for letting. The cuisine makes best use of Lincolnshire's produce and is complemented by excellent wines and real ales. A new addition to The Crown's development is the purpose-built, self-contained conference and meeting suite. The beautiful Burghley House is on the edge of the town and Rutland Water and Peterborough Cathedral are nearby. The university city of Cambridge and horseracing at Huntingdon and Newmarket are an easy drive away.

Our inspector loved: *The genuine enthusiasm and thoughtfulness of all the staff, and the well-designed bedrooms and bathrooms.*

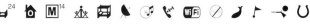

THE DOWER HOUSE HOTEL

MANOR ESTATE, WOODHALL SPA, LINCOLNSHIRE LN10 6PY

The Dower House Hotel is an elegant example of Edwardian architecture that has retained all of its period features yet has been sensitively modernised to include modern conveniences. Situated in a peaceful, secluded location adjacent to the first fairway on The Bracken Course at Woodhall Spa and surrounded by 2 acres of gardens and woodlands, this is an ideal venue for those wishing to unwind and forget the stresses of everyday living. The home-from-home atmosphere is enhanced by welcoming staff and meticulous attention to detail, and beautifully appointed bedrooms have every amenity and opulent en-suite bathrooms. Many rooms boast a walk-in power shower and some have direct access to the pretty gardens surrounding the hotel. The hotel's chef creates sumptuous dishes using the finest local ingredients in an intimate ambience, and a wide range of international wines, beers, spirits and liqueurs are served in the bar. A private room is available for small meetings and dinners. Guests may explore the woods surrounding the hotel, which are abundant in wildlife and overlook the beautiful courses of the English Golf Union's National Golf Centre. Woodhall Spa's shopping and museums are within walking distance and there are many castles and National Trust properties in the area.

Our inspector loved: The huge welcoming log fires, and the window seat under the impressive stained-glass windows depicting kings and queens.

Directions: From the central crossroads of Woodhall Spa, turn right onto Station Road and turn left into Spa Road. Turn right and The Dower House is located on the right-hand side of the private road off Manor Road.

Web: www.johansens.com/dowerhousehotel
E-mail: info@dowerhousehotel.co.uk
Tel: 0870 381 9214
International: +44 (0)1526 352588
Fax: 01526 352263

Price Guide:
single £75–£85
double £110–130
suite £150

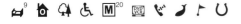

IDYLLIC COTTAGES AT VERE LODGE

SOUTH RAYNHAM, FAKENHAM, NORFOLK NR21 7HE

Directions: From Swaffham take the A1065 towards Fakenham. After 11 miles enter South Raynham. 100 yards past the village sign turn left and continue 400 yards.

Web: www.johansens.com/verelodge
E-mail: major@verelodge.co.uk
Tel: 0870 381 8961
International: +44 (0)1328 838261
Fax: 01328 838300

Price Guide: (excluding VAT)
£315–£1,488 per cottage

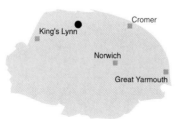

Quietly scattered amidst 8 acres of grounds, Vere Lodge offers a selection of spacious, comfortable and well-equipped self-catering cottages that suit any sized family. Some cottages have open fireplaces, their own private enclosed gardens and sunny patios while all offer microwaves, dishwashers, fridges and electrical appliances. A great deal of care has gone into making the cottages as homely as possible, with pictures and floral arrangements adding thoughtful finishing touches. There is a superb indoor leisure centre with a large heated swimming pool, sauna, solarium and games room, whilst the peaceful surroundings are a paradise for children. Each morning everybody gathers on the lawn for the animals' breakfast time, offering the opportunity to feed goats, donkey and pony, then throughout the day they can enjoy the toddlers' playground, croquet lawn, football area, tennis court and Enchanted Wood. Further afield the delightful, unspoilt landscape of Norfolk has much to offer with its beaches, innumerable castles and stately homes, bird and wildlife sanctuaries and racing at Fakenham. Upon returning to Vere Lodge, the availability of a frozen food service takes the stress out of the evening meal. Seasonal and short breaks are available.

Our inspector loved: *The beautiful away-from-it-all setting, and the excellent indoor leisure centre.*

THE KINGS HEAD HOTEL

GREAT BIRCHAM, KING'S LYNN, NORFOLK PE31 6RJ

Tall red brick chimneys and high, decorative gables are just two of the attractive exterior features of this white-faced, Grade II Listed Victorian hotel backing onto open fields in the heart of North Norfolk. Renovated, extended and refurbished to bring a touch of modern sophistication to the charming and tranquil Norfolk village of Great Bircham, it exudes a warm, comfortable, cosy ambience that guarantees a restful and relaxing stay. The décor and furniture are stylish and tasteful and the bedrooms are a delight: en suite, de luxe, spacious, individually designed and with every amenity to satisfy the most discerning visitor. The bathrooms, with handmade Norfolk toiletries, are particularly luxurious. The kitchen uses the freshest local ingredients to create innovative menus in the award-winning restaurant, which overlooks an attractive, sheltered courtyard that is an idyllic suntrap for summertime socialising and dining. Light meals and snacks are served in the contemporary-styled bar, alongside local and guest ales. A range of in-house health and beauty treatments can be arranged to order. The stately homes of Houghton Hall, Holkham Hall and Sandringham are within easy reach and for nature lovers there are bird sanctuaries and miles of unspoilt sandy beaches a short drive away.

Our inspector loved: *The thoughtfully designed interior, welcoming staff, and delicious cuisine.*

Directions: From King's Lynn take the A149 (towards Fakenham). Just after Hillington turn left onto the B1153 and continue to Great Bircham.

Web: www.johansens.com/kingsheadbircham
E-mail: welcome@the-kings-head-bircham.co.uk
Tel: 0870 381 9203
International: +44 (0)1485 578 265
Fax: 01485 578 635

Price Guide:
single £69.50–£125
double/twin £125–£200

THE GREAT ESCAPE HOLIDAY COMPANY

THE GRANARY, DOCKING, KINGS LYNN, NORFOLK PE31 8LY

The north-west Norfolk coast, sweeping towards the Wash consists mainly of a long stretch of sand and low cliffs, exposed saltings and tidal inlets. There are picturesque little harbours and villages, an abundance of birdlife and marshland stretching from King's Lynn westwards into Lincolnshire. It is a place of peace where one can believe that time stands still. Scattered along the coastline are a variety of unique and charming Great Escape holiday homes, all of which can help the visitor unwind from the pressures of everyday life. There are grand country houses, particularly attractive for corporate gatherings, charming and secluded little cottages, fascinating period houses and airy barn conversions. Some have large gardens leading down to the marshes, and boats are available for use. Others have a sunny patio, a studio or stables waiting for riding guests. The common denominator is the quality and style of décor, furnishings and service. After a personal welcome guests are provided with wine and the ingredients for a simple meal. White bed and bath linen together with first-class maid service ensure a perfect home-from-home environment. Daily staffing can be arranged. Ready to serve meal service and wine delivery. Short breaks are available.

Directions: All properties are within easy reach of A149 coast road. Directions will be supplied at time of booking.

Web: www.johansens.com/greatescape
E-mail: bookings@thegreatescapeholiday.co.uk
Tel: 0870 381 8568
International: +44 (0)1485 518717
Fax: 01485 518937

Price Guide:
£300–£3,000 per week
daily rates are available upon request

Our inspector loved: The charm and individuality of the properties, and the very personal service.

ELDERTON LODGE HOTEL & LANGTRY RESTAURANT

GUNTON PARK, THORPE MARKET, NEAR NORTH WALSHAM, NORFOLK NR11 8TZ

Ideal for those seeking a peaceful and comfortable retreat, within reach of lively Norwich City, this friendly environment is a relaxing haven surrounded by impressive views of private wooded grounds and 800 acres of deer parkland. Grade II listed, 18th century and built of local estate bricks faced with pebbles from the nearby coast, Elderton is less than 5 miles from the North Norfolk coastline and perfectly situated for visiting its numerous attractions. Formerly the shooting lodge to the adjacent Gunton Hall estate, Elderton was also a favoured retreat for Victorian beauty Lillie Langtry, who is said to have entertained Edward VII here when he was Prince of Wales. Each inviting bedroom, with modern bathroom or shower room, has been individually decorated and provides a TV and DVD player; a selection of complimentary films is available at reception. Pre-dinner drinks may be enjoyed in the lounge and bar before sampling the table d'hôte or particularly excellent value for money seasonal menu in the AA Rosette-awarded Langtry Restaurant, which is popular with guests and local residents alike. The cathedral city of Norwich, National Trust properties including Blickling and Felbrigg Halls and seaside towns of Sheringham and Cromer as well as the Norfolk Broads National Park are nearby.

Our inspector loved: *The overwhelming sense of peace and tranquillity, and beautiful views dotted with magnificent red deer.*

Directions: Leave Norwich on the B1150 and join the A149 towards Cromer. The hotel is on the left prior to entering Thorpe Market.

Web: www.johansens.com/eldertonlodge
E-mail: enquiries@eldertonlodge.co.uk
Tel: 0870 381 8502
International: +44 (0)1263 833547
Fax: 01263 834673

Price Guide:
single £65
double £100–£120

BEECHWOOD HOTEL

CROMER ROAD, NORTH WALSHAM, NORFOLK NR28 0HD

Directions: Leave Norwich on the B1150 and drive 13 miles to North Walsham. Pass under the railway bridge then turn left at the first traffic lights and right at the next set. The hotel is 150m on the left.

Web: www.johansens.com/beechwood
E-mail: enquiries@beechwood-hotel.co.uk
Tel: 0870 381 8353
International: +44 (0)1692 403231
Fax: 01692 407284

Price Guide:
single £75–£90
double £100–£160

Recipient of VisitBritain's Hotel of the Year 2003 for England, this elegant, spacious, ivy-clad house is surrounded by well laid-out gardens, dating back to 1800. For many years residents in North Walsham knew the hotel as the doctor's house; during these years an enviable society guest list was headed by Agatha Christie, a regular visitor during a 30-year period, and the Sheikh of Iraq. Individually decorated bedrooms are delightful, filled with traditional and antique furniture and feature magnificent large windows. The new Garden Wing comprises additional spacious and luxurious guest rooms, which boast Victorian-style bathrooms with freestanding "Mae West" style slipper bath. The comfortable garden lounge is well supplied with books and magazines and the lounge/bar is a relaxing haven. The exquisite "Ten-Mile Dinner" menu is served in the 2 AA Rosette awarded restaurant, which features locally reared meat and locally produced vegetables, prepared by head chef, Steven Norgate. When in season, expect to see Sheringham lobster, Cromer crab, Thornham oysters, mussels from Morston and even Norfolk cheese. One of the AA's Top 200 Hotels in Britain and Ireland and winner of the 1999 Johansens Most Excellent Value for Money Award.

Our inspector loved: *The very professional yet warm and personal welcome, and attention to detail.*

THE STOWER GRANGE

SCHOOL ROAD, DRAYTON, NORWICH, NORFOLK NR8 6EF

The Stower Grange, built of mellow Norfolk bricks under Dutch pantiles, dates back to the 17th century. In former times it was a gracious rectory. Today it offers travellers a peaceful retreat – the gardens have fine lawns with inviting shade provided by the mature trees – yet the property is only 4½ miles from the commercial and historic centre of Norwich. The Stower is owned by Richard and Jane Fannon; the atmosphere is friendly and informal and in cooler months open fires add to the welcome. There are 8 spacious individually decorated bedrooms with en-suite facilities, one with an exceptional oak four-poster bed for those in a romantic mood. The restaurant, locally renowned as a "special place" to dine, looks directly on to the gardens. The imaginative cooking of chef, David Kilmister, ensures good eating from the individually priced menus. The restaurant closes on Sunday evenings, however, residents can enjoy a steak and salad in the Lounge Bar. Places of interest nearby include Norwich, Norfolk Broads, various historic houses including Sandringham, the Norfolk Coast and horseracing at Fakenham. Seasonal breaks are available.

Our inspector loved: The warmth of the welcome, and the well-equipped and designed bedrooms.

Directions: From A11 turn left onto the inner ring road and proceed to the ASDA junction with A1067 Norwich–Fakenham Road. At approximately 2 miles to Drayton turn right at the Red Lion pub. After 80 yards bear left.

Web: www.johansens.com/stowergrange
E-mail: enquiries@stowergrange.co.uk
Tel: 0870 381 8921
International: +44 (0)1603 860210
Fax: 01603 860464

Price Guide:
single £70
double £90
suite £105

THE OLD RECTORY

103 YARMOUTH ROAD, NORWICH, NORFOLK NR7 OHF

Directions: Follow the A47 Norwich bypass towards Great Yarmouth. Take the A1042 exit and follow the road into Thorpe St Andrew. Bear left onto the A1242 and the hotel is approx 50 yards on the right after the first set of traffic lights.

Web: www.johansens.com/oldrectorynorwich
E-mail: enquiries@oldrectorynorwich.com
Tel: 0870 381 8784
International: +44 (0)1603 700772
Fax: 01603 300772

Price Guide: (special weekend rates available)
single from £78
double from £105
deluxe double from £125

Chris and Sally Entwistle extend a warm and hospitable welcome and the promise of fine personal service to guests at the Old Rectory. Dating back to 1754, their delightful Grade II listed Georgian home, clad with Wisteria and Virginia Creeper, stands in an acre of mature gardens on the outskirts of Norwich overlooking the Yare Valley. The spacious, individually furnished bedrooms, both in the hotel and the adjacent Victorian Coach House, offer quality, comfort and style. After a busy day, you can enjoy a pre-dinner drink in the elegant Drawing Room, enhanced by a roaring log fire during the winter and choose from a prix-fixe menu. The tempting 2 AA Rosette awarded menu is changed daily and is freshly prepared to order. The Wellingtonia Room and the Conservatory, overlooking the pool terrace and gardens, provide a unique venue for business meetings and private luncheons or dinners. Included in the top 200 by the AA and Johansens Most Excellent Service Award winner in 2001, The Old Rectory is the ideal base from which to explore the historic city of Norwich, the Norfolk Broads, the beautiful Broadland countryside and the Norfolk Coast. There is a self-catering 'Dowagers Cottage' in the hotel grounds available for longer stays.

Our inspector loved: *The friendly hospitality from Chris and Sally, and the very comfortable accommodation.*

THE NEPTUNE INN & RESTAURANT

85 OLD HUNSTANTON ROAD, OLD HUNSTANTON, NORFOLK PE36 6HZ

Recently acquired by new owners, this former 19th-century coaching inn has undergone a complete transformation to resemble a New England coastal property adorned with replica boats, black and white photography and attractive artwork. Situated along the picturesque North Norfolk coastline between Hunstanton and Cromer, bird and nature watchers and keen painters and photographers alike will revel in this location, amongst the most protected coastal areas in England. Each of the seven bedrooms is decorated in a minimalist style with clean lines and features white, handmade New England furniture. Every guest room is fitted with Internet access. Public rooms encourage relaxation with their mellow brown tones, displays of fresh flowers and inviting Lloyd Loom sofas and chairs. Seasonal cuisine is served in the restaurant where the talented young chef uses only the freshest local produce available. The typical American Sunday brunch must be sampled! While away the hours in the welcoming bar or simply relax in the lounge area. Nearby Holkham and Houghton feature a number of stately homes and the Queen's Norfolk retreat at Sandringham is close by.

Our inspector loved: *The warm welcome, and personal touches and beautiful linen in the bedrooms.*

Directions: From King's Lynn follow the A149.

Web: www.johansens.com/neptune
E-mail: reservations@theneptune.co.uk
Tel: 0870 381 9374
International: +44 (0)1485 532122
Fax: 01485 535314

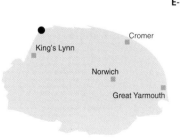

Price Guide:
single from £45
double from £70
seasonal offers available

BROVEY LAIR

CARBROOKE ROAD, OVINGTON, THETFORD, NORFOLK IP25 6SD

Self-indulgence and fabulous food combine to create an atmosphere of clandestine expectation at this superb restaurant with rooms. A relaxed lifestyle pervades Brovey Lair, which is reflected in the contemporary junior garden suites that have all the comforts and accessories of a 5-star hotel. The Café at Brovey Lair is a surprising Norfolk gastronomic gem described by Michelin as a "unique dining experience." The Good Food Guide recognises this tiny restaurant as a top destination in East Anglia daring its readers to "go with a sense of adventure," whilst Tatler's Restaurant Guide says, "plaudits pour in for Tina Pemberton's East-West fusion cooking." Dinner is a 4-course epicurean feast of exotic fish and seafood, flavoursome vegetarian soups and exquisite desserts. Chef-Patron Tina focuses on healthy ingredients and fusing spices and flavours from distant countries with fresh, local and Mediterranean produce. The original Californian/Mexican breakfast is a real treat with tropical fruit, spicy egg dishes and pancakes with sautéed bananas. On warm summer days guests may swim, have brunch on the terraces then sunbathe by the heated pool.

Directions: Allowing 2 hours from north London take the M11 to junction 9 then the A11 towards Norwich. Just north of Thetford turn left onto the A1075 towards Watton. Ovington is a right turn ½ mile north of Watton.

Web: www.johansens.com/broveylair
E-mail: thecafe@broveylair.com
Tel: 0870 381 8385
International: +44 (0)1953 882706

Price Guide:
rooms from £125

Our inspector loved: The owners' absolute passion for fabulous, intelligently sourced and innovative food.

THE GIN TRAP INN

6 HIGH STREET, RINGSTEAD, HUNSTANTON, NORFOLK PE36 5JU

This is the very epitome of a traditional country inn: wooden beams, timber, tiled floors and inglenook fireplace. A warm ambience is created by the impeccable staff in this former 17th-century coaching inn set in the sleepy village of Ringstead. There are just three bedrooms at this family-run Norfolk property and all are bedecked with pretty fabrics and two boast free-standing roll-top baths. Across the road, an original cart-shed and stable block have been transformed into self-catering cottages ideal for larger groups. Guests can enjoy a pint of real ale in the beamed bar before taking dinner in the cosy restaurant. Cuisine created from an abundance of North Norfolk coast produce features fresh oysters, mussels, samphire and fish in many of the seasonal dishes. The "Afters" menu is a must, offering indulgent but irresistible treats such as orange passion fruit tart with apricot compote and dark chocolate ice cream and accompanying liqueurs, malt whiskies, brandies or dessert wines. Afternoon distractions are plentiful and include browsing around Ringstead village, with its garden nursery and antiques shop, 2 nearby golf courses, horse-racing at Fakenham and exploring the beautiful coastline with its abundance of bird-watching and nature reserves.

Our inspector loved: The rolltop baths, the comfortable mix of old beams and chandeliers in the bedrooms, and the fine food - a lovely inn.

Directions: From King's Lynn take the A149. Just past Norfolk Lavender, Ringstead is signed to the right.

Web: www.johansens.com/gintrap
E-mail: gintrapinn@keme.co.uk
Tel: 0870 381 9376
International: +44 (0)1485 525264
Fax: 01485 525264

Cromer
King's Lynn
Norwich
Great Yarmouth

Price Guide:
single from £50
double from £80

BROOM HALL COUNTRY HOTEL

RICHMOND ROAD, SAHAM TONEY, THETFORD, NORFOLK IP25 7EX

Directions: From the roundabout, ½ mile north of Watton on the B1108 turn towards Saham Toney. The hotel is situated on the left-hand side after ½ mile.

Web: www.johansens.com/broomhall
E-mail: enquiries@broomhallhotel.co.uk
Tel: 0870 381 8384
International: +44 (0)1953 882125
Fax: 01953 885325

Price Guide:
single £65–£85
double £105–£160
seasonal breaks available

Cromer
King's Lynn
Norwich
Great Yarmouth

Situated in 15 acres of mature gardens and parkland Broom Hall is a charming Victorian country house offering peace and tranquillity. The airy and spacious bedrooms, most of which have lovely views, are individually furnished and provide guests with both comfort and a range of modern amenities. A feature of the public rooms are the ornate ceilings and in the lounge a large open fire can be enjoyed in the winter months. An indoor heated swimming pool is available for guests' use. Fresh vegetables, from Broom Hall's own garden when in season, and many old-fashioned desserts ensure that dinner, overseen by the head chef, in the dining room overlooking the garden is an enjoyable occasion. Small conferences can be arranged and the entire house can be "taken over" for your family reunion or celebration. Seasonal breaks are available. Places of interest nearby include Norwich, Cambridge, Ely and Bury St Edmunds. Sandringham and many National Trust properties, Thetford Forest, Norfolk Broads and coastline offering nature reserves and bird sanctuaries are also within easy reach.

Our inspector loved: *The lovely old fireplaces in the bedrooms and wonderful views from the huge bedroom windows.*

THE WINDMILL AT BADBY

MAIN STREET, BADBY, DAVENTRY, NORTHAMPTONSHIRE NN11 3AN

The Windmill at Badby was first established as an inn during the 17th century and is situated in the centre of the pretty village of Badby, the heart of renowned walking countryside where The Knightley Way, Fawsley Park and the ancient Badby Woods meet. The owners, with their extensive experience of hotel and pub management, have an abundance of innovative ideas and offer exclusive use of the property for house parties. An ideal weekend getaway, the hotel offers many programmes including environmental and nature conservation activities. Good food, alongside a range of cask-conditioned ales, is prepared under the skilled direction of Carl Fisher and Darren Hill in the award-winning kitchen. There is a varied range of homemade dishes on the menu, which includes an excellent value for money traditional Sunday luncheon. The finest and freshest local produce is used to create these delicious dishes; specialities include Stilton mushrooms, Gressingham duck breast and loin of lamb. A new exclusive training and meeting facility is now available, and small wedding receptions, birthday parties and functions are catered for in-house. Places to visit include Althorp House, Silverstone Grand Prix Circuit, Sulgrave Manor, Canons Ashby, Warwick and Stratford-upon-Avon.

Our inspector loved: *The delightful light and airy Henry Spencer bedroom in the Bluebell Cottage annexe.*

Directions: Situated in the centre of Badby, a village located off the A361, 2 miles south of Daventry on the Banbury road.

Web: www.johansens.com/windmillatbadby
E-mail: info@windmillinn-badby.com
Tel: 0870 381 9002
International: +44 (0)1327 702363
Fax: 01327 311521

Price Guide:
single £62.50
double £65–£79
family room £79.50

THE FALCON HOTEL

CASTLE ASHBY, NORTHAMPTONSHIRE NN7 1LF

Directions: Exit M1 junction 14 northbound or 15 southbound. Follow the signs to A428 where Castle Ashby and The Falcon are clearly signposted, 6 miles south-east of Northampton.

Web: www.johansens.com/falcon
E-mail: falcon.castleashby@oldenglishinns.co.uk
Tel: 0870 381 8512
International: +44 (0)1604 696200
Fax: 01604 696673

Price Guide:
single from £95
double/twin from £120
premier £139.50

Market Harborough

Northampton

Towcester

6 miles south of Northampton, in the heart of the Marquess of Northampton's estate, The Falcon, winner of Condé Nast Johansens Most Excellent Traditional Inn 2005, is a delightful country cottage hotel, secluded and tranquil, minutes away from the rambling acres of Castle Ashby House. The owners have invested energy and enthusiasm into transforming this once modest place into a haven of comfort, excellent food and attentive service. Bedrooms are beautifully furnished, cosy cottage style and the bathrooms have been recently upgraded. Lunch and dinner, which are created where possible from seasonal, home-grown produce, are served in the intimate restaurant which overlooks a lawn with willow trees. The cuisine, modern English in flavour,is excellent value-for-money. A fixed-price menu costs £27.50, there is also an interesting à la carte selection. The extensive wine list can be studied by guests at their leisure over pre-prandial drinks by a glowing log fire. Walk in the grounds of Castle Ashby estate. Further afield, visit Woburn, Althorp, Silverstone, Bedford and Stratford.

Our inspector loved: *The beautifully decorated rooms throughout and the warm welcome.*

THE NEW FRENCH PARTRIDGE

HORTON, NEAR NORTHAMPTON, NORTHAMPTONSHIRE NN7 2AP

This fine restaurant has been painstakingly restored by owners Tanya Banerjee and Ian Oakenfull from the former longstanding and well known French Partridge restaurant. Today, it boasts 2 going on 3, AA Rosettes, and attracts visitors from far and wide. Run as a place of hospitality since the late 1500s, it was extended in 1622 to create a traditional country manor and stands in the delightful Northamptonshire village of Horton. Its 10 en-suite bedrooms are individually and strikingly designed with luxurious bathrooms. All are equipped with high-speed, wireless free Internet connections. Several wonderfully furnished private meeting or dining rooms include the Horton and Gunning Rooms, and the newly created and surprisingly spacious Cellar Bar serves tapas. Outside, the grounds extend to 1½ acres, and there is a magical terrace garden where dining and drinks can be enjoyed in the summer. The New French Partridge is licensed for civil wedding ceremonies, and is happy to accommodate functions and business events. Northampton is 10 minutes away and Milton Keynes is a 15-minute journey.

Our inspector loved: The beautifully appointed bedrooms and bathrooms.

Directions: Situated south east of Northampton on the B526. Take the M1, junction 14 from the south. From the north take junction 15A or junction 15.

Market Harborough

Northampton

Towcester

Web: www.johansens.com/newfrenchpartridge
E-mail: info@newfrenchpartridge.co.uk
Tel: 0870 381 9201
International: +44 (0)1604 870033
Fax: 01604 870032

Price Guide:
double from £140

127

WAREN HOUSE HOTEL

WAREN MILL, BAMBURGH, NORTHUMBERLAND NE70 7EE

Directions: There are advance warning signs on the A1 both north and south. Take B1342 to Waren Mill. Hotel (floodlit at night) is on south-west corner of Budle Bay just 2 miles from Bamburgh.

Web: www.johansens.com/warenhouse
E-mail: enquiries@warenhousehotel.co.uk
Tel: 0870 381 8967
International: +44 (0)1668 214581
Fax: 01668 214484

Price Guide:
single £83–£122
double £113–£160
suite £153–£195

"To visit the North East and not to stay here, would be foolish indeed". So says one entry in a visitors book that is filled with generous and justified praise for this delightful traditional country house, which lives up to all its promises and expectations and beyond. The hotel is set in 6 acres of gardens and woodland on the edge of Budle Bay Bird Sanctuary overlooking Holy Island and 2 miles from the majestic Bamburgh Castle. The owners, Anita and Peter, do not cater for children under 14, so they are able to offer a rare commodity of peace and tranquillity even during the busy summer months. Throughout the hotel, the antique furnishings and the immaculate and well-chosen décor evoke a warm, friendly and charming ambience. Seated in the candle-lit dining room, surrounded by family pictures and portraits, guests can select dishes from the daily changing menu and wines from over 250 bins. There is a boardroom for executive meetings. Dogs by prior arrangement. Special short breaks available all year. The Farne Islands are just a boat trip away; Bamburgh, Alnwick and Dunstanburgh Castles and Holy Island are nearby. Waren House is open all year. Special breaks available.

Our inspector loved: *This delightful small hotel on the heritage coast overlooking Budle Bay.*

RESTAURANT SAT BAINS WITH ROOMS

LENTON LANE, TRENTSIDE, NOTTINGHAM, NOTTINGHAMSHIRE NG7 2SA

In a delightfully peaceful and secluded position on the banks of the River Trent, Restaurant Sat Bains is only 5 minutes from central Nottingham, 20 minutes from Nottingham East Midlands Airport and conveniently located for the M1. Michelin Star chef and Roux Scholar, Sat Bains, has introduced his unique characteristics and flavours to this completely refurbished boutique hotel. A former Victorian farmhouse, this attractive restaurant with rooms has received 3 Red Stars, 4 AA Rosettes in 2006/7 for its innovative and unique style of cooking and has just been awarded Restaurant of the Year in England by the AA Guide. The food is superb: evening meals such as roast scallop, slow-cooked belly of pork, peanut brittle and milk with Granny Smith apple and Anjou pigeon, melon, feta, mint, grapefruit and single estate chocolate will satisfy the most discerning diner. The extensive wine list comprises 120 bins, including many New World vintages. The 8 en-suite, luxurious bedrooms are individual and extremely comfortable. The Charles II room has a four poster, open fireplace and private patio. The Victorian room, which is open plan, boasts a king-size bed and a free standing slipper bath, whilst the Louis XV has walk-in wardrobes and lounge. The cookery school offers intensive 1-day courses explaining the techniques of taste, texture and temperature used in the kitchen.

Our inspector loved: The sheer excellence of the gastronomic delights.

Directions: M1/jct 24 then A453. Stay in the middle lane for the flyover then turn left at the roundabout, then left again. The hotel is then signposted.

Web: www.johansens.com/satbains
E-mail: info@restaurantsatbains.net
Tel: 0870 381 8351
International: +44 (0)115 986 6566
Fax: 0115 986 0343

Price Guide: (special accommodation and gastronomic packages available)
single from £114
double from £129
suite from £265

LANGAR HALL

LANGAR, NOTTINGHAMSHIRE NG13 9HG

Directions: Langar Hall is accessible via Bingham on the A52, or via Cropwell Bishop from the A46 (both signposted). The house adjoins the church and is hidden behind it.

Web: www.johansens.com/langarhall
E-mail: imogen@langarhall.com
Tel: 0870 381 8676
International: +44 (0)1949 860559
Fax: 01949 861045

Price Guide:
single £75–£110
double/twin £90–£210
suite £210

Worksop

Mansfield

Nottingham

Set in the Vale of Belvoir, mid-way between Nottingham and Grantham, Langar Hall is the family home of Imogen Skirving. It was built in 1837 on the site of a great historic house, the home of Admiral Lord Howe. It stands in quiet seclusion overlooking gardens, where sheep graze among the ancient trees in the park. Below the croquet lawn lies a romantic network of medieval fishponds stocked with carp. Epitomising "excellence and diversity", Langar Hall combines the standards of good hotel-keeping with the hospitality and style of country house living. The popular neighbourhood restaurant serves English dishes of local meat, poultry, game, fish and shell fish with garden vegetables in season. The en-suite bedrooms are individually designed and comfortably appointed, whilst the public rooms feature fine furnishings and most rooms afford beautiful views of the garden, park and moat. Langar Hall is an ideal venue for small boardroom meetings. It is also an ideal base from which to visit Belvoir Castle, see cricket at Trent Bridge, visit students at Nottingham University and to see Robin Hood's Sherwood Forest. Dogs can be accommodated by arrangement.

Our inspector loved: The Old World charm, the traquillity, and the imaginative food.

COCKLIFFE COUNTRY HOUSE HOTEL

BURNT STUMP COUNTRY PARK, BURNT STUMP HILL, NOTTINGHAMSHIRE NG5 8PQ

This is Robin Hood country and Cockliffe is situated in the heart of it, 6 miles north of Nottingham. A lovely, unusually designed 17th-century house with turreted-style corners it stands in 3 acres of colourful, mature gardens adjacent to the open spaces of Burnt Stump Country Park. Dane and Jane Clarke rescued the house from disrepair 12 years ago and are proud of their renovations and refurbishments, many of which are in keeping with original features. Décor and furnishings throughout are elegant and tasteful and most rooms afford splendid views over the garden. The 11 bedrooms are individually designed and comfortably appointed to reflect the needs of discerning guests. Most are Jacuzzi en-suite, with thoughtful touches, period furniture and adorned with beautiful curtain fabrics carefully chosen by Jane Clarke. The brasserie and fine dining restaurant produce excellent and imaginative menus using local produce and game when in season. The adjoining cocktail bar is popular with guests for pre-meal drinks and after dinner coffee. A conference room with high-tech facilities is available. Golf, fishing, riding and fitness and leisure can be arranged locally. Places of interest nearby include Nottingham and its castle, Sherwood Forest, 12th-century Newstead Abbey and Southwell Minster with its medieval carvings, the earliest of their kind in England.

Our inspector loved: The striking new brasserie.

Directions: Exit the M1 at junction 26 and take the A60 north from Nottingham towards Mansfield, passing through Arnold. At the Seven Mile pub turn right then right again at the top of the hill into a hidden turning. The hotel is ½mile on the left.

Web: www.johansens.com/cockliffe
E-mail: enquiries@cockliffehouse.co.uk
Tel: 0870 381 8435
International: +44 (0)1159 680179
Fax: 01159 680623

Price Guide:
single from £75
double £95–£150

131

NEW

BURFORD LODGE HOTEL & RESTAURANT

OXFORD ROAD, BURFORD, OXFORDSHIRE OX18 4PH

Directions: Burford Lodge Hotel is located at the gateway to the Cotswolds on the A40, halfway between Oxford and Cheltenham near the attractive town of Burford. Adjacent to Burford Golf Club.

Web: www.johansens.com/burfordlodge
E-mail: info@burfordlodge.com
Tel: 0870 381 8473
International: +44 (0)1993 823354

Price Guide:
single £95
double/twin £115
suite £135

Banbury
● Oxford
Henley-on-Thames

This impressive hotel and restaurant recently opened its doors following a major refurbishment programme. The warm welcome that greets guests is indicative of the standards that the hotel offers. Owners Graham and Paula Cox have taken great care with the redesign and Burford Lodge is now a hotel for the third millennium, providing an ideal place to stay for relaxing weekends, family breaks and business meetings. The bedrooms are individually decorated in a traditional style and feature antique pieces along with every modern amenity discerning guests have come to expect, from power showers to Internet access. Behind the elegant façade, cabling has been installed for a range of high-tech business equipment, including WiFi. The stylish boardroom can cater for meetings, private dining and conferences, whilst the restaurant serves a delicious seasonal menu with a European influence using fresh, local produce. Children (as well as chocoholics) will love the chocolate fountain and there is always a good selection of fresh fish on the menu delivered daily from Brixham. All-day Sunday roasts are becoming increasingly popular. Burford is a delightful village with many antique and craft shops, and this is an ideal base for guests wishing to travel to either Oxford or Cheltenham, visit local attractions or play a round of golf at the prestigious Burford Golf Course.

Our inspector loved: This eclectic hotel with its friendly welcome.

NEW

THE LAMB INN

SHEEP STREET, BURFORD, OXFORDSHIRE OX18 4LR

The Lamb Inn, set in a quiet location in the small Cotswold town of Burford, is everyone's idea of the archetypal English inn. In a peaceful setting within a pretty walled garden guests step inside and instantly recapture something of the 14th-century spirit. Flagged floors, gleaming copper, brass and silver reflect the flicker of log fires and the well-chosen antiques all enhance the sense of history. The attractive bar area with sumptuous sofas, large chairs and log fires serves a daily changing bar menu. The speciality is fresh fish, whilst the 2 AA Rosette-awarded, more formal yet appealing restaurant, offers a wider selection complemented by superb wines. In the summer, guests can dine al fresco in the tranquil walled gardens. The bedrooms provide comfortable accommodation with oak beams, chintz curtains and antique furniture. Located near the heart of the town guests can browse through antiques shops or laze by the waters of the River Windrush. Burford is within easy reach of Oxford, Cheltenham, Stow-on-the-Wold and the many attractive Cotswold villages.

Our inspector loved: *This lovely old atmospheric inn, which is chocker-block with character!*

Directions: Sheep Street is off the main street in Burford. Burford is 20 miles west of Oxford.

Web: www.johansens.com/lambinnburford
E-mail: info@lambinn-burford.co.uk
Tel: 0870 381 8674
International: +44 (0)1993 823155
Fax: +44 (0)1993 822228

Price Guide:
double £145
four poster £175

133

THE PLOUGH HOTEL, GAME & SEAFOOD RESTAURANT

BOURTON ROAD, CLANFIELD, OXFORDSHIRE OX18 2RB

Directions: The hotel is located at the junction of the A4095 and B4020 between the towns of Witney and Faringdon, some 15 miles west of Oxford.

Web: www.johansens.com/ploughatclanfield
E-mail: bookings@theploughclanfield.co.uk
Tel: 0870 381 8826
International: +44 (0)1367 810222
Fax: 01367 810596

Price Guide:
single £50–£95
double £85–£175
suite £150–£250

Banbury

Oxford

Henley-on-Thames

With its mellow stone walls decorated by climbing ivy, triple roof peaks, slim, leaded windows and pretty lawned garden, The Plough lives up to every perception of a typical English country house. Situated on the edge of the village of Clanfield, it is a classic Cotswold manor dating from 1560 and an excellent example of well-preserved Elizabethan architecture. New owners Martin and Chrissie Agius have taken great care in preserving the charm and character of this ancient building whilst at the same time have added some contemporary features. The award-winning restaurant is renowned throughout the region for superbly prepared and impeccably served game and seafood cuisine. In summer it spills out onto the front terrace and lawn for those who enjoy light meals, coffee, tea and cool drinks in open-air surrounds. 2 dining rooms and a cosy bar, complete with sofas and open fire, are ideal for entertaining, celebrating or socialising with family, friends or business colleagues. The bedrooms, some new, some old, are beautifully appointed and offer little extras such as a decanter of sherry and waffle bathrobes. The Plough is a convenient base for touring the Cotswolds, Bath and Oxford. There are many historic houses and gardens in the area, lovely riverside walks and racing at Newbury and Cheltenham.

Our inspector loved: *The feeling of satisfaction upon entering this cosy yet stylish hotel.*

FALLOWFIELDS

KINGSTON BAGPUIZE WITH SOUTHMOOR, OXON OX13 5BH

Fallowfields, home to Begum Aga Khan, dates back more than 300 years. Updated and extended throughout the decades, this is an extremely comfortable, welcoming and spacious country house hotel brimming with character. Set in 2 acres of tranquil, pretty gardens and surrounded by 10 acres of grassland, Oxford is easily accessible, 10 miles away. Each of the guest rooms is large and traditionally decorated, some with four-poster or coroneted beds. The drawing room and bar are elegant and relaxing, and even cosier in winter months with crackling log fires. The light and airy restaurant and patio, recipient of 3 RAC dining awards, has a fresh and varied menu, and lends itself to many occasions such as a romantic evening, celebration, weekend treat or important business dinner. The library is also available for private dining. The peaceful ambience of the hotel also provides an ideal environment for high-level strategy and senior management retreats. With its convenient proximity to Oxford, the A34 and M40, Fallowfields is an excellent base for the corporate guest visiting the area or a perfect location for leisure guests wishing to explore the many cultural attractions and outdoor pursuits nearby such as theatres, stately homes and glorious walks along the Thames Path or Vale of the White Horse.

Our inspector loved: *The house, gardens and owners are a complete delight*

Directions: Take the Kingston Bagpuize exit on the A420 Oxford to Swindon. Fallowfields is at the west end of Southmoor, just after the Longworth sign.

Web: www.johansens.com/fallowfields
E-mail: stay@fallowfields.com
Tel: 0870 381 8513
International: +44 (0)1865 820416
Fax: 01865 821275

Price Guide:
single £95–£145
double £120–£170

THE DASHWOOD HOTEL & RESTAURANT

SOUTH GREEN, HEYFORD ROAD, KIRTLINGTON, OXFORDSHIRE OX5 3HJ

Owners Ros and Martin Lewis and family have spared no expense in creating and refurbishing this attractive hotel and restaurant and should be applauded for bringing something rather special to the area. A Grade II Listed building, The Dashwood stands in the village of Kirtlington, just 20 minutes' drive from the centre of Oxford. Behind the hotel's attractive façade is a luxurious interior of historic charm and contemporary elegance. The 12 guest rooms, each with their own character, are beautifully decorated and presented, furnished with hand-made oak furniture and certainly providing every comfort. The emphasis is on attention to detail with exclusive toiletries in opulent bathrooms, ultra comfortable beds, slimline LCD televisions and broadband Internet access. Attractive extras are the wall artworks created by Rebecca Lewis, the daughter of the family. The bar with its deep leather sofas is a cosy delight and the oak-beamed restaurant an experience to savour. It is laid out in a contemporary style with an open-plan kitchen, which allows diners to see chef Marcel Taylor and his talented team at work. All dishes on the regularly changing menus are thoughtfully prepared with a focus on simplicity and freshness. Blenheim Palace, Bicester, Stratford and Warwick are within easy reach as is London.

Directions: From M40 junctions 9 or 10 follow signs to Kirtlington. The hotel is in the centre of the village.

Web: www.johansens.com/dashwood
E-mail: info@thedashwood.co.uk
Tel: 0870 381 8378
International: +44 (0)1869 352707
Fax: 01869 351432

Price Guide:
single £85–£120
double £110–£150
suite £120–£150

Banbury

Oxford

Henley-on-Thames

Our inspector loved: The care and attention put into creating this exceptionally pleasing hotel and restaurant.

THE JERSEY ARMS

MIDDLETON STONEY, BICESTER, OXFORDSHIRE OX25 4AD

The Jersey Arms occupies a site rich in history. As far back as 1241, the inn was listed as providing William Longsword "for 25 men of Middleton, necessaries as food and drink." It thrived in the days of coach-and-horse long-distance travel and in 1823 was a key posting house for cross-country traffic. Today, The Jersey Arms has been honed into a retreat of comfort by Donald and Helen Livingston, the third owners in 700 years. An informal, inviting ambience has been created, and old beams, antique flintlocks and homely furnishings decorate the rooms. Bedrooms, all with private access, vary in size, and blend the charm of the past with more up-to-date décor. You can request the suite in the converted old Blacksmith's shop situated through the secluded and sunny courtyard; this spacious suite still retains its original smithy's chimney. The tempting and imaginative menu in Livingstone's bar or restaurant uses local ingredients to suit all tastes and can accommodate various formal or informal occasions. Located in a rural village location, Oxford, Woodstock, Blenheim Palace and major motorway networks are all accessible. The Jersey Arms is ideal for a brief stopover to explore the area, take lunch or spend an evening with friends. Meetings catering up to 20 can be arranged.

Our inspector loved: The cosy bar and informal restaurant.

Directions: Between jct 9 and 10 of the M40 on the B430, 10 miles north of Oxford. From jct 9 take the Oxford Road. Middleton Stoney is signposted 1 mile further on. From jct 10 Middleton Stoney is signposted once past the slip road.

Web: www.johansens.com/jerseyarms
E-mail: jerseyarms@bestwestern.co.uk
Tel: 0870 381 8644
International: +44 (0)1869 343234
Fax: 01869 343565

Price Guide:
single from £85
double from £98
suite from £125

THE KINGS HEAD INN & RESTAURANT

THE GREEN, BLEDINGTON, NR KINGHAM, OXFORDSHIRE OX7 6XQ

Directions: Take the A44 Oxford–Woodstock road to Chipping Norton, then the B4450 to Bledington; or take the Oxford–Burford road to Stow-on-the-Wold and join the B4450. Nearest motorway M40 junction 11 (north) junction 9 (south).

Web: www.johansens.com/kingshead
E-mail: kingshead@orr-ewing.com
Tel: 0870 381 8654
International: +44 (0)1608 658365
Fax: 01608 658902

Price Guide:
double £75–£100
four-poster £120

The attractively situated, Kings Head Inn and Restaurant is peacefully located beside a traditional village green, complete with a bubbling brook inhabited by friendly ducks. During the summer months, Morris dancers and musicians can regularly be seen in action on the green performing the Bledington Dances. The building has always served as a hostelry and much of its historical character remains. With its exposed stone walls, original beams, inglenook fireplace and old settles, the Kings Head fulfils everyone's anticipations of a traditional English inn. The bedrooms which are in the inn or set around the cottage courtyard are comfortable and cosy. The carefully compiled menu is changed regularly and is backed up by a selection of fine wines. Excellent inventive bar food is served at lunchtime and in the evenings together with a changing selection of real ales. Traditional Sunday lunch is also served. The Kings Head Inn is situated in the heart of the Cotswolds, within easy reach of Oxford, Stratford-upon-Avon, Cheltenham and Blenheim. It is an ideal base for exploring the area or for a country weekend break.

Our inspector loved: *This lovely old traditional inn - full of character.*

THE SPREAD EAGLE HOTEL

CORNMARKET, THAME, OXFORDSHIRE OX9 2BW

The historic market town of Thame with its mile-long main street is a delightful town just 6 miles from the M40 and surrounded by beautiful countryside speckled with tiny, charming villages, many of them with cosy thatched cottages. The Spread Eagle has stood tall, square and in the heart of Thame since the 16th century and over the years has played host to Charles II, French prisoners from the Napoleonic wars, famous politicians and writers such as Evelyn Waugh. The former proprietor John Fothergill introduced haute cuisine to the provinces and chronicled his experiences in the best seller, "An Innkeeper's Diary". The book is still available at The Spread Eagle and the brasserie is named after him. It serves tasty English and French cuisine made with the freshest local produce including Oxfordshire beef. Guests have 33 traditional bedrooms to choose from, comprising 2 suites, 23 doubles, 3 twins and 5 singles. All are en-suite and in the style expected of an old coaching inn hotel. Conference, banqueting and meeting facilities are available in a self contained suite which is also suitable for weddings. The hotel has a large car park at the rear. The Spread Eagle is ideally situated for visits to many fascinating historic places such as Blenheim Palace and Waddesdon Manor.

Our inspector loved: Stepping back in time in this historic coaching inn.

Directions: Exit M40 at junction 6. Take B4009 to Chinnor and then B4445 to Thame. The hotel is on the left after the roundabout at the west end of Upper High Street. To reach car park, turn into Rooks lane at rounabout, turn right at end. Car park can be found on the right hand side.

Banbury

Oxford

Henley-on-Thames

Web: www.johansens.com/spreadeaglethame
E-mail: events.spreadeaglehotel@virgin.net
Tel: 0870 381 8902
International: +44 (0)1844 213661
Fax: 01844 261380

Price Guide:
single from £98
double/twin from £115

DUKE OF MARLBOROUGH COUNTRY INN

WOODLEYS, WOODSTOCK, OXFORD OX20 1HT

This friendly, traditional British inn is just a few minutes from the bustling town of Woodstock, and a short drive away from the university city of Oxford. Its hotel accommodation is situated in a separate rustic building, designed in keeping with the rural setting and is as ideal as a base for exploring the area, a stopover or for a corporate stay. The 13 en-suite rooms are spacious, comfortably furnished and warmly lit, with a range of facilities. Priding itself on its levels of service and hospitality, the Duke of Marlborough serves thoughtfully prepared seasonal dishes in its restaurant and the menus make good use of locally sourced produce. A section of the menu offers chefs special – wholesome steaks with a choice of delicious sauces whilst other considerations include fish, vegetarian options and a childrens menu. Visitors are also warmly welcomed into the bar, and can enjoy an extensive wine list and collection of real ales. The beer garden and patio provides a safe and secure area for youngsters when the weather is fine. Nearby Blenheim Palace, the birthplace of Winston Churchill, is well worth a visit, as are Woodstock itself, Oxford and the glorious Cotswolds.

Directions: The inn is mid-way between Oxford and Chipping Norton, and is situated on the main A44 road, north of Woodstock just past the garage.

Web: www.johansens.com/dukeofmarlborough
E-mail: sales@dukeofmarlborough.co.uk
Tel: 0870 381 9219
International: +44 (0)1993 811460
Fax: 01993 810165

Price Guide:
single £65
double/twin £85–£110

Banbury

Oxford

Henley-on-Thames

Our inspector loved: The friendly staff, large open bar and convenient location.

THE FEATHERS

MARKET STREET, WOODSTOCK, OXFORDSHIRE OX20 1SX

A 17th-century country town house, The Feathers is an independently owned and managed hotel in the heart of historical Woodstock, a few miles from central Oxford and a few minutes' walk from Blenheim Palace. Woodstock is one of England's most attractive country towns built mostly in Cotswold stone and dates back to the 12th century. Antiques, log fires and traditional English furnishings lend character, comfort and charm in winter whilst the courtyard garden offers a secluded, delightful and relaxed setting for al fresco dining during the summer months where guests can enjoy a light lunch, afternoon tea or simply indulge in a glass of champagne. Beauty treatments and revitalizing massages are available at Preen, The Feathers' beauty suite, and the Drawing Room is the perfect setting for a boardroom meeting or private dining. The Study and the Bistro are intimate and comfortable public rooms. Awarded AA Rosettes, the antique panelled restaurant is internationally renowned for its fine cuisine and is complemented by a high standard of service. The regularly changing menu offers a variety of dishes created from the finest local and seasonal produce. Ideally situated for exploring Blenheim Palace, the Cotswolds and the Spires of Oxford. Exclusive use of the hotel, special offers and weekend breaks are available throughout the year.

Our inspector loved: The character and charm of this lovely old hotel.

Directions: From London leave the M40 at junction 8. From Birmingham leave at junction 9. Take the A44 and follow signs to Woodstock. The hotel is on the left.

Web: www.johansens.com/feathers
E-mail: enquiries@feathers.co.uk
Tel: 0870 381 8519
International: +44 (0)1993 812291
Fax: 01993 813158

Price Guide:
single £99–£199
double/twin £145–£195
suite £225–£275

BARNSDALE LODGE

THE AVENUE, RUTLAND WATER, NEAR OAKHAM, RUTLAND LE15 8AH

Directions: The Lodge is on A606 Oakham–Stamford road.

Web: www.johansens.com/barnsdalelodge
E-mail: enquiries@barnsdalelodge.co.uk
Tel: 0870 381 8342
International: +44 (0)1572 724678
Fax: 01572 724961

Price Guide:
single £70–£80
double/twin £80–£110
superior £100–£130

Surrounded by the undulating green hills of England's smallest county and overlooking the rippling expanse of Rutland Water, this former 17th-century farmhouse, built of local stone quarried from the adjacent estate of the Earl of Gainsborough, is an idyllic retreat for those wishing to escape everyday bustle and enjoy the peace of unspoilt countryside. Restored and converted, every comfort and modern facility is available. Standing at the head of an impressive, tree-lined avenue, Barnsdale is located to the north of Oakham with its well-preserved market square; market days are Wednesday and Saturday. The furnishings and décor are exquisite and the well-equipped, en-suite bedrooms, offer relaxation; 2 have been specifically designed for disabled guests, some are interconnecting and many offer panoramic views south over Rutland Water. Richard Carruthers, the talented head chef of Blue Bird notoriety, brings an inspirational new bistro-style menu using organic and local produce, free-range eggs from the Gainsborough Estate and damson jam from the orchards, complemented by a cellar of fine wines. A multitude of water sports can be arranged, and Belvoir and Rockingham Castles are within easy reach. Burghley House, Stamford, Belton House (National Trust property), Grantham and the market towns of Uppingham and Oaham are close by.

Our inspector loved: *The selection of charming dining rooms.*

NEW

THE LAKE ISLE RESTAURANT & TOWNHOUSE HOTEL

16 HIGH STREET EAST, UPPINGHAM, RUTLAND LE15 9PZ

This small personally run restaurant and town house hotel is situated in the pretty market town of Uppingham, dominated by the famous Uppingham School and close to Rutland Water. The entrance to the building, which dates back to the 18th century, is via a quiet courtyard where a wonderful display of flowering tubs and hanging baskets greets you. In winter, sit in the bar where a log fire burns or relax in the upstairs lounge which overlooks the High Street. In the bedrooms, each named after a wine growing region in France and all of which are en suite, guests will find fresh fruit, homemade biscuits and a decanter of sherry. Those in the courtyard are cottage-style suites. Under the personal direction of chef Stuart Mead, the restaurant offers seasonal changing menus using fresh ingredients. There is an extensive wine list of more than 200 wines ranging from regional labels to old clarets. Special "Wine Dinners" are held throughout the year, enabling guests to appreciate this unique cellar. Burghley House, speedway in Rockingham and Belvoir Castle are within a short drive.

Our inspector loved: The quiet secluded walled garden.

Directions: Uppingham is near the intersection of A47 and A6003. The hotel is on the High Street and is reached on foot via Reeves Yard and by car via Queen Street.

Oakham

Stamford

Uppingham

Web: www.johansens.com/lakeisle
E-mail: info@lakeislehotel.com
Tel: 0870 381 8670
International: +44 (0)1572 822951
Fax: 01572 824400

Price Guide:
single £55–£75
double/twin £75–£95
suite £95–£120

PEN-Y-DYFFRYN COUNTRY HOTEL

RHYDYCROESAU, NEAR OSWESTRY, SHROPSHIRE SY10 7JD

Directions: From the A5 and Oswestry town centre take the B4580 west towards Llansiln for approximately 3 miles. After a sharp bend turn left into the village.

Web: www.johansens.com/penydyffryn
E-mail: stay@peny.co.uk
Tel: 0870 381 8809
International: +44 (0)1691 653700
Fax: 01978 211004

Price Guide:
single £82
double £106–£158

Enjoying breathtaking views of the Welsh mountains from its peaceful location high on the last hill in Shropshire, this captivating hotel offers guests a retreat in which to totally relax and unwind. The property, constructed in 1845 from local stone, was originally a Georgian rectory occupied by a Celtic scholar and is now a Grade II listed building. The owners, Miles and Audrey Hunter and their team, provide a discreet, efficient and hospitable service. An abundance of seasonal fresh flowers throughout the hotel adds to the charm and cosy ambience that has long been established here. All of the well-appointed bedrooms overlook the attractive terraced gardens and enjoy stylish décor and contemporary facilities. The superior room boasts a king-size draped bed and Japanese whirlpool. The master bedrooms in the main hotel possess spa baths whilst the 4 rooms in the coach house have their own private patios. In the restaurant, Chef David Morris has been awarded 2 AA Rosettes for the daily changing menu he creates from local, often organic, produce. To accompany the menu there is an exciting wine list with many organic wines, alongside a variety of non-alcoholic organic beverages. The Medieval towns of Chester and Shrewsbury are nearby and the local area offers hill walking, riding, golf, and trout fishing.

Our inspector loved: Sitting on the terrace enjoying the wonderful views. Always a special place to unwind.

144

SOULTON HALL

NEAR WEM, SHROPSHIRE SY4 5RS

Dating from the 15th and 17th centuries, this imposing Tudor, brick built manor with magnificent pillared courtyard and beautiful walled garden, stands in 550 acres of scenic Shropshire parkland 2 miles east of the ancient market town of Wem. Family run, it offers warmth, peace, tranquillity, privacy, discrete service and the utmost comfort. The Hall retains much of the grandeur and character of its historic bygone days, enhanced with the modern facilities a 21st-century visitor expects. The Ashton family, descendants of the first protestant Lord Mayor of London who bought Soulton Hall in 1556, have improved and refurbished the property whilst retaining many of the unique features in the 6 spacious bedrooms; 4 in the main building and 2 in the nearby coach house. Equally attractive is the recently converted Soulton Court Long Room, which forms part of a range of buildings surrounding the White Garden. Built in 1783 as stables, it has a stone-flagged floor, beams, 5 large glazed doors and is an ideal venue for meetings and events. Ann Ashton presides in the kitchen where her skills in traditional English cooking are enhanced by imagination and flair. Specialities might include hand-raised game pie and butter baked salmon served with saffron oil. Hawkstone Country Park, Nescliffe Hill, Ironbridge, Shrewsbury, Chester, Stoke and Ludlow are nearby.

Our inspector loved: This unspoilt ancient hall, and traditional dishes.

Directions: Take the M54 to the end and then the A5 to the junction with the A49. Go north on the A49 then join the B5065 west to Wem.

Web: www.johansens.com/soultonhall
E-mail: enquiries@soultonhall.co.uk
Tel: 0870 381 8899
International: +44 (0)1939 232786
Fax: 01939 234097

Price Guide:
single from £40
double from £76

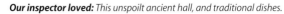

COMPTON HOUSE

TOWNSEND, AXBRIDGE, SOMERSET BS26 2AJ

Directions: From the M5 take either junction 21, A370/A371 and head towards Cheddar, or junction 22, A38 towards Bristol for 7 miles and turn right at Cross. Compton House is west of Axbridge just off the A371.

Web: www.johansens.com/comptonhouse
E-mail: info@comptonhse.com
Tel: 0870 381 8441
International: +44 (0)1934 733944
Fax: 01934 733945

Bath

Taunton   Yeovil

Price Guide:
single from £70
double/twin £95–£120

With a wealth of charm and atmosphere dating back to a less hectic era, this impressive 17th-century, Grade II listed manor house is a real gem. Beautifully and peacefully situated in historic Axbridge, at the foot of the southern slopes of scenic Mendip Hills, it commands spectacular views over the Somerset Levels to Glastonbury Tor. Delightfully designed and surrounded by an expansive and secluded lawned garden, Compton House is steeped in history. Parts of the hotel date back to Elizabethan times and there is an abundance of oak panelling, elegant mouldings and wonderful fireplaces throughout. Enthusiastic owners, Patricia and Robert Tallack, whose interest is routing local walks, have created a homely, relaxing ambience and their continual pursuit of excellence has earned the hotel a reputation for comfort, hospitality and service. Meeting facilities are available and intimate weddings can be arranged. The generous en-suite bedrooms boast many original features, and Patricia uses Fairtrade and West Country produce for the superb dishes served in the attractive dining room, following apèritifs, if desired, on the sun-catching garden terrace. Cheddar, with its fascinating gorge, is just 2 miles away, Wells and its magnificent cathedral 10 miles, Bath and Bristol, with its international airport, are both within easy reach.

Our inspector loved: *This beautiful little gem with all its welcoming surprises.*

BELLPLOT HOUSE HOTEL & THOMAS'S RESTAURANT

HIGH STREET, CHARD, SOMERSET TA20 1QB

Venture to this delightful Georgian bolt-hole, which was built back in 1729, and admire the many vestiges of the property's past. The 7 bedrooms are named after the female deed holders who once owned Bellplot and each room has en-suite facilities, crisp white linen, television and satellite as well as a computer worktop for Internet users and business guests. The décor is strongly in-keeping with the period and includes gold and royal green plus natural wood flooring throughout the ground floor. Current owners Betty and Dennis Jones pride themselves on their warm welcome afforded to all guests. Head chef Thomas Jones excels in the culinary department: after a beverage in the intimate bar, guests may relax in the AA Rosette-awarded restaurant, 1 of only 4 in Somerset to be awarded Taste of the West, and try the sumptuous cuisine such as Lyme Bay crab cake followed by whole baby spring poussin. Diners would do well to save some room for dessert with temptations such as baked lemon tart with an orange coulis and clotted cream and luxuriously warm bread and butter pudding. Use of the nearby golf and squash club, and swimming pool, sauna, Jacuzzi and tennis courts at the leisure club can be arranged. Breaks are available

Our inspector loved: This delightful small town house oozing warmth, welcome, comfort, relaxation and superb cuisine.

Directions: From the north exit the M5 at junction 25 then join the A358 signposted for Chard. From the south take the A30.

Web: www.johansens.com/bellplothouse
E-mail: info@bellplothouse.co.uk
Tel: 0870 381 8339
International: +44 (0)1460 62600
Fax: 01460 62600

Price Guide:
single from £99
double from £112

ASHWICK COUNTRY HOUSE HOTEL

DULVERTON, SOMERSET TA22 9QD

Directions: From the M5, junction 27 take the A361 to Tiverton. Take the A396 north until joining the B3222 to Dulverton and then the B3223 signposted Lynton and Exford. After a steep climb drive over a second cattle grid and turn left to Ashwick Country House Hotel.

Web: www.johansens.com/ashwickcountryhouse
E-mail: reservations@ashwickhouse.com
Tel: 0870 381 8327
International: +44 (0)1398 323868
Fax: 01398 323868

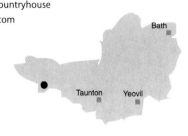

Price Guide:
single from £79
double from £118
dinner from £25

This little jewel of a hotel is hidden away in a splendid, tranquil location on the south-eastern edge of Exmoor National Park overlooking lush woodland, which enfolds the River Barle. Built in 1901 and originally decorated in William Morris style, Ashwick Country House Hotel has been tastefully furnished by new owners Barbara and Bob Clift. At the heart of the house the sumptuous Baronial-style galleried hall still displays William Morris wallpaper alongside antique and contemporary Oriental pieces, which are to be found throughout. On chillier days the large log fire and comfortable settees provide a welcome sanctuary for a winter warmer, and guests can also relax in the cosy library or take drinks in the lounge. The sweeping lawns and water gardens are frequented by deer, pheasant, foxes and rabbits and a large variety of birds. All of the hotel's rooms are well appointed, with en-suite facilities, mini bar, TV and wireless broadband. Ashwick House was proud to recently announce the arrival of award-winning Chef Dan Kings to its restaurant where visitors can enjoy his unpretentious, classic yet modern meals using the best local produce complemented by Bob's thoughtfully stocked wine cellar. Aromatherapy treatments and massage are available at the hotel upon request.

Our inspector loved: *The total transformation of this delightful, tucked away little gem – it's a must.*

THREE ACRES COUNTRY HOUSE

THREE ACRES, BRUSHFORD, DULVERTON, SOMERSET TA22 9AR

Hidden by trees in large secluded grounds on the edge of Exmoor, the peaceful Three Acres Country House is an ideal oasis in which to escape the pressures of modern day living. The spacious rooms have been decorated with relaxation and comfort in mind, with generous sofas, log fires, and a licensed bar with a sun terrace. There is no morning rush for a delicious breakfast, which includes daily specials using fresh local produce. Excellent restaurants, cafés and pubs full of character can be found in the area and the owners are very helpful with making recommendations and booking tables. Each of the luxury bedrooms has been individually decorated and styled, featuring comfortable beds, crisp white linen, superb facilities and delightful views. Bathrooms, some with free-standing baths, have fluffy white towels and delicately scented toiletries. The hotel is ideally situated for visiting the dramatic coast, local treasures and beauty spots, which are too numerous to list. The unspoilt charm of Dulverton is nearby with shops, art galleries and antiques. Exmoor National Park is a haven of wildlife including red deer, bird life and trout filled rivers. A plethora of outdoor pursuits can be arranged including cycling, horse riding, fishing and shooting.

Our inspector loved: The feel of space and comfort inside and out. The fabulous countryside.

Directions: From Exmoor Visitors Centre follow the main Tiverton Road (B3222) out of Dulverton. Follow this road until you reach Brushford. Turn right at the Carnarvon Arms garage. After 300 yards turn right at a small crossroads. The hotel is just ahead.

Web: www.johansens.com/threeacres
E-mail: enquiries@threeacrescountryhouse.co.uk
Tel: 0870 381 9229
International: +44 (0)1398 323730

Price Guide:
single £50–£65
double/twin £70–£100

149

FARTHINGS COUNTRY HOUSE HOTEL & RESTAURANT

HATCH BEAUCHAMP, NEAR TAUNTON, SOMERSET TA3 6SG

Directions: Take the M5, junction 25 and join the A358. Go through Henlade and travel for approximately 1 mile then turn left signed Hatch Beauchamp. From the A303, at Ilminster take the A358 to Taunton, travel approximately 5 miles, turn right signed Hatch Beauchamp

Web: www.johansens.com/farthings
E-mail: farthing1@aol.com
Tel: 0870 381 8515
International: +44 (0)1823 480664
Fax: 01823 481118

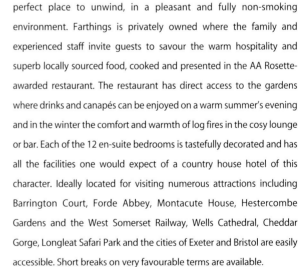

Price Guide:
guest bedrooms from £110
master bedrooms from £155

Farthings Country House Hotel & Restaurant is situated in the delightful village of Hatch Beauchamp, a quiet and peaceful location in the heart of Somerset, yet only 5 miles from Taunton and the M5. The hotel overlooks the village green and enjoys 3 acres of private and peaceful gardens. With a wonderfully relaxing and informal atmosphere it is the perfect place to unwind, in a pleasant and fully non-smoking environment. Farthings is privately owned where the family and experienced staff invite guests to savour the warm hospitality and superb locally sourced food, cooked and presented in the AA Rosette-awarded restaurant. The restaurant has direct access to the gardens where drinks and canapés can be enjoyed on a warm summer's evening and in the winter the comfort and warmth of log fires in the cosy lounge or bar. Each of the 12 en-suite bedrooms is tastefully decorated and has all the facilities one would expect of a country house hotel of this character. Ideally located for visiting numerous attractions including Barrington Court, Forde Abbey, Montacute House, Hestercombe Gardens and the West Somerset Railway, Wells Cathedral, Cheddar Gorge, Longleat Safari Park and the cities of Exeter and Bristol are easily accessible. Short breaks on very favourable terms are available.

Our inspector loved: *The very tasteful, newly refurbished lounge bar and restaurant.*

BERYL

WELLS, SOMERSET BA5 3JP

This 19th-century Gothic mansion is a true little gem, set in 13 acres of parkland and gardens, which have been lovingly restored with great skill. Tastefully furnished with antiques, it also offers hospitality of the highest order. Holly Nowell and her daughter Mary-Ellen are charming hostesses, and take pride in the great attention to detail evident throughout the house. Guests are invited to use the honesty bar in the Green Room or enjoy drinks and wines on the lawn in summer. Holly and Mary-Ellen are happy to organise group bookings and make reservations for overnight guests at the many first-class restaurants and pubs situated nearby. The en-suite bedrooms have interesting views and offer all modern comforts. Places of interest nearby include Wells Cathedral (1 mile), Wookey Hole Caves, Cheddar Gorge, Glastonbury Abbey, Longleat House, Stourhead, Farleigh Castle, The Roman Baths at Bath, and many more fascinating places. For more active guests, there is Beryl's outdoor pool (May to September), marvellous golf, fishing, riding, excellent walking and a nearby leisure centre.

Our inspector loved: *The wonderful feeling of being welcomed as if an old friend.*

Directions: Leave Wells on Radstock Road B3139. Follow the signs to "The Horringtons" and after the church turn left into Hawkers Lane (not Beryl Lane). Beryl is signed at the top with a leafy 500-yard drive to the main gate.

Web: www.johansens.com/beryl
E-mail: stay@beryl-wells.co.uk
Tel: 0870 381 8358
International: +44 (0)1749 678738
Fax: 01749 670508

Price Guide:
single £60–£80
double £85–£120

GLENCOT HOUSE

GLENCOT LANE, WOOKEY HOLE, NEAR WELLS, SOMERSET BA5 1BH

Impressive and majestic inside and out, this late Victorian mansion, built in grand Jacobean style with enchanting mullioned windows, it is a true gem. Situated at the foot of the Mendip Hills, Glencot House is idyllically set in 18 acres of lovingly tended gardens and parkland with a gently meandering trout-filled river in a wonderful, secluded position only 1½ miles from the medieval cathedral city of Wells. A Grade II listed building, the house has been sensitively renovated and restored to provide comfortable and luxurious country house accommodation with all the amenities of modern-day living. The atmosphere is welcoming and homely, the ambience peaceful and tranquil and the service is impeccable. A wealth of beautiful features include carved ceilings and dressers, walnut panelling, huge fireplaces, crystal chandeliers and superb antiques. Each of the comfortable en-suite bedrooms enjoys views over the garden or surrounding countryside and has been individually decorated and furnished with period pieces; many have four-poster beds. Evening relaxation can be enjoyed in the cosy drawing room or library before sampling a delicious set menu in the elegant dining room. Enjoy garden walks, fishing, the sauna and indoor jet stream pool, and snooker room, or visit nearby Wookey Hole Caves, Cheddar Gorge, Glastonbury and Longleat.

Directions: From the M5 exit at junction 21 if travelling from the north or junction 22 from the south then follow the signs towards Wells and Wookey Hole for approximately 20 miles on the A371.

Web: www.johansens.com/glencothouse
E-mail: relax@glencothouse.co.uk
Tel: 0870 381 8552
International: +44 (0)1749 677160
Fax: 01749 670210

Price Guide:
double £165–£295

Our inspector loved: This magnificent mansion in breathtaking grounds.

KARSLAKE COUNTRY HOUSE & RESTAURANT

HALSE LANE, WINSFORD, EXMOOR NATIONAL PARK, SOMERSET TA24 7JE

Originally a 15th-century Malthouse, Karslake House was subsequently named after Sir John Burgess Karslake, a prominent lawyer and member of Parliament during the 1860s. Nestling in the wooded hills of Exmoor, Karslake is ideally located for exploring the north and south of Devon's coast. Nick and Juliette Mountford, resident owners for 6 years, have invested their time and devotion to create a peaceful haven in this exquisite area of Exmoor where views of the Exe Valley and the hotel's garden can be seen from 3 of the 5 en-suite bedrooms. The four-poster guest room offers total luxury. Awarded a Rosette each year, the restaurant uses seasonal, local produce, and homemade bread, jams and marmalades at breakfast. The wine list is comprehensive and the bar is well-stocked. The beautiful sitting room invites guests to relax in its deep-seated sofas by the wood burner alternatively, clay pigeon shooting can be arranged as well as pony trekking along the rolling moorland and walking trips, complete with packed-lunch provided by the hotel. 1, 2 or 3-day courses of fly-fishing, salmon or trout fishing can also be organised; day-tickets are available for experienced fishermen. Relaxation treatments such as aromatherapy, lymphatic drainage massage and cranio-sacral therapy are provided by Karslake's complementary health therapist.

Directions: Exit the M5, junction 27. Follow the A361 for approximately 3 miles to the roundabout. Take the first exit signed Dulverton (A396) then follow signs to Minehead and turn left at the first Winsford sign.

Web: www.johansens.com/karslake
E-mail: enquiries@karslakehouse.co.uk
Tel: 0870 381 9134
International: +44 (0)1643 851242
Fax: 01643 851242

Price Guide:
single £55-£70
double £75-£110

Our inspector loved: *Taking a restful break at this relaxing country house.*

NEW

THE ICKWORTH HOTEL AND APARTMENTS

HORRINGER, BURY ST EDMUNDS, SUFFOLK IP29 5QE

Directions: From the A14 at Bury St Edmunds (junction 42), follow the brown signs for Ickworth.

Web: www.johansens.com/ickworth
E-mail: ickworth@ickworthhotel.com
Tel: 0870 381 8678
International: +44 (0)1284 735350
Fax: 01284 736300

Price Guide:
single/double/suite £185–£420

Ickworth is the perfect retreat for couples and families alike. An impressive country house and estate surrounded by 1,800 acres of glorious deer park and gardens, Ickworth was created by the Earl Bishop of Bristol in the 18th century and today the east wing comprises the hotel. The airy rooms of the interior have been decorated in a delightful mix of classic, traditional and contemporary furnishings, which bring a dash of style and warmth whilst respecting its traditions. Bedrooms are diverse in size and design but all come with beautiful bathrooms and combine comfort and luxury. The Dower House, a short bicycle ride across the estate, houses stunning apartments that offer spacious accommodation and self-catering facilities for large families or groups of friends. Guests can eat in the fine dining restaurant, Frederick's, more informally in Café Inferno, in The Conservatory or al fresco in the garden. There are many activities on offer from swimming, tennis and horse riding to pampering at the Aquae Sulis Retreat. Children are special guests at the Ickworth: there is a crèche for the younger children and Club/Blu for those who are older, which features table football, table tennis and computer games. Bury St Edmunds is a 5-minute drive away and Newmarket Racecourse and Cambridge are within easy reach.

Our inspector loved: *The specially commissioned artwork in Frederick's Restaurant.*

CLARICE HOUSE

HORRINGER COURT, HORRINGER ROAD, BURY ST EDMUNDS SUFFOLK IP29 5PH

Clarice House is a residential spa housed within a beautifully refurbished neo-Jacobean mansion. Set within 20 acres of Suffolk countryside its grounds include ancient woodland and a protected site of scientific interest. Inside, an air of calm relaxation pervades. Guests are welcomed in the large lounge with lovely panelling and carved wood whilst informal meals are served in the bar. The excellent restaurant is open to residents and non-residents alike. For those choosing to stay for bed and breakfast, bedrooms are comfortable and well-appointed with luxurious en-suite bathrooms. A variety of Spa Break packages are available which also include dinner and of course full use of the spa facilities, prices start from £145 per person. The gym comprises hi-tech equipment with computerised personal programme management. There is a team of dedicated instructors and a full programme of classes run daily. A beautiful 20-metre indoor swimming pool leads into a spa bath, steam room and sauna. The suite of beauty salons offers a huge range of indulgent treatments from the more traditional facials, manicures and pedicures to holistic treatments such as reflexology, reiki and Indian head massage. The hotel is within easy reach of the racing at Newmarket, the university city of Cambridge and glorious Constable country. Fly fishing and clay pigeon shooting can also arranged.

Our inspector loved: *The combination of modern comfort within the period surroundings.*

Directions: About 1 mile outside Bury St Edmunds, situated on the A143 towards Haverhill.

Web: www.johansens.com/clarice
E-mail: bury@claricehouse.co.uk
Tel: 0870 381 8431
International: +44 (0)1284 705550
Fax: 01284 716120

Price Guide:
single £55–£75
double/twin £85–£100

NEW

GREAT TANGLEY MANOR

WONERSH COMMON, WONERSH, NEAR GUILDFORD, SURREY GU5 0PT

Directions: Take exit A3 for Guildford and then the A281 towards Shalford. At the roundabout take the A248 towards Cranleigh and after 1 mile take the left-hand drive onto Wonersh Common. Great Tangley Manor is approximately 500 yards up the track on the left.

Web: www.johansens.com/greattangley
E-mail: info@GreatTangleyManor.co.uk
Tel: 0870 381 8677
International: +44 (0)20 7526 4852
Fax: 020 7526 4853

Heathrow
Egham
Kingston upon Thames
Epsom
Guildford
Gatwick

Price Guide:
Short breaks from £180 per person
Per week from £4200

Creatively and lovingly restored by Glyn and Anne Powell-Evans, this stunning property is available on a weekly-let/winter weekend basis and makes an ideal base for 1 or 2 families looking to explore this beautiful corner of Surrey. The Grade I listed Moated Manor is a breathtaking example of history with its medieval hall, Elizabethan dining room, whose timbers are reputedly from the Armada fleet and Arts & Craft library. The magical Victorian gardens include a large lake. Modern amenities and comforts such as the walnut kitchen and all glass breakfast room are recent additions to the property, and every room seems to look out onto its own patch of garden where lazy afternoons and family picnics can be spent. There are 5 bedrooms affording comfortable accommodation for 10 people, whilst sofa beds allow for extra numbers. Each bathroom boasts a piece of history from the art deco to the more kitsch "Harrods". The cobbled town of Guildford, with its medieval castle and dramatic cathedral, is within easy access, whilst trains run every 10 minutes into London. Hampton Court Palace, Ascot, RHS Wisley, Sandown Park racing and Wimbledon tennis are all within a 30-minute drive and Denbies Wine Estate is a great day trip. Glyn and Anne live unobtrusively next door and are on-hand to answer any questions.

Our inspector loved: *The beautiful restoration, and the grounds.*

CHASE LODGE

10 PARK ROAD, HAMPTON WICK, KINGSTON-UPON-THAMES, SURREY KT1 4AS

Chase Lodge is situated in a quiet conservation area of architectural merit adjacent to Bushy Park. Originally built in 1870 as an artisan's house, the Lodge is now a very successful, bustling small hotel run by its owner, Denise Dove and her young staff. The interiors have been designed to a high standard, with particular regard to the bijou nature of the building and with well chosen items of furniture complementing bold décor and fabrics. The bedrooms are cosy and the most recently refurbished bathrooms all feature either a Jacuzzi bath or a steam shower. The conservatory-style restaurant, with its cane furniture and marble topped tables, looks onto the tiny courtyard garden. Its proximity to many major events in the English social season makes Chase Lodge an outstanding choice for value: Wimbledon tennis; the Oxford and Cambridge Boat Race; horse racing at Kempton Park, Epsom Downs, Sandown Park and Royal Ascot; rugby at Twickenham; and now the annual flower show at Hampton Court. Central London with its shops and theatres is a short train ride away. Other places of interest nearby are Richmond and Syon Park, Windsor Castle, Ham House and Kew Gardens.

Our inspector loved: Its individual character and the imaginative use of space within a tiny town house setting.

Directions: From the M3, junction 1 or Kingston take the A308. At the western end of Kingston Bridge is the Hampton Wick roundabout, take the White Hart exit into High Street (the A310), then left at The Forresters into Park Road.

Web: www.johansens.com/chaselodge
E-mail: info@chaselodgehotel.com
Tel: 0870 381 8419
International: +44 (0)20 8943 1862
Fax: 020 8943 9363

Price Guide:
single from £65
double from £71

THE HOPE ANCHOR HOTEL

WATCHBELL STREET, RYE, EAST SUSSEX TN31 7HA

Dating back to the mid-18th century, The Hope Anchor was featured in Malcolm Saville's children's books and with its beautiful old timbers, nooks and crannies and secret passages it possesses immense character and charm. An enviable position in one of Rye's most enchanting and interesting cobbled streets means it boasts stunning views across Romney Marsh, Camber Castle and the rivers Brede and Tillingham. Individually furnished bedrooms offer a range of double and family accommodation and all are en-suite with tea and coffee making facilities and direct dial telephones. The hotel comprises a bar, lounge and an excellent restaurant that welcomes residents and non-residents alike. Menus portray an imaginative use of fresh, seasonally available local ingredients. Rye itself was described as, "about as perfect as a small town can get," by the Daily Telegraph and landmarks such as Mermaid Street, Church Square, St Mary's Church, Lamb House and the 13th-century Ypres Tower are all within a few minutes' stroll.

Our inspector loved: *The spacious Admiral's Apartment with its private terrace and amazing views across the marshes to neighbouring Winchelsea and the sea beyond.*

Directions: From the A268 circumnavigate Rye clockwise via the A259. Turn right by the Heritage Centre and straight up Mermaid Street. Turn right into West Street, right into Church Square and right again into Watchbell Street. The Hope Anchor Hotel is at the end of the street.

Web: www.johansens.com/hopeanchor
E-mail: info@thehopeanchor.co.uk
Tel: 0870 381 8607
International: +44 (0)1797 222216
Fax: 01797 223796

Ashford Int.
Uckfield
Hastings
Brighton
Eastbourne

Price Guide:
double/twin £100–£160
suite £160–£210

THE MILL HOUSE HOTEL

MILL LANE, ASHINGTON, WEST SUSSEX RH20 3BX

This enchanting Grade II listed country house exudes warmth and character, quietly tucked away in the pretty West Sussex countryside. Vestiges of the past are evident throughout the interior: many interesting antiques can be found in the public rooms and beautiful original paintings adorn the walls, forming a lasting testament to their 17th-century origins. After extensive renovation and careful refurbishment, the house combines an authentic charm of a bygone era with the convenience of modern facilities, complemented by traditional, attentive service. Individually decorated bedrooms are warm and comfortable with stylish décor, and the attractive gardens are ideal for relaxing in the sunshine. Gastronomes will be impressed with the excellent cuisine, expertly prepared from the finest local ingredients served with a good selection of wines, liqueurs and cognacs. Accommodating up to 48 people, the meeting room is perfect for small conferences and private dining. Heritage enthusiasts will be delighted with the location of this property as Parham House and Arundel Castle and Cathedral are within easy reach. Petworth, Chichester and Brighton offer good shopping, restaurants, entertainment and antique hunting. There are many beautiful beaches nearby.

Our inspector loved: The new owner's many improvements to this delightful country hideaway.

Directions: Ashington is west of the A24 and north of the junction with the A283. If travelling from the north, follow the large brown signs.

Web: www.johansens.com/millhousehotelashington
E-mail: info@millhousehotelsussex.co.uk
Tel: 0870 381 8735
International: +44 (0)1903 892426
Fax: 01903 893846

Gatwick
East Grinstead
Midhurst
Chichester
Brighton

Price Guide:
single from £52
double from £92
suite from £110

CROUCHERS COUNTRY HOTEL & RESTAURANT

BIRDHAM ROAD, APULDRAM, NEAR CHICHESTER, WEST SUSSEX PO20 7EH

This former farmhouse, set just ½ a mile from the Yacht Basin and 2 miles from the centre of Chichester, has been re-styled into a fine country hotel and awarded 3 AA stars for its 18 bedrooms, good food and most attentive service. The new, spacious open-plan ground floor impresses guests the moment they arrive at reception and the bedrooms, most of which are located in the converted coach house and barn, do not disappoint. However, it is the newly designed public areas which will excite approval: the bar and lounge areas and the fine new 60 seat restaurant have transformed Crouchers. Dishes, freshly prepared from the very finest ingredients and the inspiration of chef Gavin Wilson, have already won the first Rosette recognition. Meals are complemented by a carefully constructed and interesting wine list, reflecting the family's connections with South Africa. Crouchers Country Hotel will delight those wishing merely to relax and escape the pressures of a hectic lifestyle. In the summer months a tranquil ambience envelopes the courtyard as guests sip chilled drinks and laze in the sun.

Our inspector loved: *The splendid conservatory extension to the restaurant.*

Directions: From the M27, junction 12 take the A27 to Chichester and then the A286 south towards The Witterings. Crouchers Country Hotel and Restaurant is on the left.

Web: www.johansens.com/crouchersbottom
E-mail: crouchers@btconnect.com
Tel: 0870 381 8462
International: +44 (0)1243 784995
Fax: 01243 539797

Price Guide:
single £65-£95
double £95-£130

NUTHURST GRANGE
HOCKLEY HEATH, WARWICKSHIRE B94 5NL

The most memorable feature of this friendly country house hotel is its outstanding restaurant. Linda and Stephen Pike and their head chef have won many accolades for their imaginative menus, described as "English, cooked in the light French style". Diners can enjoy their superb cuisine in one of the 3 adjoining rooms which comprise the restaurant and form the heart of Nuthurst Grange. The rest of the house is no less charming – the spacious bedrooms have a country house atmosphere and are appointed with extra luxuries such as an exhilarating air-spa bath, mini-bar, a trouser press, hairdryer and a safe for valuables. For special occasions there is a room furnished with a four-poster bed and a marble bathroom. There are fine views across the 7½ acres of landscaped gardens. Executive meetings can be accommodated at Nuthurst Grange – within a 12 mile radius of the hotel lie central Birmingham, the NEC, Stratford-upon-Avon, Coventry and Birmingham International Airport. Sporting activities available nearby include golf, canal boating and tennis.

Our inspector loved: *The elegant interlinked dining rooms and their superb cuisine.*

Directions: From M42 take exit 4 then A3400 for Hockley Heath (2 miles, south). Nuthurst Grange Lane is ¼ mile south of the village. Also, M40 (exit 16, southbound only), take the first left. The entrance is 300 yards.

Web: www.johansens.com/nuthurstgrange
E-mail: info@nuthurst-grange.com
Tel: 0870 381 8776
International: +44 (0)1564 783972
Fax: 01564 783919

Price Guide:
single £139
double/twin £159–£179
suite £189

NEW

BEECHFIELD HOUSE

BEANACRE, WILTSHIRE SN12 7PU

Directions: From the M4 junction 17 take the A350 towards Poole. On entering the village of Beanacre (approximately 10 miles / 15 minutes from the motorway) the hotel is well signposted and can be found on the left.

Web: www.johansens.com/beechfieldhouse
E-mail: reception@beechfieldhouse.co.uk
Tel: 0870 381 8643
International: +44 (0)1225 703700
Fax: 01225 790118

Price Guide:
single from £85
double from £100
family from £125

Malmesbury
Swindon
Bath
Warminster
Salisbury

Beechfield House stands in 8 acres of secluded grounds and gardens and is an impressive example of late Victorian architecture. Built in 1878, it is privately owned and run as a welcoming country house hotel with emphasis on retaining the essential warmth and atmosphere of a family home. All 18 bedrooms are comfortable, spacious and well appointed with en-suite facilities. Elsewhere, guests can relax and unwind in either the Morning room, Drawing room or The Orangery, all of which are beautifully presented with elegant furnishings and period colour schemes. There are several private dining rooms as well as The Bay Tree Restaurant which seats 45 people and overlooks the walled garden and heated outdoor swimming pool. Menus feature a wide variety of dishes using locally sourced quality produce. In addition the hotel can cater for functions, small or large, business or pleasure, as well as being licensed for civil weddings and partnerships. There are many local attractions nearby including the National Trust village of Lacock which is approximately 2 miles away. The Roman city of Bath and Longleat House are also close by, and the Cotswolds, Somerset and Dorset are all easily accessible.

Our inspector loved: *The classical façade of this late Victorian house set in elegant grounds.*

WIDBROOK GRANGE

WIDBROOK, BRADFORD-ON-AVON, NEAR BATH, WILTSHIRE BA15 1UH

Widbrook Grange, home of resident owners Jane and Peter Wragg, is an elegant 250-year-old Georgian country house, peacefully located in 11 acres of grounds amidst rolling countryside yet only 17 minutes from the city of Bath. The hotel has an atmosphere of warmth and informality with cosy lounges and a log fire burning on cold winter nights. The service is attentive yet unobtrusive and for this, Widbrook Grange has been named RAC Little Gem Hotel of the Year. The spacious, tastefully decorated bedrooms in the main house, courtyard and gardens include romantic four-posters, family rooms and facilities for the disabled. Families relax in the heated indoor swimming pool, as do delegates who use the hotel's conference suite. The intimate, AA Rosette award-winning Medlar Tree Restaurant serves fine British regional cuisine using fresh, home-grown produce, complemented by an interesting selection of New and Old World wines. Walks from the hotel lead to Kennet and Avon canal with its picturesque narrow boats, then on to the Saxon Tithe Barn and Church in the medieval town of Bradford-on-Avon. Longleat, Stonehenge and Lacock Abbey are all within easy driving distance, and for the more energetic, golf, horse riding and boat and cycle hire can be arranged.

Our inspector loved: The friendly and informal atmosphere.

Directions: From Bradford-on-Avon take the A363 Trowbridge Road. Widbrook Grange is 200 metres on the right after the Kennet and Avon Canal.

Web: www.johansens.com/widbrookgrange
E-mail: stay@widbrookgrange.com
Tel: 0870 381 8996
International: +44 (0)1225 864750/863173
Fax International: +44 (0)1225 862890

Price Guide:
single £95–£110
double £110–£120
four poster £130
family rooms from £150

THE OLD MANOR HOTEL

TROWLE, NEAR BRADFORD-ON-AVON, WILTSHIRE BA14 9BL

Directions: The hotel is on the A363 towards Trowbridge, 1½ miles from Bradford-on-Avon.

Web: www.johansens.com/oldmanorbath
E-mail: romanticbeds@oldmanorhotel.com
Tel: 0870 381 8782
International: +44 (0)1225 777393
Fax: 01225 765443

Price Guide:
single £70–£90
double/twin £90–£95
four poster £110
suite £130

Set on Trowle Common on the outskirts of Bradford-on-Avon, The Old Manor Hotel is 20 minutes from the centre of Bath. To William the Conqueror's surprise, following the completion of the Doomsday Book, he discovered that he owned it. Today, this tranquil Georgian-style hotel, and converted surrounding farm, is rather special: a working farm until 20 years ago, many of the old buildings such as the milking parlour, barn and stables remain standing. These historic buildings now house the dining room, bar and charming bedrooms; 4 guest rooms are located in the main manor house whilst the remaining bedrooms are in a variety of old farm buildings within the grounds. It is necessary to walk outside to reach the restaurant and bar from some bedrooms. All bedrooms are en suite, individually decorated, have refurbished antique beds and feature interesting antiques and pictures collected by the owner Tim Burnham; some feature low ceilings with old beams. 3 years ago the stables were converted into 4 fabulous suites with integral lounge area; each has a large en-suite bathroom with walk-in shower and bath, 3 have 6ft wide king-size beds with Victorian carved oak bedheads. The fourth has twin double beds, low light switches and disabled facilities in the bathroom. The extension to the dining room boasts a lovely garden room/conservatory, and there is a pub-style bar.

Our inspector loved: *The abundance of quirky features throughout.*

STANTON MANOR HOTEL & GALLERY RESTAURANT

STANTON SAINT QUINTIN, NEAR CHIPPENHAM, WILTSHIRE SN14 6DQ

A wide, columned entranceway welcomes guests to this attractive stone-built hotel, which lies in the delightful village of Stanton Saint Quintin on the edge of the Cotswolds. Listed in the Doomsday book, and once owned by Lord Burghley, chief minister to Queen Elizabeth I, the property was rebuilt in 1840 and stands in 7 acres of landscaped gardens. Refurbished in 2005 by owners Robert and Linda Davis, the modern facilities and comforts combine successfully with those of the past, which include magnificent Tudor fireplaces and stone flooring. The en-suite rooms are spacious and individually designed with toning fabrics and comfortable furniture. 4 rooms have four-poster beds and their own themes such as Oriental and Provençal; comfortable family rooms are also available. Head Chef Jean-Paul Giraud and his team use local quality produce to create traditional English and Continental cuisine in the elegant Gallery Restaurant that overlooks the gardens. The restaurant exhibits an eclectic collection of art by prominent Oriental artists. Light snacks are served in the cosy bar or lounge and may be enjoyed al fresco on the patio. Ideally situated close to the historic city of Bath and a short distance from Cheltenham, Lacock, Castle Combe and other stunning Cotswold villages. Stanton Manor Hotel will be opening a new 200-seat Conference Suite/Wedding Barn in spring 2007.

Our inspector loved: The excellent food in comfortable surroundings.

Directions: Exit the M4 at junction 17 and join the A429 towards Cirencester. After approximately 200 yards, turn left to Stanton Saint Quintin. Stanton Manor Hotel is on the left in the village.

Web: www.johansens.com/stantonmanor
E-mail: reception@stantonmanor.co.uk
Tel: 0870 381 8910
International: +44 (0)1666 837552
Fax: 01666 837022

Price Guide:
single £110–£115
double £135–£175
double superior deluxe £210

THE LAMB AT HINDON

HIGH STREET, HINDON, WILTSHIRE SP3 6DP

Directions: Situated off the A303 and A350, less than a 2-hour drive from London.

Web: www.johansens.com/lambathindon
E-mail: info@lambathindon.co.uk
Tel: 0870 381 9208
International: +44 (0)1747 820 573
Fax: 01747 820 605

Price Guide:
single £70
double/twin £99–£135

The Lamb dates back to approximately the 12th century at which time it traded as a public house. By 1870 it was a well established inn for coaches travelling between London and the West Country. Its character and many original features remain, from the inglenook fireplaces to the flag stone floors and wooden beams. Antique furniture and rich colours complemented by tartan fabrics feature throughout the inn and the individually furnished 14 spacious and charming bedrooms; 3 have four-poster beds. There are ample spaces to relax, such as the Whisky & Cigar Bar, the solid oak table, which seats 10 people and the cosy Snug with its comfortable armchairs and a sofa. Food on offer includes sandwiches and bar snacks as well as the full à la carte selection. Fresh ingredients are sourced, whenever possible, from the best local or Scottish suppliers, alongside wines from the award-winning Boisdale selection, many rarely seen in the UK. In addition to the real ales the malt whisky menu is reputedly the largest in Wiltshire. The unspoilt village of Hindon is just 20 minutes from Salisbury, and is well placed for exploring Stonehenge, Wilton, Longleat and the surrounding county, much of which has been designated as an area of Outstanding Natural Beauty.

Our inspector loved: *The warm, cosy atmosphere throughout this old coaching inn.*

THE GEORGE INN

LONGBRIDGE DEVERILL, WARMINSTER, WILTSHIRE BA12 7DG

A warm welcome awaits guests to this friendly inn. All rooms have been refurbished, and there is a public bar as well as a cosy residents lounge with a good selection of books and games to while away a lazy afternoon. The inn can cater for conferences, weddings and parties. The welcoming Kingston Restaurant and the Longbridge Bar, which is warmed by an open fire, serve an excellent à la carte menu and a good selection of mouth-watering home-cooked dishes that might include tender lamb shank braised in a rich red wine and redcurrant jus or oven-baked Dover sole with lemon and herb butter. Outside the Riverside Garden, which is set in 2 acres of gardens and has plenty of car parking, is a popular venue during the warmer months. Active guests can explore the surroundings on foot or by bicycle, whilst golf and fishing can also be arranged. The George Inn is the ideal base from which to explore nearby Longleat and Bath, Stourhead, Wookey Hole Caves, Stonehenge and Wardour Castle.

Our inspector loved: The friendly staff, and good food.

Directions: From the A303 take the A350 towards Warminster; The George Inn is on the left. From the A36 take the A350 towards Shaftesbury; The George Inn is on the right.

Web: www.johansens.com/georgewarminster
Tel: 0870 381 8542
International: +44 (0)1985 840396
Fax: 01985 841333

Price Guide:
single £45
double/twin £70–£95
family room £80–£85

NEW

THE PEACOCK INN

WORCESTER ROAD, BORASTON, TENBURY WELLS, WORCESTERSHIRE WR15 8LL

Directions: On the A456 Kidderminster to Tenbury Wells Road.

Web: www.johansens.com/peacockboraston
E-mail: thepeacockinn001@aol.com
Tel: 0870 381 8514
International: +44 (0)1584 810506
Fax: 01584 811236

Price Guide:
single £55
double £75

The Peacock Inn is a high quality public house situated in the valley of the River Teme. Owner Robert Cheadle was once maître d' on the *QE2*, and today aims to create the ambience and welcoming atmosphere of the traditional British inn. A fine selection of ales, lagers and wines can be enjoyed in the charming bar and lounge areas with their original oak beams, wood-panelled walls and roaring open fires. Excellent meals are created from the freshest ingredients and menus include dishes such as mille feuilles of black pudding and apple, goats cheese and truffle oil crostinis, noisettes of lamb with artichoke hearts and Aberdeen Angus steaks. A pleasant patio area is available for al fresco drinks or dining in the summer months. Attention to detail is carried through into the accommodation and the 6 luxury en-suite rooms also boast oak beams, tea and coffee making facilities and individual styling. 2 rooms have local, hand-crafted oak four-poster beds, one has a Colonial bed, and the double de luxe room houses an original 125-year-old roll-top bath. A full English breakfast is included for overnight guests. The inn has an exclusive fishing area for guests' use only on the Teme just 100 yards away. Nearby places of interest include Tenbury Wells, Kidderminster and Worcester.

Our inspector loved: *The exposed beams throughout the property; especially in the dining area located in the old stables.*

THE BROADWAY HOTEL

THE GREEN, BROADWAY, WORCESTERSHIRE WR12 7AA

The Broadway Hotel stands proudly in the centre of the picturesque Cotswold village of Broadway where every stone evokes memories of Elizabethan England. Once used by the Abbots of Pershore, the hotel was formerly a 16th-century house, as can be seen by its architecture which combines the half timbers of the Vale of Evesham with the distinctive honey-coloured and grey stone of the Cotswolds. It epitomises a true combination of Olde Worlde charm and modern day amenities with friendly, efficient service. All bedrooms provide television, telephone and tea and coffee making facilities. Traditional English dishes and a peaceful ambience are offered in the beamed Courtyard Restaurant. There is an impressive variety of à la carte dishes complemented by good wines. The congenial Jockey Club bar is a pleasant place to enjoy a drink. The hotel overlooks the village green at the bottom of the main street where guests can browse through shops offering an array of fine antiques. On a clear day, 13 counties of England and Wales can be viewed from Broadway Tower. Snowshill, Burford, Chipping Campden, Bourton-on-the-Water, Stow-on-the-Wold and Winchcombe as well as larger Cheltenham, Worcester and Stratford are within easy reach.

Our inspector loved: *The open wood burning stove and massive Cotswold stone fireplace.*

Directions: From London M40 to Oxford, A40 to Burford, A429 through Stow-on-the-Wold, then A44 to Broadway.

Web: www.johansens.com/broadwayworcestershire
E-mail: info@broadwayhotel.info
Tel: 0870 381 8381
International: +44 (0)1386 852401
Fax: 01386 853879

Price Guide:
single £80–£105
double/twin £130–£145
superior £150–£165

THE OLD RECTORY

IPSLEY LANE, IPSLEY, NEAR REDDITCH, WORCESTERSHIRE B98 0AP

Directions: From the M42 take junction 3 and follow the A435 towards Redditch. Keep on this road until you reach the island at Mappleborough Green. Turn right, go straight over the first island and then left at the second island onto Icknield Street Drive. Take the first left into Ipsley Lane and the hotel is on the left.

Web: www.johansens.com/oldrecipsley
E-mail: ipsleyoldrectory@aol.com
Tel: 0870 381 9169
International: +44 (0)1527 523000
Fax: 01527 517003

Price Guide:
single from £102
double/twin from £120

The Old Rectory has stood for over 500 years, though it was "modernised" in 1812 by the great-grandson of Sir Christopher Wren, who lived in the house for 40 years. The site itself is steeped in history; the Domesday Book listed a building here, and along one boundary of the grounds runs the original Roman built Icknield Street. Today the emphasis is on hospitality and creating a relaxed, warm atmosphere and memorable stay for guests. All of the comfortable bedrooms – one of which is reputedly haunted – differ in shape, size and décor, with some featuring exposed beams, and one with a barrel ceiling. Dinner is served each night in the conservatory and the restaurant prides itself on preparing everything possible on the premises from the freshest seasonal produce. Coffee and liqueurs may be enjoyed in the welcoming snug or lounge, whilst the beautiful gardens with their rhododendrons, Portuguese laurel, old oak, cedar, silver birch and weeping ash trees beckon to be explored. In the heart of the beautiful Midlands, The Old Rectory is a 20-minute drive from Stratford-upon-Avon, Warwick and Birmingham, and within easy reach of the Cotswolds, Cheltenham and Oxford. The hotel is non-smoking throughout, but guests are welcome to make use of the grounds.

Our inspector loved: *The fascinating working mechanism of the tower clock.*

170

COLWALL PARK

COLWALL, NEAR MALVERN, WORCESTERSHIRE WR13 6QG

This delightful country house style hotel is situated on the sunny western side of the breathtaking Malvern Hills, close to the centre of peaceful Colwall village where its famous water is bottled. Surrounded by beautiful gardens, there are footpaths from the hotel leading directly onto the Malvern Hills, where views over the surrounding countryside are spectacular. Efficient, knowledgeable and very friendly staff, winners of the prestigious AA Courtesy and Care Award, will show guests to one of the 22 bedrooms and suites. All are individually furnished and decorated to a very high standard and every room is en suite and features trouser press, satellite TV, direct dial telephone with data port, coffee and tea making facilities as well as home-made biscuits. The highly acclaimed, award-winning Seasons Restaurant (Michelin, Egon Ronay, Birmingham Restaurant of the Year, AA 2 Rosette) is a contemporary furnished oak-panelled room and serves delicious gourmet food. The popular Lantern Bar, a meeting place for locals and residents alike, features a crackling log fire during winter and offers real ales, superb house wines and an exciting menu of freshly made meals and snacks. Local attractions include Gloucester, Worcester, Hereford and Cheltenham and the historic market town of Ledbury.

Our inspector loved: The bar: warm décor, warm fire, warm welcome.

Directions: Take the M5, junction 7, the A442 then the A449. Colwall village is on the B4218 between Malvern and Ledbury.

Web: www.johansens.com/colwallpark
E-mail: hotel@colwall.com
Tel: 0870 381 8437
International: +44 (0)1684 540000
Fax: 01684 540847

Price Guide:
single £79-£89
double/twin £120–£140
suite £150–£170

171

THE WHITE LION HOTEL

HIGH STREET, UPTON-UPON-SEVERN, NEAR MALVERN, WORCESTERSHIRE WR8 0HJ

Henry Fielding wrote part of his novel "The History of Tom Jones" way back in 1749 where he described the hotel as "the fairest Inn on the street" and "a house of exceedingly good repute". The owners Jon and Chris Lear have committed themselves to upholding this tradition with good old-fashioned hospitality along with examples of the finest cuisine in the area cooked for the popular Pepperpot Brasserie, which has been awarded an AA Rosette, RAC Dining Awards and the CAMRA Good Beer Award. Using only the finest ingredients Jon and his team produce an imaginative menu served with flair – and homemade treats – which have attracted the attention of a discriminating local clientele. A lunch time menu with lighter meals may be enjoyed in the lounge or in the congenial bar. All 13 bedrooms are from varying periods dating from 1510, the Rose Room and the Wild Goose Room at the White Lion are named in a Fielding book. The White Lion is central for visiting The Malvern Hills, The Three Counties Show Ground, the market town of Ledbury, Tewkesbury's Norman Abbey, Worcester, Cheltenham and Gloucester. The Cotswolds, Black Mountains and Stratford-upon-Avon are all within an easy drive.

Directions: From M5/jct 8 follow M50 and exit at jct 1 onto A38 north. After 3 miles turn left onto A4104. Go over the bridge, turn left, then right. Parking is at the rear.

Web: www.johansens.com/whitelionupton
E-mail: info@whitelionhotel.biz
Tel: 0870 381 8989
International: +44 (0)1684 592551
Fax: 01684 593333

Price Guide:
single £70–£90
double £92.50–£135
four-poster £125–£150
multiple days negotiable

Our inspector loved: Jon Lear's imaginative blackboard menu in the friendly bar.

THE AUSTWICK TRADDOCK

AUSTWICK, VIA LANCASTER, NORTH YORKSHIRE LA2 8BY

Standing in 2 acres of peaceful, landscaped gardens in the heart of the Yorkshire Dales National Park is this fine Georgian country house hotel and restaurant, which oozes character, charm and the friendliest of hospitality. It is an ideal location for those wishing to enjoy dramatic scenery, spectacular walks, tranquillity and the freshest of country air. Surrounding the unspoilt village of Austwick is some of the most sensational limestone scenery in Europe, including the Ingleborough Cave with its dazzling stalagmites and stalagatites. Close by are the 3 famous peaks of Whernside, Pen-y-ghent and Ingleborough and within a short walk of the nearby market town of Settle are caves which have yielded finds from pre-history. Guests at the Austwick Traddock can relax after walking and sightseeing tours in a comfortable bar and lounge, warmed in winter by open log fires or enjoy a quiet nap in their bedroom. Each is individually designed, delightfully decorated and like the remainder of the building, beautifully furnished with English antiques. Chef, Tom Eunson, produces excellent Anglo-French cuisine in the restaurant, which has been awarded an AA Rosette and Organic Restaurant of the Year 2006, complemented by an extensive wine list. Special breaks are available.

Directions: Austwick is a mile north west of Settle on the A65, midway between Skipton and junction 36 of the M6.

Web: www.johansens.com/austwick
E-mail: info@austwicktraddock.co.uk
Tel: 0870 381 8331
International: +44 (0)15242 51224
Fax: 015242 51796

Price Guide:
single £80–£100
double/twin £130–£180

Our inspector loved: The delicious dinner at this family-run hotel.

STOW HOUSE HOTEL

AYSGARTH, LEYBURN, NORTH YORKSHIRE DL8 3SR

Directions: Stow House is situated on the A684 at the edge of the village of Aysgarth, which is midway between Leyburn and Hawes.

Web: www.johansens.com/stowhouse
E-mail: info@stowhouse.co.uk
Tel: 0870 381 8920
International: +44 (0)1969 663635

Price Guide:
single £44–£55
double/twin £72–£96

Tall, charming and attractive, this stone-built former Victorian Vicarage stands impressively in 2 acres of mature grounds. It is a 10-minute walk from famous Aysgarth Falls in the heart of beautiful Wensleydale, watered by the Ure, the most open and wooded of the Yorkshire Dales. Built in 1876 for Fenwick William Stow, Rural Dean of Wensleydale and over the years lovingly and sympathetically restored, it has 9 en-suite bedrooms, all individually decorated and furnished with every comfort. 2 luxury guest rooms, one with a four-poster, are slightly larger and offer panoramic views over the Dale, although all rooms have a lovely outlook. There is a cosy bar and a comfortable lounge which opens onto a garden that features an impressive selection of trees dating from the mid 19th century and a stunning view towards Bishopdale. Excellent meals can be enjoyed in the intimate dining room and chef, Michael Sullivan, uses the freshest of local produce. A croquet lawn and lawn tennis court are available during the summer months. Stow House specialises in house parties and shooting parties where guests are able to take over the whole hotel for their own special celebration. There are wonderful walks direct from the door and the area abounds in historic castles, abbeys and stately homes. There are 3 golf courses locally.

Our inspector loved: The panoramic views over Wensleydale from the four-poster bed.

THE DEVONSHIRE FELL

BURNSALL, SKIPTON, NORTH YORKSHIRE BD23 6BT

The Devonshire Fell is lucky to have one of those rare locations where the views from the hotel are simply stunning. Step inside to be met by bold bright colours where The Duchess of Devonshire's imagination has made its mark. Large comfortable sofas, an enormous wood burning stove and original contemporary art combine to create a warm and inviting atmosphere. This small boutique hotel is very much "city chic in the countryside" and prides itself on the impeccable standards of service and friendliness it provides. Freshly prepared food is sourced locally, wherever possible, and from the kitchen gardens at its sister hotel in Bolton Abbey. The 10 bedrooms and 2 family suites incorporate fresh and vivid colours and are well equipped with CD/DVD players and flat-screen TVs, big bottle toiletries and all the little extras to make each stay as enjoyable as possible and, of course, look out to breathtaking views. Guests have complimentary use of the spa and leisure facilities at The Devonshire Health Spa at nearby Bolton Abbey. Places of interest include Bolton Abbey Estate, Skipton Castle, Grassington, Malham Cove, Harrogate and the World Heritage Site of Fountains Abbey and Studley Royal Park. The Dalzell Room is available for private events.

Our inspector loved: The bright, vivid colours of the décor, and the magnificent views.

Directions: Take exit A1M, junction 47 then the A59 towards Skipton. At Bolton Bridge turn right for the B6160 for Burnsall. The hotel is on the left upon approaching the village.

Web: www.johansens.com/devonshirefell
E-mail: reservations@thedevonshirearms.co.uk
Tel: 0870 381 8554
International: +44 (0)1756 729111
Fax: 01756 710564

Price Guide:
single £75–£130
double/twin £125–£195

175

THE RED LION

BY THE BRIDGE AT BURNSALL, NEAR SKIPTON, NORTH YORKSHIRE BD23 6BU

Beamed ceilings, creaky floors and log fires in winter greet you at this former 16th-century Ferryman's Inn on the banks of the River Wharfe in the picturesque Yorkshire Dales village of Burnsall. Owned and run by the Grayshon family, it is surrounded by glorious open countryside. Guests can step out for numerous walks straight from the front door. The hotel is actually on the "Dalesway". The bedrooms are all slightly different yet traditionally furnished, many with antiques and most have wonderful views over the village green, river and Burnsall Fell. The restaurant has been awarded an AA Rosette for serving food that is delicious and varied, imaginatively cooked and well-presented. Table d'hôte dishes such as local rabbit braised in ale and served with herb dumplings, or partridge with apricot seasoning and game chips, are complemented by international wines. Special half-board terms and winter warmer breaks are available. Bolton Abbey and Priory, the historic market town of Skipton with its medieval castle and the Settle to Carlisle Railway. The Red Lion has private fishing on the River Wharfe, 7 miles of trout and grayling fishing and offers partridge and pheasant shooting over 3000 acres on the nearby Grimwith Estate. Skipton and Ilkley golf courses are 11 miles away. 3 self-catering cottages are also available.

Directions: Burnsall is north of Skipton on B6160 between Grassington and Bolton Abbey. The inn is in the village centre by the bridge.

Web: www.johansens.com/redlionburnsall
E-mail: redlion@daelnet.co.uk
Tel: 0870 381 8850
International: +44 (0)1756 720204
Fax: 01756 720292

Price Guide:
single £60–£115
double £125–£155

Scarborough
Ripon
Harrogate   York

Our inspector loved: Lunch on the terrace overlooking the River Wharfe.

HOB GREEN HOTEL, RESTAURANT & GARDENS

MARKINGTON, HARROGATE, NORTH YORKSHIRE HG3 3PJ

Set in 870 acres of farm and woodland this charming "country house" hotel is only a short drive from the spa town of Harrogate and the ancient city of Ripon. The restaurant has an excellent reputation locally with only the finest fresh local produce being used, much of which is grown in the hotel's own garden. The interesting menus are complemented by an excellent choice of sensibly priced wines. All 12 bedrooms have been individually furnished and tastefully equipped to suit the most discerning guest. The drawing room and hall, warmed by log fires in cool weather, are comfortably furnished with the added attraction of fine antique furniture, porcelain and pictures. Situated in the heart of some of Yorkshire's most dramatic scenery, the hotel offers magnificent views of the valley beyond from all the main rooms. York is only 23 miles away. There is a wealth of cultural and historical interest nearby with Fountains Abbey and Studley Royal water garden and deer park a few minutes' drive. The Yorkshire Riding Centre is in Markington Village. Simply relax in this tranquil place where your every comfort is catered for. Special breaks available.

Our inspector loved: *Strolling around the large lovingly tended Victorian walled herb, vegetable and cutting flower garden.*

Directions: Turn left signposted Markington off the A61 Harrogate to Ripon road, the hotel is 1 mile after the village on the left.

Web: www.johansens.com/hobgreen
E-mail: info@hobgreen.com
Tel: 0870 381 8600
International: +44 (0)1423 770031
Fax: 01423 771589

Price Guide:
single £95–£118
double/twin £110–£155
suite £135–£175

NEW

THE WENSLEYDALE HEIFER

WEST WITTON, WENSLEYDALE, NORTH YORKSHIRE DL8 4LS

Directions: On the A684 trans-pennine road between Leyburn and Hawes.

Web: www.johansens.com/wensleydaleheifer
E-mail: info@wensleydaleheifer.co.uk
Tel: 0870 381 8625
International: +44 (0)1969 622322
Fax: 01969 624183

Price Guide:
single £80
double/twin £98–£120

Conveniently located on the A684, The Wensleydale Heifer is situated between Leyburn and Hawes in the Yorkshire Dales National Park and offers the ultimate in comfort within beautiful surroundings. Charming themed bedrooms are elegantly decorated and some provide mini-suites and four-poster beds. No luxury is spared: each room has Egyptian cotton sheets, Molton Brown toiletries and luxurious bath towels. Staff are experienced and offer excellent service. In the Whiskey Club Lounge, guests can relax and enjoy a morning coffee with a newspaper or in the evenings, taste one of the many hand-picked malt whiskeys available. There is a huge open fireplace, snug armchairs of the softest leather and an atmosphere that is both intimate and romantic. Owner/Chef David Moss, oversees the award-winning gastronomy. In the Fish Bar, which is decorated with rattan chairs and a sea grass flooring, there is a sumptuous selection of seafood dishes sourced entirely from the British Isles. The award-winning restaurant is perfect for a special occasion and has a refined atmosphere; most of the meat is locally reared and the ingredients are of the best quality. The menu changes weekly so a delectable surprise is always guaranteed. On finer days meals are served al fresco in the garden. The Yorkshire Dales has plenty to offer with picturesque villages and delightful scenery.

Our inspector loved: *This totally refurbished inn, and delicious food.*

DUNSLEY HALL

DUNSLEY, WHITBY, NORTH YORKSHIRE YO21 3TL

Dunsley Hall hotel stands in 4 acres of magnificent landscaped gardens in the North Yorkshire Moors National Park and has remained virtually unaltered since being built at the turn of the 20th century. Most of the individually decorated bedrooms, some with four-poster beds, benefit from a fantastic view over the sea, which is only a few minutes walk away, and have rich, luxurious fabrics and fine furniture. All rooms are non-smoking. Mellow oak panelling, a handsome Inglenook carved fireplace and stained glass windows enhance the drawing room's relaxing and restful features. From the Oak Room, Terrace Suite or Pyman Bar, guests can savour the Rosette award-winning regional dishes and seafood specialities made from only the freshest of ingredients. There is a hard-surface tennis court and a 9-hole putting green. Places of interest nearby include Castle Howard, Robin Hood's Bay, the North Yorkshire Moors Steam Railway and the birthplace of Captain Cook. Guests enjoy reduced green fees at Whitby Golf Course. There is also a self catering holiday cottage available.

Our inspector loved: The stained glass windows in the drawing room and the peacock strutting around the garden.

Directions: From the A171 Whitby–Teeside road, turn right at the signpost for Newholme, 3 miles north of Whitby. Dunsley Hall is the first turning on the left, 1 mile further on the right.

Web: www.johansens.com/dunsleyhall
E-mail: reception@dunsleyhall.com
Tel: 0870 381 8494
International: +44 (0)1947 893437
Fax: 01947 893505

Price Guide:
single £87.50–£130
double/twin £140–£190

HEY GREEN COUNTRY HOUSE HOTEL

WATERS ROAD, MARSDEN, WEST YORKSHIRE HD7 6NG

Directions: From Huddersfield, take A62 Oldham road to Marsden. Drive through the village and after approximately 1 mile the Hey Green is signed on the right.

Web: www.johansens.com/heygreen
E-mail: info@heygreen.com
Tel: 0870 381 8652
International: +44 (0)1484 844235
Fax: 01484 847605

Price Guide:
single £79-£149
double £109-£179

A solidly built, traditional West Yorkshire hotel with an imposing pillared entranceway, Hey Green Country House stands in superb landscaped grounds overlooking the spectacular countryside of the Colne Valley, midway between Huddersfield and Oldham. It is a peaceful, tranquil location just over 6 miles from the shops and entertainment of either town but with a multitude of historic and natural attractions within easy reach and a preponderance of green pastures, drystone walls and little grey farms in the surrounds. Style, good taste and a welcoming ambience personify the hotel with relaxation and attentiveness high on the list of staff priorities. Each en-suite bedroom has character and charm, every home comfort, little extra personal touches and most offer panoramic scenic views. An excellent 2 AA Rosette á la carte menu featuring modern British cuisine is served in an attractive restaurant situated in the oldest part of the hotel, built about 1710. It has a superb flagstone floor and an open fire burning throughout winter months. A large, comfortable conservatory is popular for pre and after-dinner social chats. Corporate meeting and event facilities available.

Our inspector loved: This peaceful retreat in The Last of the Summer Wine country.

For further information on the Channel Islands, please contact:

Visit Guernsey
PO Box 23, St Peter Port, Guernsey GY1 3AN
Tel: +44 (0)1481 723552
Internet: www.visitguernsey.com

Jersey Tourism
Liberation Square, St Helier, Jersey JE1 1BB
Tel: +44 (0)1534 500777
Internet: www.jersey.com

Sark Tourism
The Visitors Centre, The Avenue, Sark, GY9 0SA
Tel: +44 (0)1481 832345
Internet: www.sark.info

Herm Tourist Office
The White House Hotel, Herm Island via Guernsey GY1 3HR
Tel: +44 (0)1481 722377
Internet: www.herm-island.com

or see **pages 228-230** for details of
local attractions to visit during your stay.

Images from www.britainonview.com

THE WHITE HOUSE

HERM ISLAND, GUERNSEY, CHANNEL ISLANDS GY1 3HR

Directions: Herm is reached by boat from St Peter Port, Guernsey.

Web: www.johansens.com/whitehouseherm
E-mail: hotel@herm-island.com
Tel: 0870 381 8988
International: +44 (0)1481 722159
Fax: 01481 710066

Price Guide: (including dinner)
double/twin £150–£220

As wards of Herm Island, Adrian and Pennie Heyworth assume responsibility for the wellbeing of all visitors to their island home which is for all to enjoy at leisure. For an island just 1½ miles long its diversity is remarkable and during a 2-hour stroll that takes in its cliff walks, white sandy coves and abundant wildlife no two moments are the same. The magic starts to work from the moment of arrival at the pretty harbour, for in the absence of cars on Herm a tractor laden with guests' luggage chugs up from the jetty to The White House, winner of the Condé Nast Johansens Most Excellent Coastal Hotel Award 2005. Here, relaxation is the key, and guests can enjoy afternoon tea or a drink in its succession of homely lounges, in the bar or on the poolside patio. In keeping with a cherished tradition there are no televisions, no clocks nor telephones in the hotel's 40 bedrooms, the best of which have balconies and sea views. Appointments are nonetheless faultless and all include spacious up-to-date private bathrooms. Families are made particularly welcome and high tea is a popular event with younger guests. Seafood plays a prominent part on the wonderful menus: Guernsey lobster, scallops and crab are landed regularly. Self-catering holiday cottages are also available.

Our inspector loved: *Wonderful beaches, inviting walks and good food into the bargain.*

LA SABLONNERIE

LITTLE SARK, SARK, CHANNEL ISLANDS GY9 0SD

Owner and manager Elizabeth Perrée considers La Sablonnerie an oasis of good living and courtesy rather than a luxury hotel. It is truly that – and more! It is an hotel of rare quality situated in a time warp of simplicity on a tiny, idyllic island where no motor cars are allowed and life ambles along at a peaceful, unhurried pace. A vintage horse-drawn carriage collects guests from Sark's tiny harbour to convey them in style to the islands' southernmost tip - Little Sark. Crossing la Coupée, a narrow isthmus, guests can enjoy breathtaking views of the coast. Tranquil cosiness, friendliness and sophistication characterise this hotel with its low ceilings and 400-year-old oak beams. Opened in 1948 and retaining many of the characteristics of the old farmhouse, La Sablonnerie has been extended and discreetly modernised to provide 22 bedrooms which are charmingly individual in style and offer every amenity. The granite-walled bar, with its open fire, is a comfortable extra lounge where pre-dinner drinks can be enjoyed before sampling the delights of the candle-lit restaurant. The hotel has a reputation for superb cuisine. Many of the dishes are prepared from produce grown on its own farm and gardens and enhanced by locally caught lobster and oysters.

Our inspector loved: *The place to stay on this exceptional little island retreat – bring sensible shoes for excellent walking.*

Directions: By air or sea to Guernsey and then by ferry from St Peter Port.

Web: www.johansens.com/lasablonnerie
Tel: 0870 381 8666
International: +44 (0)1481 832061
Fax: 01481 832408

Grandes Rocques
Herm
St Peter Port
Sark
Airport

Price Guide: (including dinner)
single from £78
double/twin £156–£196

The King and I

For further information on Ireland, please contact:

The Irish Tourist Board
(Bord Fáilte Éireann)
Baggot Street Bridge
Dublin 2
Tel: +353 (0)1 602 4000
Internet: www.ireland.ie

Northern Ireland Tourist Information
Belfast Welcome Centre
47 Donegall Place
Belfast, BT1 5AD
Tel: +44 (0)28 9024 6609
Internet: www.gotobelfast.com

or see **pages 228-230** for details of
local attractions to visit during your stay.

Images from Fáilte Ireland

NEW

St Clerans Manor House

CRAUGHWELL, CO GALWAY, IRELAND

Directions: On Galway-Dublin road N6, take 2nd left after passing through Craughwell. Follow road for 2 miles until you come to black gates of house on your right (30 minutes from Galway City).

Web: www.johansens.com/stclerans
E-mail: stclerans@iol.ie
Tel: 00 353 91 846555
Fax: 00 353 91 846600

Price Guide: (Euro)
double €225–€350

A very warm and friendly welcome awaits guests at the magnificent St Clerans Manor House. Set in 45 acres of beautiful rural countryside, this two-storey 18th-century house is a truly magical place, where life seems to be lived at a different pace. Built in 1784 by the Burke family, the house has been carefully restored to its original splendour by its present owner, Merv Griffin, who has created a wonderfully luxurious and relaxing ambience. Art treasures from around the world adorn the rooms, and elegant period furnishings can be found throughout the house. Each of the 12 luxurious guest rooms is individually decorated, equipped with every modern amenity including high-speed Internet access, and offers breathtaking views of the surrounding countryside. Meals are served in the manor's splendid dining room, which has been host to several kings, princes and Hollywood celebrities. Renowned Japanese chef Hisashi Kumagai, known as "Kuma", creates both European and Oriental cuisine with unique inspirational flair. Situated 2km outside the village of Craughwell, 32km east of Galway, St. Clerans Manor House is ideally located for exploring this beautiful region, and offers numerous activities such as golf, sea, lake and river fishing, horse riding, horse racing and clay pigeon shooting.

Our inspector loved: *The peace and tranquillity of the 45 acres surrounding the manor house*

NEW

BROOK LANE HOTEL

KENMARE, CO KERRY, IRELAND

This delightfully quirky little boutique hotel, just a short walk from the picturesque town of Kenmare, offers a truly unique stay in a friendly and relaxed environment. The 20 individually decorated bedrooms are simply wonderful, with under-floor bathroom heating, large beds and soft, fluffy pillows ensuring a good night's sleep. Food is a real passion here, and the inviting bar/bistro with its sumptuous armchairs, is the perfect place to meet friends and enjoy the mouth-watering range of classic dishes with a modern twist. The stylish, comfortable dinging room can be hired exclusively for private or corporate events and other occasions. Brook Lane Hotel offers up-to-date business facilities, WI-FI and high speed wired internet access, light airy rooms and a generous working space and is particularly suitable for small business meetings, presentations and private parties. It is also a very popular location for romantic weddings. The roads around Kenmare are ideal for cycling – bikes are available locally, whilst Glen Inchaquin Park, with its breathtaking landscapes, waterfalls, woodlands and lakes, is a paradise for birdwatchers and nature lovers. Golf enthusiasts will enjoy the two scenic golf courses nearby, Kenmare Golf Course and the Ring of Kerry Golf & Country Club. After an exciting day outdoors, guests may gather at the hotel bar and listen to some local traditional live music.

Our inspector loved: The great big beds and heated bathroom floors.

Directions: On the N70 just a short walk from the pretty town of Kenmare.

Web: www.johansens.com/brooklanehotel
E-mail: info@brooklanehotel.com
Tel: 00 353 64 42077
Fax: 00 353 64 40869

Price Guide: (Euro)
double/twin €65–€95
suite €130–€150

Tralee
Dingle
Killarney

COOPERSHILL HOUSE

RIVERSTOWN, CO SLIGO, IRELAND

Directions: Leave N4 Sligo–Dublin road at Drumfin follow signs for Coopershill. 1 mile on, turn left.

Web: www.johansens.com/coopershillhouse
E-mail: ohara@coopershill.com
Tel: 00 353 71 9165108
Fax: 00 353 71 9165466

Price Guide: (Euro)
single from €134
double from €224

Winner of Johansens 1995 Country House Award, Coopershill is a fine example of a Georgian family mansion. Home to 7 generations of the O'Hara family since 1774, it combines the spaciousness and elegance of an earlier age with modern comforts. Public rooms are furnished in period style with gilt-framed portraits, hunting trophies and antiques. 6 of the bedrooms have four-poster or canopy beds and all have private bathrooms. Dinner is served by candlelight in the elegant dining room, where good cooking is complemented by a wide choice of wines. Open log fires and personal attention from owners Brian and Lindy O'Hara and their son Simon help to create the warm atmosphere and hospitality that typify Coopershill. Out of season the house is open to parties of 12 to 16 people at a special rate. The River Arrow winds through the 500-acre estate; trout and coarse fishing are available. Shooting is not permitted, leaving the abundant wildlife undisturbed. There is an excellent hard tennis court and also a croquet lawn. There are marvellous mountain and lakeside walks to enjoy in the area. Closed 1st November to 1st April.

Our inspector loved: *"Penny" the parrot who lives in the drinks cabinet.*

Recommendations in Scotland appear on pages 190-208

For further information on Scotland, please contact:

Visit Scotland
Ocean Point 1, 94 Ocean Drive, Edinburgh, EH6 6JH
Tel: +44 (0)131 332 2433
Internet: www.visitscotland.com

or see **pages 228-230** for details of
local attractions to visit during your stay.

Images from www.britainonview.com

CASTLETON HOUSE HOTEL

GLAMIS, BY FORFAR, ANGUS DD8 1SJ

Directions: From Edinburgh, take M90 Juntion 11; take A90 through Dundee, then A928 to Glamis, left on to A94. 3 miles on right.

Web: www.johansens.com/castletonhouse
E-mail: hotel@castletonglamis.co.uk
Tel: 0870 381 8411
International: +44 (0)1307 840340
Fax: 01307 840506

Price Guide:
single £120–£140
double/twin £180–£220
four-poster £240

This elegant 3 AA Rosette Edwardian hotel lies in the beautiful vale of Strathmore, a lush enclave beneath the Angus glens. Built in 1902, it stands on the site of a 12th-century fortification, the surrounding ditch being presumed to be a former defensive moat. Recently completely refurbished by its new owners, it now has an ambience of relaxed elegance where attention to detail and personal service are paramount. Each of the 6 bedrooms has been individually furnished, whilst the Regency four-poster suite has an additional dressing room housed in the turret. Guests may dine in the beautiful period dining room or the more informal conservatory; in either location a carefully planned menu of local ingredients with a winning combination of traditional and contemporary dishes is served. Glamis Castle is just 3 miles away and a must for every visitor. The family home of the late Queen Mother, it is surprisingly free of rope restricted areas and has a number of family photographs as well as 2 resident ghosts! Dundee and Perth are within easy driving distance and Blairgowrie lies just 15 minutes away. Beyond Rosemount lies the route to the Highlands for true historians and the more adventurous. One of the AA's top 200 hotels in the UK

Our inspector loved: *The top class, personal service and wonderful innovative cooking in this miniature grand hotel.*

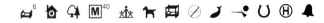

HIGHLAND COTTAGE

BREADALBANE STREET, TOBERMORY, ISLE OF MULL PA75 6PD

Highland Cottage is a delightful, intimate hotel that sits above Tobermory, a picturesque town on the Isle of Mull. Set in a quiet conservation area of the town, it evokes feelings of restful tranquillity yet is only a 5-minute walk from the town's main streets and Fisherman's Pier. Comfortable chairs in the sunny public rooms are perfect to relax and read the paper in. The cottage also has a large selection of books. Themed bedrooms, which are decorated in an island style, are cheerful and uplifting with homely touches and carefully chosen furniture for a truly comfortable stay. The hotel's restaurant is recognised for its high quality and has been awarded with 2 highly acclaimed AA Rosettes as well as the prestigious RAC Gold Ribbon award and AA Top Hotel status. Exceptionally delicious and imaginative dishes are prepared using top quality, locally produced ingredients. Seafood often comes direct from the Tobermory boats, caught by local divers and fishermen and the meat is of West Highland stock. The beautiful Isle of Mull has lots to offer and is completely different from any other Scottish island, with a fascinating character and picturesque landscape. A car is essential as public transport on the island is not good and there are many scenic drives to enjoy.

Our inspector loved: *The friendly reception at this haven in the most picturesque location in Western Scotland.*

Directions: There are frequent crossings from the mainland each day. When entering Tobermory on the main Salen road, go straight across at the mini roundabout, over the narrow stone bridge and immediately turn right. This is Breadalbane Street and the hotel is on the right opposite the Fire Station.

Isle of Mull   Oban

Dunoon

Glasgow

Campbelltown

Web: www.johansens.com/highlandcottage
E-mail: davidandjo@highlandcottage.co.uk
Tel: 0870 381 9184
International: +44 (0)1688 302030

Price Guide:
single from £100
double £135–£175

BALCARY BAY HOTEL

AUCHENCAIRN, NR CASTLE DOUGLAS, DUMFRIES & GALLOWAY DG7 1QZ

Directions: Located off the A711 Dumfries–Kirkcudbright road, 2 miles out of Auchencairn on the Shore Road.

Web: www.johansens.com/balcarybay
E-mail: reservations@balcary-bay-hotel.co.uk
Tel: 0870 381 8334
International: +44 (0)1556 640217/640311
Fax: 01556 640272

Price Guide:
single £66
double/twin £115–£135

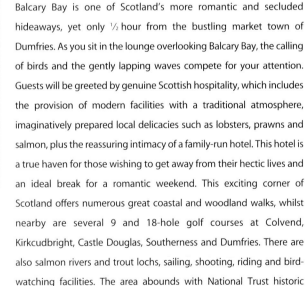

Enjoying a very warm climate due to its proximity to the Gulf Stream, Balcary Bay is one of Scotland's more romantic and secluded hideaways, yet only ½ hour from the bustling market town of Dumfries. As you sit in the lounge overlooking Balcary Bay, the calling of birds and the gently lapping waves compete for your attention. Guests will be greeted by genuine Scottish hospitality, which includes the provision of modern facilities with a traditional atmosphere, imaginatively prepared local delicacies such as lobsters, prawns and salmon, plus the reassuring intimacy of a family-run hotel. This hotel is a true haven for those wishing to get away from their hectic lives and an ideal break for a romantic weekend. This exciting corner of Scotland offers numerous great coastal and woodland walks, whilst nearby are several 9 and 18-hole golf courses at Colvend, Kirkcudbright, Castle Douglas, Southerness and Dumfries. There are also salmon rivers and trout lochs, sailing, shooting, riding and bird-watching facilities. The area abounds with National Trust historic properties and gardens. Seasonal short breaks and reduced inclusive rates are available for 3 and 7 night stays.

Our inspector loved: The views from this hotel, which complete the feeling of total escape.

NEW

THE PEAT INN

PEAT INN, BY CUPAR, FIFE KY15 5LH

Originally a coaching inn dating from the 1700s, for over 30 years The Peat Inn has enjoyed a reputation for being one of the finest restaurants in Scotland. It was recently taken over by the former head chef of étain, Terence Conran's Glaswegian enterprise, award-winning chef Geoffrey Smeddle and his charming wife Katherine. They have created a refined yet friendly and relaxed atmosphere where everything is dedicated to the unhurried and unpretentious enjoyment of good food and wine. There is a large sitting room with comfortable sofas and a big stone open fireplace, whilst the restaurant occupies three dining rooms and has a strong French style in furnishings and décor. Dishes are based on the best of what is locally and seasonally available: game, beef and lamb from the Highlands, vegetables from abundant Fife and fresh fish from the sea. Menus are modern and interesting, and complemented by a fantastic wine list featuring over 400 bins. A Bordeaux-based friend of the family acts as consultant for the list and cellar. 25 yards to the rear of the restaurant is The Residence, providing eight bedroom suites with views over the surrounding farmland; all are split-level apart from one for disabled guests, and decorated in a French style with Italian marble bathrooms.

Our inspector loved: *This legendary restaurant with rooms that have been given a new lease of life.*

Directions: The Peat Inn lies 6½ miles to the south-west of St Andrews by the A915 and B940.

Web: www.johansens.com/thepeatinn
E-mail: stay@thepeatinn.co.uk
Tel: 0870 381 8673
International: +44 (0)1334 840206
Fax: 01334 840530

Price Guide:
single £125
double/twin £165

CORRIEGOUR LODGE HOTEL

LOCH LOCHY, BY SPEAN BRIDGE, INVERNESS-SHIRE PH34 4EA

Directions: 17 miles north of Fort William on the A82, on the south side of Loch Lochy, between Spean Bridge and Invergarry on the way to Skye.

Web: www.johansens.com/corriegour
E-mail: info@corriegour-lodge-hotel.com
Tel: 0870 381 8447
International: +44 (0)1397 712685
Fax: 01397 712696

Price Guide: (including dinner)
double/twin £176–£191
special seasonal breaks are available

Surrounded by 9 acres of woodland and gardens, with views over Loch Lochy, this former Victorian hunting lodge enjoys one of the finest settings in the "Great Glen", an area steeped in history. Recently refurbished, the warm, tasteful décor features large comfy sofas and log fires that create a welcoming atmosphere, particularly in the lounge and restaurant. The cosy bedrooms feature handmade furniture, imported lights, silk drapes and designer carpets; many have state-of-the-art bathrooms and views of the loch. Service is friendly and relaxed and nothing is ever too much trouble. Winner of the coveted Taste of Scotland Award, the Loch View Restaurant and conservatory offers exquisite cuisine, based on finest local produce such as venison, salmon and Highland lamb. Savour assiette of organic lamb with gratin potatoes, Provençal vegetables and a lamb and rosemary jus followed by an iced Baileys parfait with coffee poached pear. The area is the gateway to the Highlands and west coast, and a true paradise for nature lovers or those simply wishing to recharge their batteries. Outdoor pursuits include fishing, cycling, pony trekking and skiing. A small lochside beach with its own jetty is nearby. Although Loch Ness is not far away, Lizzie, Nessie's 3-humped cousin, has been sighted in Loch Lochy!

Our inspector loved: The continual improvements, interesting food, and lovely setting of this understated hotel.

THE BRIDGE HOTEL

DUNROBIN STREET, HELMSDALE, SUTHERLAND KW8 6JA

Situated in the heart of Helmsdale, The Bridge Hotel was taken over by new owners Lorraine and Ronnie Dunnet in 2006 and remains an unpretentious, smart and stylish venue. The ground floor is entirely finished in Caithness slate and the interiors feature an extraordinary array of stuffed deer heads, from roe to red deer, moose and reindeer. Accommodation is excellent value and comfortable with cosy beds and bathrooms, but do not feature televisions, telephones or tea and coffee making facilities. In a drive to build on the enviable reputation the hotel and restaurant has established for its food, the Dunnets have appointed a new Head Chef who brings new flair to the cuisine. The best Scottish produce, some sourced locally from Helmsdale Harbour, is combined to create dishes such as pan fried wood pigeon, locally caught dressed Helmsdale crab, Scotch rump steak and oven baked fresh local lobster gratin. Breakfast, lunch, dinner and relaxed Sunday roasts are served in the restaurant, which is also open to non-residents all year round. The Bridge is happy to organise events for private celebrations or business organisations and has a state-of-the-art conference room that can cater up to 30 people theatre style or for private dining.

Our inspector loved: *The unexpected pleasure of coming across this splendid inn, in such a far flung location.*

Directions: Take the A9 coastal road and The Bridge Hotel is in the centre of Helmsdale village.

Web: www.johansens.com/thebridgehelmsdale
E-mail: mail@bridgehotel.net
Tel: 0870 381 8645
International: +44 (0)1431 821100

Price Guide:
single £50–£60
double/twin £65–£95
suite £100–£150

John O'Groats
Portree
Inverness
Fort William
Glasgow

DUNAIN PARK HOTEL

INVERNESS, IV3 8JN

Directions: 2 miles south west of the city centre, on the A82.

Web: www.johansens.com/dunainpark
E-mail: info@dunainparkhotel.co.uk
Tel: 0870 381 8433
International: +44 (0)1463 230512
Fax: 01463 224532

Price Guide:
double £138–£198

Guests are welcomed with afternoon tea at this relaxed and informal hotel where visitors would be forgiven for thinking they had entered a private home. Secluded in six acres of gardens and woodlands this Georgian country house provides 11 comfortable bedrooms; each has an Italian marble bathroom and six bedrooms have been fitted with traditional furnishings and are very spacious. Many of the original rooms have four-poster beds and the suites boast king-size beds and separate lounges. The Coach House is exceptionally private: converted into two cottages, each comprises two beds and a lounge. Particular care is taken to choose quality produce to create delicious meals and the herbs, soft fruits and vegetables on the menu are grown on the premises. Salmon, scallops, venison, lamb and game are bought locally. The menu is traditionally Scottish with a French influence and the wine list consists of over 70 selections; more than 200 malt whiskies are also available. There are over 20 golf courses nearby, trout fishing can be arranged and walks around the Victorian gardens or nearby Caledonian Canal are recommended.

Our inspector loved: *The traditional comforts and isolation from urban bustle.*

THE STEADINGS AT THE GROUSE & TROUT

FLICHITY, FARR, SOUTH LOCH NESS, INVERNESS IV2 6XD

Set amidst the striking Upper Strathnairn countryside replete with lochs and heathered lands, stands this delightful, unpretentious hotel full of charm and rustic character. Built in 1860, the property was originally outbuildings and part of Flichity Inn, which was destroyed in 1964. Today, quality accommodation in relaxed and peaceful surroundings are on offer. The comfortable conservatory lounge enables guests to sit back and enjoy the wonderful panaromic scenery and wildlife. This is the ideal base from which to explore the whisky trail, castles, lochs and glens of the hidden Scottish Highlands. The area boasts an abundance of wildlife including herds of deer, wild goats, beautiful grouse and sedate heron landing on the Flichity Loch, and privileged guests may even spot osprey collecting a trout from the Loch or a stoat playing with the resident hare family on the hotel's lawn. South Loch Ness is a unique location that harmoniously couples wildness with tranquillity, and the awe-inspiring landscape beckons to be discovered. Enjoy local and international beers in The Grouse & Trout Lounge Bar and sumptuous Scottish and international cuisine prepared from local produce accommpanied by an excellent wine list and an array of fine Scottish malt whiskies.

Our inspector loved: The wonderful location of this ever improving, intimate hotel.

Directions: Leave Inverness southwards on the A9. After 5 miles turn right onto the B851 signposted Fort Augustus. The hotel is a further 7½ miles along this road.

Web: www.johansens.com/steadings
E-mail: stay@steadingshotel.co.uk
Tel: 0870 381 9138
International: +44 (0)1808 521314
Fax: 01808 521741

Price Guide:
single £68
double £95

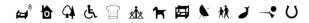

GRESHORNISH HOUSE HOTEL

EDINBANE, BY PORTREE, ISLE OF SKYE IV51 9PN

Directions: 61/2 miles north east of Dunvegan on the A850. The hotel is signposted to the north off the main road and lies 2 miles further on along its own drive.

Web: www.johansens.com/greshornishhouse
E-mail: info@greshornishhouse.com
Tel: 0870 381 8656
International: +44 (0)1470 582266
Fax: 01470 582345

Price Guide:
single £50–£150
double £100–£150

Described as "a typical Skye manor house," Greshornish House Hotel occupies a secluded lochside site amidst 10 acres of gardens and wooded grounds. The oldest part of the building dates back to the mid-18th century and today the door of this family-run hotel is always open, in accordance with the hospitable tradition of the island. There are 9 distinctive and comfortable en-suite bedrooms, one of which is allegedly haunted. Some boast stunning views across Loch Greshornish to Trotternish or overlook the Victorian walled garden and hills beyond. Four-poster, double and twin rooms are available. In the intimate candle-lit dining room, innovative menus are served and feature an abundance of local seafood, game, Skye lamb, Scotch beef and exceptional Scottish cheeses. Following dinner, guests can enjoy a game of snooker, chess or a quiet book by the drawing room fire with a good malt whisky. The hotel has a tennis court and croquet lawn and acts as the perfect base for exploring the island's ancient brochs, local museums, potteries, craft shops and galleries or more famous attractions such as Dunvegan Castle, Skyeskyns Tannery and the Talisker Distillery.

Our inspector loved: *The peaceful location, great improvements, and the personal attention of the charming new owners.*

HOTEL EILEAN IARMAIN

SLEAT, ISLE OF SKYE IV43 8QR

Hotel Eilean Iarmain stands on the small bay of Isle Ornsay in the South of Skye with views over the Sound of Sleat. The hotel prides itself on its log fires, inventive cooking and friendly staff. 1997/8 accolades include the RAC Restaurant Award, RAC Merit Award for Hospitality, Comfort and Restaurant, AA Rosette for Restaurant, AA Romantic Hotel of Great Britain and Ireland Award, Les Routiers Corps d'Elite Wine Award and Macallan Taste of Scotland, runner-up Hotel of the Year Award. There are 12 indivdiually decorated bedrooms and 4 light and airy suites, each with a double bedroom and cosy sitting room with a sofa bed. Log fires warm the reception rooms and the wood-panelled dining room where candle-lit dinners can be enjoyed overlooking the bay and the island of Ornsay. The menu features game when in season and fresh seafood landed at the pier. Premier cru clarets feature on the extensive wine list, and a large selection of malt whiskies includes local Poit Dhubh and Talisker. Clan MacDonald Centre, Armadale Castle and Talisker Distillery are close by. Sports include sea-fishing, shooting and walking.

Our inspector loved: *This delightful, informal hostelry, quite magically situated, unpretentious food, charming staff and lovely fresh bright rooms.*

Directions: The hotel is in Sleat, between Broadford and Armadale on the A851. 20 minutes from Skye Bridge; linked by ferry to Mallaig Station and is 35 minutes by road from Lochalsh Railway Station over Skye Bridge.

John O'Groats

Portree

Inverness

Fort William

Glasgow

Web: www.johansens.com/eileaniarmain
E-mail: hotel@eileaniarmain.co.uk
Tel: 0870 381 8619
International: +44 (0)1471 833332
Fax: 01471 833275

Price Guide:
single £75–£95
double £90–£190
suite £150–£250

TORAVAIG HOUSE

KNOCK BAY, SLEAT, ISLE OF SKYE IV44 8RE

Directions: By the Skye Bridge take A87 to Broadford. Turn left to Armadale, Sleat (A851) on approach to Broadford. Continue towards Armadale for approx.10 miles. The hotel is less than 1 mile from the Tarskavaig junction on the main A851 and on the left hand side of the road.

Web: www.johansens.com/toravaig
E-mail: info@skyehotel.co.uk
Tel: 0870 381 9344
International: +44 (0)1471 833231
Fax: 01471 833231

Price Guide:
single £69.50
double £129–£160

Amidst 2 acres in a secluded part of the island, overlooking the Sound of Sleat, Toravaig House has been totally transformed into a welcoming small hotel by owners Anne Gracie and Kenneth Gunn. The extensive refurbishment programme has created one of the island's most exclusive and luxurious retreats, offering first-class service at an affordable price, and has received many accolades including: 2005 winner of Scottish Island Hotel of the Year by Hotel Review Scotland, 2006 winner of Condé Nast Johansens Most Excellent Service Award and 2006 Scottish Council for Development and Industry Excellence in Tourism Award. The tastefully furnished bedrooms have every amenity, and exquisite cuisine, served in the elegant Iona restaurant, is created from fresh local produce, alongside fine wines and malts. Small weddings and functions can be accommodated by the dedicated staff, and the house is ideally situated for exploring the Isle of Skye, a nature lover's paradise with fantastic low-level walking and climbing in the Cuillin Mountains. Daily skippered charters on the hotel's yacht, "Solus," a 36' Jeanneau Sun Odyessy, offers cruising in some of the best sailing waters in the world around the south of Skye and the mainland. Sleat, known for its unique Highland culture, has acquired an excellent reputation for its musical events, and a splendid Feis is held in mid-July.

Our inspector loved: *The bright airiness of this revitalised hotel.*

RUDDYGLOW PARK

LOCH ASSYNT, BY LAIRG, SUTHERLAND IV27 4HB

This small, quiet country house is located in the beautiful north-west Highlands of Scotland, and is owned and run by Patricia Filmer-Sankey, a native of the parish of Assynt. Its unusual name dates back to the National Hunt racehorse, "Ruddyglow," ridden by Patricia's father, the late Captain Filmer-Sankey, in the 1920s. Ruddyglow won over 27 races and a painting, by an artist of the times, hangs in the dining room depicting his last Grand Military Gold cup win. The house has a superb elevated position with spectacular views from the terraces: over 4½ acres of much loved and well tended woodland gardens, majestic mountains and Scottish lochs. Bedrooms are traditional and feature Egyptian cotton bed linen and pure Hungarian goose down duvets. Lavish bathrooms, with Jacuzzi baths and power showers, thick, velvety bathrobes and bathroom accessories ensure a truly indulgent stay. An extensive organic Continental buffet and traditional full Scottish breakfasts are served daily, and by prior arrangement, flavoursome dinners created from organic, local produce can be prepared. Nestled between the foothills of Quinag, and the edge of Loch Assynt, this tranquil location offers luxurious accommodation with outstanding service.

Our inspector loved: *This mini villa "par excellence" with its splendid antiques and fabulous views.*

Directions: The house lies 6 miles east of Lochinver on the A837 and is clearly signposted.

Web: www.johansens.com/ruddyglowpark
E-mail: info@ruddyglowpark.com
Tel: 0870 381 8457
International: +44 (0)1571 822216
Fax: 01571 822216

Price Guide:
rooms £70–£120

John O'Groats

Portree

Inverness

Fort William

Glasgow

FORSS HOUSE HOTEL

FORSS, NEAR THURSO, CAITHNESS KW14 7XY

Directions: Located west of Thurso 4½ miles on the A836.

Web: www.johansens.com/forsshousehotel
E-mail: anne@forsshousehotel.co.uk
Tel: 0870 381 8321
International: +44 (0)1847 861201
Fax: 01847 861301

Price Guide:
single £70–£85
double/twin £105–£135

Lovers of the open spaces and grand landscapes of the Scottish Highlands will adore this stately, traditional old house. Built 200 years ago, the owners have been gradually restoring the building to its original splendour, just as they excellently refurbished Ackergill Tower, which stands testament to their good taste and flair for design. The bedrooms in the main house have been carefully decorated with luxurious soft furnishings and are accompanied by elegant and carefully-tiled bathrooms. The conservatory is a beautifully light and airy space in which to enjoy a refreshing morning breakfast, and the more classic dining-room is an intimate and welcoming venue for evening dinner. Each meal is prepared with a simplicity that enables the true flavours of the finest local ingredients, sourced from surrounding estates, rivers and the coastline of Forss, to be retained. This sumptuous selection of seasonal and freshest Highland fish and meat is served alongside an extensive and inspiring wine collection. The house lies in the most spectacular setting that is quintessentially the Highlands: nestling gently in a tree-lined glen with its own swirling river for fishing. The area is a haven for history enthusiasts and a great place to really enjoy the tradition of the British great outdoors.

Our inspector loved: Civilisation in the wilderness.

KNOCKOMIE HOTEL

GRANTOWN ROAD, FORRES, MORAYSHIRE IV36 2SG

Dating back some 150 years, this elegant house owes much of its defining style to the Arts and Crafts movement, which in 1914 transformed the house into what it is today. Paying guests are recorded as early as the 1840s, although its metamorphosis into a stylish hotel is somewhat more recent! With just 16 bedrooms, the hotel has a winning combination of personal service and intimate atmosphere combined with an extremely stylish and elegant interior that ensures guests can relax from the moment they arrive and enjoy the local hospitality. This is Malt Whisky country and Knockomie has a fine collection for guests to savour, although a trip to one of the local distilleries is a must. It is a beautiful region with Loch Ness on the west and Speyside to the east. Country pursuits are plentiful including shooting, fishing and golf which can all be arranged by the hotel, whilst the less sporting can enjoy trips to nearby Brodie and Cawdor castles. At the end of such a day, guests can look forward to a relaxing drink in the comfortable surroundings of the bar, followed by a carefully prepared dinner from a menu that boasts a successful balance of traditional Scottish ingredients and lighter recipes.

Our inspector loved: *The unexpected pleasure of coming across this stylish hotel nicely positioned outside the town.*

Directions: Knockomie Hotel is located 1 mile south of Forres on the A940 to Grantown on Spey.

Web: www.johansens.com/knockomiehotel
E-mail: stay@knockomie.co.uk
Tel: 0870 381 8663
International: +44 (0)1309 673146
Fax: 01309 673290

Elgin

Keith

Auchnarrow

Price Guide:
single £110–£140
double/twin £160–£200

 16 M 40

CAIRN LODGE HOTEL

ORCHIL ROAD, AUCHTERARDER, PERTHSHIRE PH3 1LX

The Cairn Lodge is a hotel of distinctive quality. Sitting in the heart of the splendid Perthshire countryside, it is easy to forget that Glasgow and Edinburgh are both only 1 hour away. Service at Cairn Lodge is second-to-none while ingredients gathered from the Scottish countryside contribute to the superb cuisine. Scottish hospitality is guaranteed to provide an unforgettable experience. The bedrooms are beautifully appointed, all are en-suite and have tea and coffee making facilities, colour television and private telephone. Apart from the famous Gleneagles courses, golfers are within easy reach of St Andrews and Carnoustie, there are also a host of local courses. Alternative activities include fishing, horse riding, clay pigeon and game shooting, falconry and hill walking. Less energetic, but no less breathtaking, is simply relaxing and taking in the beauty of the surrounding Perthshire countryside.

Directions: On the western outskirts of town, the hotel is signposted off the main road on the link road to Crieff.

Web: www.johansens.com/cairnlodge
E-mail: info@cairnlodge.co.uk
Tel: 0870 381 9284
International: +44 (0)1764 662634
Fax: 01764 664866

Price Guide:
single £95–£155
double/twin £110–£230

Our inspector loved: The air of spaciousness and cheerful ambience.

THE FOUR SEASONS HOTEL

LOCHSIDE, ST FILLANS, PERTHSHIRE PH6 2NF

This rambling, white hotel is delightfully situated on the eastern edge of Loch Earn, which has been described as the jewel in the crown of Perthshire lochs. All around is unspoilt Southern Highland landscape, steep hillsides and towering, rugged mountains whose lower slopes are covered with deep green woodland. It is an area of scenic splendour, about 30 miles west of the historic city of Perth. The Four Seasons Hotel, supervised by resident owner Andrew Low, is excellent in every way and is superb value for money. The furnishings and décor are simple yet tasteful and open fires and several lounges add to the interior charm. Guests may choose to savour fine dining in the 2 Rosette-awarded restaurant or in the more informal Bistro. The team of chefs create imaginative modern European cuisine featuring the best local produce. The bedrooms are beautifully proportioned and cosy; all are on the first floor and each has a private bathroom and home-from-home comforts. Six fully-equipped chalets on the hillside behind the hotel are suitable for families with one or two children or for visitors seeking extra privacy. When not enjoying the magnificent views and changing colours from the hotel's south-facing terrace, guests can enjoy walking at Ben Vorlich or visiting the picturesque Southern Highland's villages.

Our inspector loved: The fine views, relaxed atmosphere, and emphasis on good food.

Directions: Take the A85 west from Perth.

Web: www.johansens.com/fourseasons
E-mail: info@thefourseasonshotel.co.uk
Tel: 0870 381 8528
International: +44 (0)1764 685 333
Fax: 01764 685 444

Price Guide:
(closed in January and early February)
double £106–£126

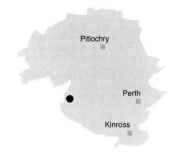

CASTLE VENLAW

EDINBURGH ROAD, PEEBLES EH45 8QG

Directions: From Edinburgh, follow the A703 to Peebles. After 30mph sign, the hotel drive is signposted on the left. From Peebles follow the A703 to Edinburgh the Hotel is on the right after .75 mile.

Web: www.johansens.com/venlaw
E-mail: stay@venlaw.co.uk
Tel: 0870 381 8410
International: +44 (0)1721 720384
Fax: 01721 724066

Price Guide:
double/twin £120–£170
four poster £170–£185
romantic suite £180–£230

Just 40 minutes from the city of Edinburgh, yet within the peaceful Borders countryside, the Castle sits majestically on the slopes of Venlaw Hill overlooking the royal and ancient town of Peebles. Originally built as a private house in 1782, it is now recognised as one of the leading 4-star hotels in the area maintaining country house tradition and offering an air of elegance and relaxed informality. From the welcoming Library with its oak panelling and log fire to the 12 bedrooms – all named after Scotland's finest malt whiskies – great care has been taken to preserve the Castle's charm and character. Guests choose from a range of suites, including the recent additions of 2 dedicated romantic suites and, at the top of the tower, a family suite complete with a children's den. The spacious and airy 2 AA Rosette restaurant provides the perfect ambience in which to enjoy menus where delicious local produce such as Borders salmon, lamb and game are given an international flavour. Outside, acres of beautiful woodland grounds can be explored, golf or fishing enjoyed, and the history in the ruined Abbeys and historic houses can be appreciated. Edinburgh, Glasgow and Stirling are within easy reach. Short breaks including dinner, are available throughout the year starting from £70.

Our inspector loved: The peace, the quiet, the stylish friendly service and the fantastic romantic suites.

CULZEAN CASTLE – THE EISENHOWER APARTMENT

MAYBOLE, AYRSHIRE KA19 8LE

Situated in the heart of one of Scotland's most magnificent country parks and dramatically perched on a cliff top with breathtaking views, Culzean Castle is the ideal base for a golfing trip in an area that boasts some of Scotland's finest links courses. The Eisenhower Apartment is a presidential retreat for guests bored with 5-star hotels. The 6-bedroom upper floor of Culzean was retained for General Eisenhower when the Castle was handed over to The National Trust for Scotland in 1945. Now, guests can enjoy the style and comfort once reserved for the General and his family. Guests staying in the apartment can either enter the Castle through the impressive armoury at the front door, or use the private lift at the side door. When you arrive on the top floor you are entering a rather splendid home and the friendly welcome from the staff simply amplifies this feeling. Whether you are travelling on your own, as a couple, or maybe wishing to book all the rooms for that special party, the Castle will make you feel most welcome. Guests have access to the Castle during opening hours and can explore the 560-acre country park with its woodlands, deer park and newly recreated Victorian Vinery situated in the enchanting Walled Garden.

Our inspector loved: *The unbelievable location and feeling of luxury amongst such history.*

Directions: From Glasgow, take the M77/ A77 south towards Ayr. Culzean Castle is 12 miles south of Ayr on the A719.

Web: www.johansens.com/culzeancastle
E-mail: culzean@nts.org.uk
Tel: 0870 381 8469
International: +44 (0)1655 884455
Fax: 01655 884503

Price Guide:
single from £140
double from £250

NEW

AMHUINNSUIDHE CASTLE

AMHUINNSUIDHE CASTLE ESTATE, ISLE OF HARRIS HS3 3AS

Directions: 12 miles north west of Tarbert by the A859 and B887.

Web: www.johansens.com/amhuinnsuidhe
E-mail: info@amhuinnsuidhe.com
Tel: 0870 381 8408
International: +44 (0)1859 560200
Fax: 01859 560263

Price Guide:
(please contact the castle for a
comprehensive price guide)

Stornoway

● Tarbert

Rodel

There can be few more breathtaking settings than that of this magnificent stately castle. Built in an attractive baronial style the granite building stands at the western shores of the Isle of Harris with views over the Sound of Taransay. There is an abundance of wildlife - otters frolicking in the turquoise waters, stag roaming the glens, and eagles soaring above. The castle itself can sleep up to 20 guests in 12 elegant first-floor bedrooms, where comfort and luxury are paramount - each has its own private bathroom and unrivalled views. The wood-panelled dining room is simply stunning and an impressive backdrop for dinner, be it communal dining amongst guests or when the castle is hired exclusively for a private function. The castle's own loch is the source of its delicious bottled water that complements the local and seasonal ingredients used in the outstanding cuisine. Seafood is freshly caught on the island, whilst venison, trout and salmon come from the castle's own stocks. Fishing and shooting are very popular, and with ownership rights on 6 river systems and 55000 trust-owned acres it is a huntsman's paradise. Ghillies are on hand to offer instruction or share professional tips. Golf, cookery classes, guided nature walks and visits to tweed-weaving sheds can be arranged. Closed November to March.

Our inspector loved: This idyllic, fairytail castle with its cordon of white sand and turquoise water.

For further information on Wales, please contact:

Wales Tourist Board
Brunel House, 2 Fitzalan Road, Cardiff CF24 0UY
Tel: +44 (0)29 2049 9909
Web: www.visitwales.com

North Wales Tourism
77 Conway Road, Colwyn Bay, Conway LL29 7LN
Tel: +44 (0)1492 531731
Web: www.nwt.co.uk

Mid Wales Tourism
The Station, Machynlleth, Powys SY20 8TG
Tel: (Freephone) 0800 273747
Web: www.visitmidwales.co.uk

South West Wales Tourism Partnership
The Coach House, Aberglasney, Carmarthenshire SA32 8QH
Tel: +44 (0)1558 669091
Web: www.swwtp.co.uk

or see **pages 228-230** for details of
local attractions to visit during your stay.

Images from www.britainonview.com

THE INN AT THE ELM TREE

ST BRIDES, WENTLOOGE, NR NEWPORT NP10 8SQ

Directions: From Newport, exit M4 at junction 28 and take B4239 for approximately 3 miles.

Web: www.johansens.com/elmtree
E-mail: inn@the-elm-tree.co.uk
Tel: 0870 381 8637
International: +44 (0)1633 680225
Fax: 01633 681035

Price Guide:
single £80–£90
double/twin £90–£130

This is a warm, welcoming and extremely relaxing place. Situated in a little known coastal village just a 15-minutes drive from Cardiff and Newport, the Inn at the Elm Tree is described by owner's Shaun and Donna Ellis as a 21st-century inn with traditional values. Surrounded by the flat river meadows of the Seven Estuary it is an ideal venue in which to escape from the noise and pressures of everyday life. Peace and tranquillity abound in an area of special scientific interest teeming with bird and wildlife, offering protection to rare and varied flora and fauna. The inn's bedrooms are excellent: designed to the highest standards of quality and comfort, homely and appealing whilst offering every facility, plus personal touches and little luxuries characteristic of a leading hotel. They have king-sized beds, iron and brass beds and four-posters, beamed ceilings, chunky pine furniture and rocking chairs. 2 ground-floor rooms can be booked as a family suite with its own entrance. The intimate, AA Rosette award-winning candle-lit restaurant with adjoining Café Bar, which opens onto a Tropical Courtyard, serves traditional favourites alongside the varied and seasonal European cuisine. Open fires burn during cooler months. Golf, horse riding, clay shooting, sea, trout and course fishing are all nearby.

Our inspector loved: *The spacious bedrooms with an abundance of extra touches and the warmth and friendly service from Shaun and his team.*

Ty Mawr Country Hotel

BRECHFA, CARMARTHENSHIRE SA32 7RA

Nestled in the glorious Welsh countryside in the beautiful Brechfa Forest, this charming 15th-century house is an ideal base for a country retreat. Literally meaning "big house" Ty Mawr is steeped in history and retains many original features such as thick stone walls, low ceilings and old beams. The bedrooms are well appointed with antique pine furnishings and have bathrooms with Italian tiled floors and claw-foot baths. In colder months log fires create a cosy hideaway from the chilly outdoors and guests can warm up with a hearty dish from the delicious supper menu. Welsh black beef might be the obvious choice but the freshly caught seafood from Cardigan Bay is definitely worth a try! In the summer visitors enjoy dining al fresco in the attractive lawned gardens with the River Marlais running through. The refurbished, adjacent former bakery now houses the Flock Inn, a microbrewery. Using a range of traditional floor malts from Warminster and hops from Charles Faram, 3 types of beer are produced: Bois Baaach, Shear Delight and Ewe-reek-a! Brewery tours can be arranged and microbrewery/hotel packages are available. This area is renowned for its spectacular castles and National Botanic Gardens. Carmarthen is less than 20 minutes away and a little further afield is the Victorian seaside resort of Tenby. Alternatively, walk or cycle through the breathtaking forest valleys.

Our inspector loved: The welcome by hosts Annabel and Stephen.

Directions: Located 14 miles north-east of Carmarthen on the B4310.

Web: www.johansens.com/tymawr
E-mail: info@wales-country-hotel.co.uk
Tel: 0870 381 9318
International: +44 (0)1267 202332

Price Guide:
single £65-£70
double/twin £95–£105

CONRAH COUNTRY HOUSE HOTEL

RHYDGALED, CHANCERY, ABERYSTWYTH, CEREDIGION SY23 4DF

Directions: The Conrah lies 3 miles south of Aberystwyth on the A487.

Web: www.johansens.com/conrahcountryhouse
E-mail: enquiries@conrah.co.uk
Tel: 0870 381 8444
International: +44 (0)1970 617941
Fax: 01970 624546

Price Guide:
single £85–£100
double/twin £130–£170

One of Wales's much loved country house hotels, the Conrah is tucked away at the end of a rhododendron-lined drive, only minutes from the spectacular rocky cliffs and sandy bays of the Cardigan coast. Set in 22 acres of rolling grounds, the Conrah's magnificent position gives views as far north as the Cader Idris mountain range. Afternoon tea and Welsh cakes or pre-dinner drinks can be taken at leisure in the quiet writing room or one of the comfortable lounges, where antiques and fresh flowers add to the relaxed country style. The acclaimed restaurant uses fresh local produce, together with herbs and vegetables from the Conrah kitchen garden, to provide the best of both classic and modern dishes. The hotel is owned and run by the Heading family who extend a warm invitation to guests to come for a "real taste of Wales", combined with old-fashioned, high standards of service. For recreation, guests may enjoy a game of table tennis in the summer house, croquet on the lawn or a walk around the landscaped gardens. Those wishing to pay in euro's are welcome to do so. Golf, pony-trekking and sea fishing are all available locally, whilst the university town of Aberystwyth and home of the national library of Wales is only 3 miles away. Closed Christmas.

Our inspector loved: *The timeless charm.*

TAN-Y-FOEL COUNTRY HOUSE

CAPEL GARMON, NR BETWS-Y-COED, CONWY LL26 0RE

This contemporary bijou-style house, built of magnificent Welsh stone has won many plaudits as an outstanding small country house that blends finest country elegance with innovative interior design. The intimate reception rooms styled in earth tones offer a calming and tranquil atmosphere. Set in breathtaking surroundings, it commands views of the verdant Conwy Valley and the rugged peaks of Snowdonia. Once inside Tan-y-Foel a "no smoking" policy prevails. Each extremely comfortable bedroom has its own strikingly individual style, thoughtful small touches add to their charm and the bathrooms are delightfully appointed. Celebrated for her impeccable cuisine, Janet, a member of "The Master Chefs of Great Britain", sources the best local produce, fresh fish, Welsh black beef and organically grown vegetables for her creatively composed nightly menus, which have been recognised with 3 AA Rosettes. This, combined with an outstanding selection of wines, will ensure an experience to savour. The personal welcome, which perfectly complements the nature of the Pitmans' unique house, has resulted in them receiving the Condé Nast Johansens – Most Excellent Country House 2006 award, and the accolade of 5 Star Country House Guest Accommodation with the Welsh Tourist Board

Our inspector loved: Sitting in the restaurant listening to guests commenting on the truly delicious menu. Superb comments, well deserved.

Directions: From Chester, A55 to Llandudno, A470 towards Betws-y-Coed. 2 miles south from Llanrwst fork left towards Capel Garmon. Tan-y-Foel is just over a mile uphill on the left.

Web: www.johansens.com/tanyfoel
E-mail: enquiries@tyfhotel.co.uk
Tel: 0870 381 8938
International: +44 (0)1690 710507
Fax: 01690 710681

Price Guide:
single £99–£150
double £145–£170

SYCHNANT PASS HOUSE

SYCHNANT PASS ROAD, CONWY LL32 8BJ

Idyllically situated in the foothills of Snowdonia National Park in North Wales, Sychnant Pass House has won many accolades as an outstanding small country house that perfectly blends charm, comfort and elegance with an overall atmosphere of conviviality and relaxation. Located 2 miles from Conwy and just a 45-minute drive via the A55 Express Way to the Ireland connections at Holyhead, it stands in 3 acres of lawns, trees, a wild garden, featuring ponds, and a little stream . Rural beauty with unfenced roads, wandering sheep and roaming wild ponies surrounds the hotel. Owners Bre and Graham Carrington Sykes are fastidious about standards and are renowned for their welcoming, warm personalities. Guests choose from a variety of rooms; each is delightfully decorated and furnished, fitted to the highest criteria. 2 ground floor bedrooms feature French windows leading onto a terrace and 4 suites have sitting rooms. Some rooms have galleries and terraces and all boast mountain and countryside views towards the nearby medieval walled town of Conwy. There are bedrooms specifically suited for children and pets, please contact the house for advice. Graham prepares excellent and imaginative cuisine in the candle-lit restaurant. Leisure facilities include an indoor heated swimming pool, a gym, sauna, hot tub and, of course, good walking and sightseeing opportunities.

Directions: From the A55 take the Conwy turning. Follow signs for the town centre, pass Conwy Visitor Centre and take the second left into Upper Gate Street. Sychnant Pass House is on the right, 2 miles out of Conwy.

Web: www.johansens.com/sychnant
E-mail: bresykes@sychnant-pass-house.co.uk
Tel: 0870 381 8936
International: +44 (0)1492 596868

Llandudno
● Conwy
Chester
Betws-y-Coed
Snowdonia

Price Guide:
single £75-£160
double/twin £95-£170
suite £140-£180

Our inspector loved: *The Welsh/Irish mix of hospitality. Always a joy.*

EGERTON GREY

PORTHKERRY, NR CARDIFF, VALE OF GLAMORGAN CF62 3BZ

A distinguished former rectory dating from the early 19th century, Egerton Grey was opened as a small luxury hotel in 1988. Tucked away in 7 acres of gardens in a secluded, wooded valley in the Vale of Glamorgan, no other houses or roads are visible; instead guests can savour glorious views towards Porthkerry Park and the sea. The house's historic character has been carefully preserved with interior design that complements its architectural features. An Edwardian drawing room has intricate plaster mouldings, chandeliers, an open fireplace and oil paintings, whilst a quiet library overlooks the garden. All 9 immaculately presented bedrooms are extremely comfortable and several have Victorian baths and brasswork. The main restaurant, once a billiard room, creates an air of intimacy with its original Cuban mahogany panelling and candle-lit tables. Owners Richard Morgan-Price and Huw Thomas take great pride in presenting high-quality cuisine and fine wines. Riding can be arranged and there is a pitch and putt course a short stroll away by the sea. The Welsh Folk Museum, Castle Coch and Cardiff Castle are nearby.

Our inspector loved: The abundance of personal touches throughout and the extremely warm welcome from your hosts Richard and Huw.

Directions: From the M4, junction 33, take the A4050. Follow airport signs for 10 miles then take the A4226 towards Porthkerry. After 400 yards turn into the lane between 2 thatched cottages, the hotel is at end of the lane.

Web: www.johansens.com/egertongrey
E-mail: info@egertongrey.co.uk
Tel: 0870 381 8501
International: +44 (0)1446 711666
Fax: 01446 711690

Price Guide:
single £90–£120
double/twin £130–£150

215

PORTH TOCYN COUNTRY HOUSE HOTEL

ABERSOCH, PWLLHELI, GWYNEDD LL53 7BU

Directions: The hotel is 2 miles from Abersoch on the Sarn Bach road. Watch for bilingual signs – Gwesty/hotel – then the hotel name.

Web: www.johansens.com/porthtocyn
E-mail: bookings@porthtocyn.fsnet.co.uk
Tel: 0870 381 8832
International: +44 (0)1758 713303
Fax: 01758 713538

Price Guide: (incl. continental breakfast)
single from £67
double/twin from £90

This is a rare country house seaside hotel – family-owned for 3 generations, the first of whom had the inspiration to transform a row of miners' cottages into an attractive, low white building, surrounded by enchanting gardens, with glorious views over Cardigan Bay and Snowdonia. The Fletcher-Brewer family have created a unique ambience that appeals to young and old alike. Children are welcome; the younger ones have their own sitting room and high tea menu. Nonetheless, Porth Tocyn's charm is appreciated by older guests, with its Welsh antiques and delightful, comfortable sitting rooms. Most of the pretty en-suite bedrooms have sea views, some are family-oriented and 3 on the ground floor are ideal for those with mobility problems. Enjoy cocktails in the intimate bar, anticipating a fabulous meal, for dining at Porth Tocyn is a memorable experience every day of the week. Scrumptious dishes and mellow wines are served in great style on antique tables. Lunch is informal, on the terrace or by the outdoor pool which is heated from May to September. There is a dining area for children and an excellent conservatory with Playstations, games, toys and outside an area for playing football. Glorious beaches, water sports, golf, tennis, riding and exploring the coast provide activities for all ages.

Our inspector loved: *The ongoing continuity of this delightful property, always a pleasure to stay.*

BAE ABERMAW

PANORAMA HILL, BARMOUTH, GWYNEDD LL42 1DQ

First time visitors to this hillside hotel overlooking the lovely Mawddach Estuary and backed by Snowdonia National Park are in for a surprise. Its exterior is a somewhat subdued, traditional, grey-stone Victorian edifice, but behind the myriad of white-framed windows are stunning rooms. Now in their third year of ownership, Richard and Connie Drinkwater have created an impressive, contemporary, stylish and truly welcoming retreat. Every care has been taken to ensure that the hotel offers the best of everything and sets itself above the label of "seaside hotel". Cool neutral colours - white, cream, flax, beige - stripped floorboards and streamlined sofas suggest a minimalist feel, while deep blue curtains and chairs add colour to the smart restaurant which has a reputation for excellence. The cuisine has some modern and exciting interpretations of classic British dishes with a French influence. Local produce is much in use, particularly Welsh black beef, marsh lamb and sea bass and there are imaginative vegetarian options. Bedrooms are decorated in soft cream and honey tones, delightfully furnished and feature deep baths and luxurious toiletries. Superb cliff top walks and beach pursuits are on the doorstep. The national mountain biking course at Coedybrenis, Portmeirion Village and the Ffestiniog Railway are nearby.

Our inspector loved: Minimal it may be, but it has traditional warmth and excellent balance. Totally charming with wonderful views.

Directions: From Dolgellau take the A496 to Barmouth. At Barmouth turn right, signposted Bae Abermaw.

Web: www.johansens.com/baeabermaw
E-mail: enquiries@baeabermaw.com
Tel: 0870 381 8332
International: +44 (0)1341 280550
Fax: 01341 280346

Price Guide:
single £86–£107
double/twin £126–£158

Plas Dolmelynllyn

GANLLWYD, DOLGELLAU, GWYNEDD LL40 2HP

In their fourth year, Janet Anderson-Kaye and Barry Green welcome guests to Plas Dolmelynllyn, quietly situated overlooking the Mawddach Valley. One of Europe's top mountain bike centres, at Coed y Brenin, is only a couple of miles away - described by journalists as "awesome" and "a great experience". Ideal for a relaxing weekend and perfectly situated for business travellers en route between north and south Wales, the house has 9 guest rooms ranging from the lovely en-suite standards to the Mawddach room, with four-poster bed and views of the valley towards Cader Idris. All rooms are traditional and individually furnished. The origins of the building, dating back to Tudor times, are in evidence, such as the Old Hall with huge log fire and beamed ceilings. The Shelley Restaurant, named after the poet who stayed here, offers an excellent breakfast complemented with a gourmet dinner menu; vegetarians are well catered for. The sumptuous lounge displays elegant Arts and Crafts influenced oak-wood panelling. Private, special and corporate occasions can be organised and exclusive use of the property can be personalised to guests' requirements, ideal for weddings, anniversaries and Christmas and New Year celebrations. In season, salmon and sea-trout fishing can be enjoyed and tuition arranged at extra cost. There are numerous walks and Fairbourne, Barmouth and Portmeirion/Porthmadog are nearby.

Directions: Plas Dolmelynllyn is off the main A470 Dolgellau - Porthmadog road, 5 miles north of Dolgellau, 2 miles south of the new Coed y Brenin visitor centre.

Web: www.johansens.com/plasdolmelynllyn
E-mail: info@dolly–hotel.co.uk
Tel: 0870 381 8825
International: +44 (0)1341 440273
Fax: 01341 440640

Price Guide:
single £75–£155
double £100–£180

Bangor

Pwllheli

Snowdonia
National Park

Dolgellau

Our inspector loved: *The Old Hall when set up for an exclusive gathering.*

HOTEL MAES-Y-NEUADD

TALSARNAU, NEAR HARLECH, GWYNEDD LL47 6YA

Amidst spectacular scenery, with views across Snowdonia National Park, this 14th-century Welsh manor house has won many awards including Top AA Hotel in 2005/2006. Owned and managed by the Jackson and Payne families, the house has been sympathetically restored to provide comfort and luxury. Furnished and equipped to a very high standard, the individual bedrooms reflect the various periods during which the house was built. Features include dormer windows, high-ceilinged Georgian rooms, 16th-century beams and even two 14th-century rooms. The sunlit conservatory is perfect for enjoying morning coffee or afternoon tea, whilst the terrace offers the magnificent spectacle of the sun setting over the Lleyn Peninsula. Delicious regional dishes, awarded 2 Rosettes, are served in the elegant restaurant where Chef Patron Peter Jackson uses the succulent fresh produce for which Wales is renowned. An excellent choice of Welsh or English breakfasts are available. The hotel's 2 walled kitchen gardens are currently being restored and provide the kitchens with salads, vegetables, herbs and fruit. The perfect venue for small meetings and exclusive use, the grounds provide a wonderful backdrop for weddings. Smoking is only allowed in the bar area. Explore numerous attractions nearby such as the North Wales coast, Portmeirion and the Ffestiniog Railway.

Our inspector loved: The amazing views and delicious dining.

Directions: Hotel is 3½ miles north of Harlech, off the B4573, signposted at the end of the lane.

Web: www.johansens.com/maesyneuadd
E-mail: maes@neuadd.com
Tel: 0870 381 9332
International: +44 (0)1766 780200
Fax: 01766 780211

Price Guide: (including dinner)
double/twin from £180–£270

Bangor

Pwllheli

Snowdonia
National Park

Dolgellau

THE BELL AT SKENFRITH

SKENFRITH, MONMOUTHSHIRE NP7 8UH

Directions: Leave the M4 (J24) take the A449 (A40) north. At the roundabout in Monmouth, turn left and then right at the traffic lights torwards Hereford. Travel 4 miles and turn left onto B4521 towards Abergavenny. The Bell is 3 miles on the left.

Web: www.johansens.com/bellskenfrith
E-mail: enquiries@skenfrith.co.uk
Tel: 0870 381 8354
International: +44 (0)1600 750235
Fax: 01600 750525

Price Guide:
single £75–£120 (not available at weekends)
double/twin £100–£155
four-poster £180

Situated in a tiny picturesque village on the edge of the River Monnow and surrounded by unspoilt Monmouthshire countryside, The Bell, a carefully renovated 17th-century coaching inn and recently voted the Best Place to Stay in Wales by the tourist board, is an oasis for visitors. The inn looks out over the historic arched bridge as well as the old castle ruins and mill. Beautifully designed in a classical style, there are roaring log fires, flagstone floors and stunning oak beams complemented by antiques, sumptuous sofas and tasteful décor. Cosy bedrooms are homely and welcoming with beautiful Welsh blankets, crisp linen, all modern amenities and sweeping views over the rolling hills or river. Guests may enjoy sipping a glass of wine or real ale in the relaxed atmosphere of the bar with its open log fire, before enjoying the imaginative contemporary dishes created by the 2 AA Rosette-awarded chef in the attractive restaurant overlooking the terrace and gardens. All meals are based on local, organic produce; a children's organic menu is also available. A private room can accommodate up to 40 for celebration meals and meetings. The Skenfrith area is rich in cultural and historical heritage and is an ideal base for many walks. It is now totally smoke free throughout the inn.

Our inspector loved: *The warm relaxing welcome with superb food, good wine and tasteful furnishings throughout.*

THE CROWN AT WHITEBROOK

WHITEBROOK, MONMOUTHSHIRE NP25 4TX

This is the perfect base for exploring a countryside that has been justifiably designated an area of outstanding natural beauty. It is an unpretentious, restful and gastronomic hideway not easy to find on the enveloping wooded slopes of the serene Wye Valley. The Crown claims to be Wales's first restaurant with rooms and has an increasing reputation for cuisine, wine, comfort and service, a welcoming retreat from 21st-century noise in a small village just 5 miles from Monmouth. Its surrounds are 3 acres of gardens leading out to green pastures and rugged limestone outcrops including the popular Wye Valley Walk and Offas's Dyke path. Meandering through is the gently flowing river whose banks are a haven for summertime picnickers. The early parts of this former inn were built between 1670 and 1707 and it has been carefully restored, refurbished and modernised to incorporate the best of the past with the amenities of today. The extremely comfortable lounge and elegant restaurant are situated in the original inn. Cuisine is superb classic French, imaginative, and to the taste of the most discerning diner. Service is attentive and appropriately relaxed. Each en-suite guest room has a character of its own and all hi-tech facilities. Walks, fishing and golf nearby.

Our inspector loved: The state-of-the-art bathrooms and fabulous cuisine, a superb dining experience.

Directions: Whitebrook is situated between the A466 and the B4293 approximately 5 miles south of Monmouth.

Web: www.johansens.com/crownatwhitebrook
E-mail: info@crownatwhitebrook.co.uk
Tel: 0870 381 8563
International: +44 (0)1600 860254
Fax: 01600 860607

Price Guide:
single £90
double £100–£120

WOLFSCASTLE COUNTRY HOTEL & RESTAURANT

WOLF'S CASTLE, HAVERFORDWEST, PEMBROKESHIRE SA62 5LZ

This former vicarage, situated in glorious Pembrokeshire countryside, offers a friendly and welcoming atmosphere. The owner/manager of 27 years, Andrew Stirling, is supported by a close network of staff, several of whom have been at Wolfscastle for many years. The charming non-smoking bedrooms, including 4 luxurious Executive Suites, have undergone recent refurbishment and now combine elegant period décor with modern conveniences; all have en-suite bathrooms, televisions and refreshment facilities. The exceptional cuisine is based on fresh local produce and the restaurant provides an exemplary service, whilst maintaining its relaxed, country hotel ambience. During the winter, the cosy bar is complete with blazing log fire. Both dining areas offer an à la carte and bar menu. The delightful premises are ideal for conferences and social events. The main function room opens out onto a magnificent patio/garden area, and guests have use of a private bar. A popular venue for smaller parties is the Barclay Suite, named after the retired pianist. The surrounding landscape is steeped in history, with Pembroke and Carew castles nearby, and St David's Cathedral and Bishop's Palace only 20 minutes away. Explore the beautiful coastline on foot or take an exhilarating boat ride to see local wildlife.

Directions: Located on the A40, in the village of Wolf's Castle, 7 miles from Haverfordwest. The hotel is on the left.

Web: www.johansens.com/wolfscastle
E-mail: enquiries@wolfscastle.com
Tel: 0870 381 9162
International: +44 (0)1437 741225
Fax: 01437 741383

Price Guide:
single £65–£80
double/twin £90–£125s

Our inspector loved: The inviting bar and the warm, welcoming home-away-from-home atmosphere created by the owner and staff.

GLANGRWYNEY COURT

GLANGRWYNEY, NR CRICKHOWELL, POWYS NP8 1ES

Christina and Warwick Jackson offer visitors a warm welcome to their splendid Georgian house amidst parkland in the scenic Usk Valley in the Brecon Beacons National Park. Traditional country house hospitality makes guests feel at home from the moment they step into the impressive entrance hall. Glangrwyney Court is a majestic bed and breakfast house offering relaxed country living with a richly decorated interior that combines superior comfort with a charming lived-in quality. There are antiques and family bric-a-brac, colourful rugs, a curved staircase, a grand piano and open log fires in the main sitting rooms. All bedrooms have en-suite facilities, the master suite has a king-size bed, en-suite steam shower and deep bath, whilst 1 twin room has a private Jacuzzi bathroom. The charming, well-equipped Gardner's Cottage has its own facilities. All bedrooms offer views over the beautiful gardens, which are a delight to explore, and the surrounding countryside. There are excellent restaurants nearby. Tennis, croquet and boules can be enjoyed on site; riding, fishing, shooting and wonderful walks are on the doorstep. This is the perfect venue for small weddings and business meetings that require a less formal arrangement in a quality setting.

Our inspector loved: So much, the quintessence of country living, delightful and blissful.

Directions: Glangrwyney is just off the A40 approximately 4 miles north west of Abergavenny.

Web: www.johansens.com/glangrwyneycourt
E-mail: info@glancourt.co.uk
Tel: 0870 381 8547
International: +44 (0)1873 811288
Fax: 01873 810317

Price Guide:
single from £50
double/twin from £65
suite from £85

Condé Nast Johansens are delighted to recommend over 300 properties across Great Britain and Ireland.

These properties can be found in *Recommended Hotels & Spas - GB & Ireland*.

Call 0800 269 397 or see the order forms on page 271 to order Guides.

England

The Bath Priory Hotel and Restaurant	B&NE Somerset	0870 381 8345
The Bath Spa Hotel	B&NE Somerset	0870 381 8346
Dukes Hotel	B&NE Somerset	0870 381 8357
Homewood Park	B&NE Somerset	0870 381 8605
Hunstrete House	B&NE Somerset	0870 381 8630
The Park	B&NE Somerset	0870 381 8394
The Royal Crescent & Bath House Spa	B&NE Somerset	0870 381 8874
Moore Place Hotel	Bedfordshire	0870 381 8745
The Bear Hotel	Berkshire	0870 381 8430
Cliveden	Berkshire	0870 381 8432
The Crab at Chieveley	Berkshire	0870 381 8318
Donnington Valley Hotel & Golf Club	Berkshire	0870 381 8484
Fredrick's – Hotel Restaurant Spa	Berkshire	0870 381 8531
The French Horn	Berkshire	0870 381 8532
The Great House	Berkshire	0870 381 8374
Oakley Court Hotel	Berkshire	0870 381 8322
The Regency Park Hotel	Berkshire	0870 381 8852
The Vineyard At Stockcross	Berkshire	0870 381 8965
New Hall	Birmingham	0870 381 8756

Danesfield House Hotel and Spa	**Buckinghamshire**	**0870 381 8474**
Hartwell House Hotel, Restaurant & Spa	Buckinghamshire	0870 381 8585
Stoke Park Club	Buckinghamshire	0870 381 8915
Hotel Felix	Cambridgeshire	0870 381 9056
The Alderley Edge Hotel	Cheshire	0870 381 8307
The Chester Grosvenor and Spa	Cheshire	0870 381 9264
Green Bough Hotel	Cheshire	0870 381 8571
Hillbark Hotel	Cheshire	0870 381 9128
Mere Court Hotel	Cheshire	0870 381 8727
Nunsmere Hall	Cheshire	0870 381 8772
Rowton Hall Hotel, Health Club & Spa	Cheshire	0870 381 8871
Alverton Manor	Cornwall	0870 381 9152
Budock Vean - The Hotel on the River	Cornwall	0870 381 8392
Fowey Hall Hotel & Restaurant	Cornwall	0870 381 8529
The Garrack Hotel & Restaurant	Cornwall	0870 381 8536
Hell Bay	Cornwall	0870 381 8591
The Idle Rocks Hotel	Cornwall	0870 381 8324
The Lugger Hotel	Cornwall	0870 381 8708
Meudon Hotel	Cornwall	0870 381 8730
The Nare Hotel	Cornwall	0870 381 8755
The Rosevine Hotel	Cornwall	0870 381 8867
St Michael's Hotel & Spa	Cornwall	0870 381 8399
Talland Bay Hotel	Cornwall	0870 381 8937
Treglos Hotel	Cornwall	0870 381 8951
The Well House	Cornwall	0870 381 8975
Armathwaite Hall Hotel	Cumbria	0870 381 8478

Farlam Hall Hotel	Cumbria	0870 381 8581
Gilpin Lodge	Cumbria	0870 381 8546
Holbeck Ghyll Country House Hotel	Cumbria	0870 381 8601
The Inn on the Lake	Cumbria	0870 381 8640
Lakeside Hotel on Lake Windermere	Cumbria	0870 381 8672
Linthwaite House Hotel	Cumbria	0870 381 8694
The Lodore Falls Hotel	Cumbria	0870 381 9314
Lovelady Shield Country House Hotel	Cumbria	0870 381 8705
Netherwood Hotel	Cumbria	0870 381 8729
Rampsbeck Country House Hotel	Cumbria	0870 381 8848
Rothay Manor	Cumbria	0870 381 8869
Sharrow Bay Country House Hotel	Cumbria	0870 381 8891
Tufton Arms Hotel	Cumbria	0870 381 8956
Callow Hall	Derbyshire	0870 381 8400
East Lodge Country House Hotel	Derbyshire	0870 381 8496
Hassop Hall	Derbyshire	0870 381 8586
The Izaak Walton Hotel	Derbyshire	0870 381 8642
The Peacock at Rowsley	Derbyshire	0870 381 8805
Riber Hall	Derbyshire	0870 381 8854
The Arundell Arms	Devon	0870 381 8323
Bovey Castle	Devon	0870 381 9286
Buckland-Tout-Saints	Devon	0870 381 8391
Burgh Island	Devon	0870 381 9207
Combe House Hotel & Restaurant	Devon	0870 381 8440
Gidleigh Park	Devon	0870 381 8545
The Horn of Plenty Country House Hotel & Restaurant	Devon	0870 381 8584
Hotel Riviera	Devon	0870 381 8624
Ilsington Country House Hotel	Devon	0870 381 8635
Langdon Court Hotel & Restaurant	Devon	0870 381 9157
Lewtrenchard Manor	Devon	0870 381 9177
Northcote Manor Country House Hotel	Devon	0870 381 8767
Orestone Manor & The Restaurant at Orestone Manor	Devon	0870 381 8794
The Palace Hotel	Devon	0870 381 8798
Soar Mill Cove Hotel	Devon	0870 381 8897
The Tides Reach Hotel	Devon	0870 381 8947
Watersmeet Hotel	Devon	0870 381 8972
Woolacombe Bay Hotel	Devon	0870 381 9007
Avonmouth Hotel and Restaurant	Dorset	0870 381 9333
Moonfleet Manor	Dorset	0870 381 8744
Norfolk Royale Hotel	Dorset	0870 381 8765
Plumber Manor	Dorset	0870 381 8829
The Priory Hotel	Dorset	0870 381 8841
Stock Hill Country House	Dorset	0870 381 8567
Summer Lodge Country House Hotel, Restaurant & Spa	Dorset	0870 381 8926
Headlam Hall	Durham	0870 381 8590
Five Lakes Hotel, Golf, Country Club & Spa	Essex	0870 381 8524
Burleigh Court	Gloucestershire	0870 381 8664
Calcot Manor Hotel & Spa	Gloucestershire	0870 381 8398
Corse Lawn House Hotel	Gloucestershire	0870 381 8448
Cotswold House Hotel	Gloucestershire	0870 381 8449
The Dial House	Gloucestershire	0870 381 9296
The Grapevine Hotel	Gloucestershire	0870 381 8564
The Greenway	Gloucestershire	0870 381 8574
The Hare and Hounds Hotel	Gloucestershire	0870 381 8302
Hotel On The Park	Gloucestershire	0870 381 8623
Lords of the Manor Hotel	Gloucestershire	0870 381 8704
Lower Slaughter Manor	Gloucestershire	0870 381 8706
The Noel Arms Hotel	Gloucestershire	0870 381 8763
The Painswick Hotel & Old Rectory Restaurant	Gloucestershire	0870 381 8797
Stonehouse Court Hotel	Gloucestershire	0870 381 8631
The Swan Hotel At Bibury	Gloucestershire	0870 381 8931
Washbourne Court Hotel	Gloucestershire	0870 381 8970
Thornbury Castle	South Gloucestershire	0870 381 8944
Audleys Wood	Hampshire	0870 381 8497

MINI LISTINGS GREAT BRITAIN & IRELAND

Condé Nast Johansens are delighted to recommend over 300 properties across Great Britain and Ireland.
These properties can be found in *Recommended Hotels & Spas - GB & Ireland*.
Call 0800 269 397 or see the order forms on page 271 to order Guides.

Careys Manor Hotel & Senspa	Hampshire	0870 381 8405
Chewton Glen	Hampshire	0870 381 8427
Chilworth Manor	Hampshire	0870 381 9057
Esseborne Manor	Hampshire	0870 381 8506
Lainston House Hotel	Hampshire	0870 381 8667
Le Poussin at Whitley Ridge	Hampshire	0870 381 8994
The Montagu Arms Hotel	Hampshire	0870 381 8743
New Park Manor & Bath House Spa	Hampshire	0870 381 8761
Passford House Hotel	Hampshire	0870 381 8804
Tylney Hall	Hampshire	0870 381 8958
Castle House	Herefordshire	0870 381 9206
Down Hall Country House Hotel	Hertfordshire	0870 381 8489
The Grove Hotel	Hertfordshire	0870 381 8646
St Michael's Manor	Hertfordshire	0870 381 8906
Sopwell House	Hertfordshire	0870 381 8898
West Lodge Park Country House Hotel	Hertfordshire	0870 381 8978
The Priory Bay Hotel	Isle of Wight	0870 381 8839
Eastwell Manor	Kent	0870 381 8498
The Spa	Kent	0870 381 8901
Eaves Hall	Lancashire	0870 381 9198
The Gibbon Bridge Hotel	Lancashire	0870 381 8544
Stapleford Park Country House Hotel & Sporting Estate	Leicestershire	0870 381 8912
41	London	0870 381 8300
51 Buckingham Gate	London	0870 381 8301
Beaufort House	London	0870 381 8350
Cannizaro House	London	0870 381 8402
The Capital Hotel & Restaurant	London	0870 381 8527
The Cranley	London	0870 381 8456
Dorset Square Hotel	London	0870 381 8488
The Egerton House Hotel	London	0870 381 8559
Grim's Dyke Hotel	London	0870 381 8486
Hendon Hall Hotel	London	0870 381 8518
Jumeirah Carlton Tower	London	0870 381 9326
Jumeirah Lowndes Hotel	London	0870 381 9285
Kensington House Hotel	London	0870 381 8648
The Mandeville Hotel	London	0870 381 8344
The Mayflower Hotel	London	0870 381 9195
The Milestone Hotel & Apartments	London	0870 381 8732
The Richmond Gate Hotel and Restaurant	London	0870 381 8855
The Royal Park	London	0870 381 9289
Sofitel St James	London	0870 381 9185
The Sumner	London	0870 381 8608
Twenty Nevern Square	London	0870 381 8957
Etrop Grange	Greater Manchester	0870 381 8507
Congham Hall	Norfolk	0870 381 8443
The Hoste Arms	Norfolk	0870 381 8415
Fawsley Hall	Northamptonshire	0870 381 8516
Rushton Hall	Northamptonshire	0870 381 8383
Whittlebury Hall	Northamptonshire	0870 381 8995
Marshall Meadows Country House Hotel	Northumberland	0870 381 8721
Matfen Hall	Northumberland	0870 381 8724
Tillmouth Park	Northumberland	0870 381 8948
Colwick Hall Hotel	Nottinghamshire	0870 381 8594
Lace Market Hotel	Nottinghamshire	0870 381 9325
Le Manoir Aux Quat' Saisons	Oxfordshire	0870 381 8682
Phyllis Court Club	Oxfordshire	0870 381 8822
The Springs Hotel & Golf Club	Oxfordshire	0870 381 8904
Weston Manor	Oxfordshire	0870 381 8981
Hambleton Hall	Rutland	0870 381 8582
Dinham Hall	Shropshire	0870 381 8482
Bindon Country House Hotel	Somerset	0870 381 8364
The Castle at Taunton	Somerset	0870 381 8538
Combe House Hotel	Somerset	0870 381 8621
Mount Somerset Country House Hotel	Somerset	0870 381 8750
Ston Easton Park	Somerset	0870 381 8916

Hoar Cross Hall Spa Resort	Staffordshire	0870 381 8598
Brudenell Hotel	Suffolk	0870 381 9182
Hintlesham Hall	Suffolk	0870 381 8595
Ravenwood Hall Country Hotel & Restaurant	Suffolk	0870 381 8849
Seckford Hall	Suffolk	0870 381 8890
The Swan Hotel	Suffolk	0870 381 8929
The Swan Hotel	Suffolk	0870 381 9280
The Westleton Crown	Suffolk	0870 381 8479
Foxhills	Surrey	0870 381 8530
Grayshott Spa	Surrey	0870 381 8466
Great Fosters	Surrey	0870 381 8569
Lythe Hill Hotel & Spa	Surrey	0870 381 8709
Pennyhill Park Hotel & The Spa	Surrey	0870 381 8815
Ashdown Park Hotel and Country Club	East Sussex	0870 381 8325
Dale Hill	East Sussex	0870 381 8471
Deans Place Hotel	East Sussex	0870 381 8576
The Grand Hotel	East Sussex	0870 381 8560
Horsted Place Country House Hotel	East Sussex	0870 381 8609
Lansdowne Place, Boutique Hotel & Spa	East Sussex	0870 381 8606
Newick Park	East Sussex	0870 381 8762
The PowderMills	East Sussex	0870 381 8835
Rye Lodge	East Sussex	0870 381 8367
Amberley Castle	West Sussex	0870 381 8312
Bailiffscourt Hotel & Health Spa	West Sussex	0870 381 8333
Millstream Hotel	West Sussex	0870 381 8739
Ockenden Manor	West Sussex	0870 381 8780
The Spread Eagle Hotel & Health Spa	West Sussex	0870 381 8903
The Vermont Hotel	Tyne & Wear	0870 381 8962
Ardencote Manor Hotel, Country Club & Spa	Warwickshire	0870 381 8320

▼

Billesley Manor	**Warwickshire**	**0870 381 8363**
Ettington Park	Warwickshire	0870 381 8508
The Glebe at Barford	Warwickshire	0870 381 8548
Mallory Court	Warwickshire	0870 381 8713
Nailcote Hall	Warwickshire	0870 381 8752
The Shakespeare Hotel	Warwickshire	0870 381 8611
Wroxall Abbey Estate	Warwickshire	0870 381 9013
Bishopstrow House & Spa	Wiltshire	0870 381 8365
Howard's House	Wiltshire	0870 381 8627
Lucknam Park, Bath	Wiltshire	0870 381 8707
The Pear Tree At Purton	Wiltshire	0870 381 8806
Whatley Manor	Wiltshire	0870 381 9197
Woolley Grange	Wiltshire	0870 381 8425
Brockencote Hall	Worcestershire	0870 381 8382
Buckland Manor	Worcestershire	0870 381 9175
The Cottage in the Wood	Worcestershire	0870 381 8452
Dormy House	Worcestershire	0870 381 8487
The Elms	Worcestershire	0870 381 8304
The Evesham Hotel	Worcestershire	0870 381 8510
Willerby Manor Hotel	East Riding of Yorkshire	0870 381 8998

Mini Listings Great Britain & Ireland

Condé Nast Johansens are delighted to recommend over 300 properties across Great Britain and Ireland.

These properties can be found in *Recommended Hotels & Spas - GB & Ireland*.

Call 0800 269 397 or see the order forms on page 271 to order Guides.

The Boar's Head Hotel	North Yorkshire	0870 381 8370
The Crown Spa Hotel	North Yorkshire	0870 381 8550
The Devonshire Arms Country House Hotel & Spa	North Yorkshire	0870 381 8480
The Feversham Arms Hotel	North Yorkshire	0870 381 9283
The Grange Hotel	North Yorkshire	0870 381 8561
Grants Hotel	North Yorkshire	0870 381 8562
Hackness Grange	North Yorkshire	0870 381 8578
Hob Green Hotel, Restaurant & Gardens	North Yorkshire	0870 381 8600
Judges Country House Hotel	North Yorkshire	0870 381 9165
Middlethorpe Hall Hotel, Restaurant & Spa	North Yorkshire	0870 381 8731
Monk Fryston Hall Hotel	North Yorkshire	0870 381 8741
The Pheasant	North Yorkshire	0870 381 8821
The Royal Hotel	North Yorkshire	0870 381 9277
Rudding Park	North Yorkshire	0870 381 8879
Simonstone Hall	North Yorkshire	0870 381 8895
The Worsley Arms Hotel	North Yorkshire	0870 381 9011
Wrea Head Country Hotel	North Yorkshire	0870 381 9012
Whitley Hall Hotel	South Yorkshire	0870 381 8993
42 The Calls	West Yorkshire	0870 381 8737
Holdsworth House Hotel & Restaurant	West Yorkshire	0870 381 8603

Channel Islands

The Atlantic Hotel and Ocean Restaurant	Jersey	0870 381 8330
The Club Hotel and Spa	Jersey	0870 381 8313
Longueville Manor	Jersey	0870 381 8436

Northern Ireland

Bushmills Inn Hotel	Antrim	028 2073 3000

Ireland

Gregans Castle	Clare	00 353 65 7077005
Longueville House & Presidents' Restaurant	Cork	00 353 22 47156

Harvey's Point	**Donegal**	**00 353 74 972 2208**
Rathmullan House	Donegal	00 353 74 915 8188
Merrion Hall Hotel	Dublin	00 353 1 668 1426
The Schoolhouse Hotel	Dublin	00 353 1 667 5014
Cashel House	Galway	00 353 95 31001
Renvyle House Hotel	Galway	00 353 95 43511
Ballygarry House	Kerry	00 353 66 7123322
Cahernane House Hotel	Kerry	00 353 64 31895
Park Hotel Kenmare & Sámas	Kerry	00 353 64 41200
Parknasilla Hotel	Kerry	00 353 1 2144800
Sheen Falls Lodge	Kerry	00 353 64 41600
Killashee House Hotel & Villa Spa	Kildare	00 353 45 879277

Mount Juliet Conrad	Kilkenny	00 353 56 777 3000
Ashford Castle	Mayo	00 353 94 95 46003
Knockranny House Hotel & Spa	Mayo	00 353 98 28600
Nuremore Hotel and Country Club	Monaghan	00 353 42 9661438
Marlfield House	Wexford	00 353 53 94 21124

Scotland

Darroch Learg	Aberdeenshire	0870 381 8477
Ardanaiseig	Argyll & Bute	0870 381 8319
Loch Melfort Hotel & Restaurant	Argyll & Bute	0870 381 8699
Kirroughtree House	Dumfries & Galloway	0870 381 8659
Channings	Edinburgh	0870 381 8413
Le Monde Hotel	Edinburgh	0870 381 8610
Mar Hall Hotel & Spa	Glasgow	0870 381 8612
One Devonshire Gardens	Glasgow	0870 381 9146

Bunchrew House Hotel	**Highland**	**0870 381 8393**
Cuillin Hills Hotel	Highland	0870 381 8467
Culloden House	Highland	0870 381 9137
Drumossie Hotel	Highland	0870 381 8577
Inverlochy Castle	Highland	0870 381 9278
Loch Torridon Country House Hotel	Highland	0870 381 9136
Rocpool Reserve	Highland	0870 381 8434
Royal Marine Hotel	Highland	0870 381 9133
Dalhousie Castle and Spa	Midlothian	0870 381 8472
Ballathie House Hotel	Perth & Kinross	0870 381 8337
Cromlix House	Perth & Kinross	0870 381 8460
Kinnaird	Perth & Kinross	0870 381 9124
The Royal Hotel	Perth & Kinross	0870 381 8875
Cringletie House	Scottish Borders	0870 381 9279
Glenapp Castle	South Ayrshire	0870 381 8551

Wales

Miskin Manor Country House Hotel	Cardiff	0870 381 8740
Falcondale Mansion Hotel	Ceredigion	0870 381 9235
Bodysgallen Hall & Spa	Conwy	0870 381 8372
St Tudno Hotel & Restaurant	Conwy	0870 381 8907
Wild Pheasant Hotel	Denbighshire	0870 381 8633
Palé Hall	Gwynedd	0870 381 8799
Penmaenuchaf Hall	Gwynedd	0870 381 8813
Allt-Yr-Ynys Hotel	Monmouthshire	0870 381 8309
Llansantffraed Court Hotel	Monmouthshire	0870 381 8697
Lamphey Court Hotel	Pembrokeshire	0870 381 8675
Penally Abbey	Pembrokeshire	0870 381 8810
Warpool Court Hotel	Pembrokeshire	0870 381 8968
The Lake Country House and Spa	Powys	0870 381 8668
Lake Vyrnwy Hotel	Powys	0870 381 8671
Llangoed Hall	Powys	0870 381 8696

HISTORIC HOUSES, CASTLES & GARDENS

Incorporating Museums & Galleries

We are pleased to feature over 140 places to visit during your stay at a Condé Nast Johansens recommended hotel.

England

Bedfordshire

▼
Woburn Abbey - Woburn, Bedfordshire MK17 9WA.
Tel: 01525 290333

Berkshire

Mapledurham House - The Estate Office, Mapledurham,
Reading, Berkshire RG4 7TR. Tel: 01189 723350

Buckinghamshire

Doddershall Park - Quainton, Aylesbury,
Buckinghamshire HP22 4DF. Tel: 01296 655238

Nether Winchendon Mill - Nr Aylesbury,
Buckinghamshire HP18 0DY. Tel: 01844 290199

Stowe Landscape Gardens - Stowe, Buckingham,
Buckinghamshire MK18 5EH. Tel: 01280 822850

Waddesdon Manor - Waddesdon, Nr Aylesbury,
Buckinghamshire HP18 0JH. Tel: 01296 653226

Cambridgeshire

The Manor - Hemingford Grey, Huntingdon,
Cambridgeshire PE28 9BN. Tel: 01480 463134

Oliver Cromwell's House - 29 St Mary's Street, Ely,
Cambridgeshire CB7 4HF. Tel: 01353 662062

Cheshire

Arley Hall & Gardens - Arley, Northwich, Cheshire CW9
6NA. Tel: 01565 777353

Dorfold Hall - Nantwich, Cheshire CW5 8LD.
Tel: 01270 625245

Rode Hall and Gardens - Rode Hall, Scholar Green,
Cheshire ST7 3QP. Tel: 01270 873237

Co Durham

The Bowes Museum - Barnard Castle,
Co Durham DL12 8NP. Tel: 01833 690606

Raby Castle - Staindrop, Darlington, Co Durham DL2 3AH.
Tel: 01833 660202

Cumbria

Isel Hall - Cockermouth, Cumbria CA13 0QG.

Muncaster Castle , Gardens & Owl Centre-
Ravenglass, Cumbria CA18 1RQ.
Tel: 01229 717614

Derbyshire

Haddon Hall - Bakewell, Derbyshire DE45 1LA.
Tel: 01629 812855

Melbourne Hall & Gardens - Melbourne,
Derbyshire DE73 8EN. Tel: 01332 862502

Renishaw Hall Gardens - Renishaw, Nr Sheffield,
Derbyshire S21 3WB. Tel: 01246 432310

Devon

Bowringsleigh - Kingbridge, Devon TQ7 3LL.
Tel: 01548 852014

Downes Estate at Crediton - Devon EX17 3PL.
Tel: 01392 439046

Dorset

Moignes Court - Moreton Road, Owermoigne, Dorchester,
Dorset DT2 8HY. Tel: 01305 853 300

Essex

The Gardens of Easton Lodge - Warwick House, Easton
Lodge, Gt Dumnow, Essex CM6 2BB. Tel: 01371 876979

Ingatestone Hall - Hall Lane, Ingatestone, Essex CM4 9NR.
Tel: 01277 353010

Gloucestershire

Cheltenham Art Gallery & Museum - Clarence Street,
Cheltenham, Gloucestershire GL50 3JT.
Tel: 01242 237431

Hardwicke Court - Nr Gloucester, Gloucestershire GL2 4RS.
Tel: 01452 720212

Mill Dene Garden - Blockley,
Moreton-in-Marsh, Gloucestershire GL56 9HU.
Tel: 01386 700 457

Sezincote - Nr Moreton-in-Marsh, Gloucestershire
GL56 9AW. Tel: 01386 700444

Hampshire

Beaulieu - John Montagu Building, Beaulieu,
Hampshire SO42 7ZN. Tel: 01590 612345

Beaulieu Vineyard and Estate - Beaulieu Estate, John
Montagu Building, Beaulieu, Hampshire SO42 7ZN.
Tel: 01590 612345

Gilbert White's House and The Oates Museum - Selborne,
Nr Alton, Hampshire GU34 3JH. Tel: 01420 511275

Greywell Hill House - Greywell, Hook,
Hampshire RG29 1DG. Tel: 01256 703565

Pylewell House - South Baddesley, Lymington,
Hampshire SO41 5SJ. Tel: 01725 513004

Herefordshire

Kentchurch Court - Kentchurch, Nr Pontrilas, Hereford,
Herefordshire HR2 0DB. Tel: 01981 240228

Hertfordshire

Ashridge - Ringshall, Berkhamsted, Hertfordshire HP4 1NS.
Tel: 01442 841027

Hatfield House, Park & Gardens - Hatfield,
Hertfordshire AL9 5NQ. Tel: 01707 287010

Isle of Wight

Deacons Nursery - Moor View, Godshill,
Isle of Wight PO38 3HW. Tel: 01983 840750

Kent

Belmont House and Gardens - Belmont Park, Throwley,
Nr Faversham, Kent ME13 0HH. Tel: 01795 890202

Cobham Hall - Cobham, Kent DA12 3BL.
Tel: 01474 823371

Groombridge Place Gardens - Groombridge, Tunbridge
Wells, Kent TN3 9QG. Tel: 01892 861444

Hever Castle & Gardens - Hever, Nr Edenbridge, Kent
TN8 7NG. Tel: 01732 865224

Knole - Sevenoaks, Kent TN15 ORP. Tel: 01732 462100

Marle Place Gardens and Gallery - Marle Place Road,
Brenchley, Nr Tonbridge, Kent TN12 7HS.
Tel: 01892 722304

Mount Ephraim Gardens - Hernhill, Nr Faversham,
Kent ME13 9TX. Tel: 01227 751496

The New College of Cobham - Cobhambury Road,
Cobham, Nr Gravesend, Kent DA12 3BG.
Tel: 01474 814280

Penshurst Place & Gardens - Penshurst, Nr Tonbridge,
Kent TN11 8DG. Tel: 01892 870307

Lancashire

Stonyhurst College - Stonyhurst, Clitheroe,
Lancashire BB7 9PZ. Tel: 01254 827084/826345

Townhead House - Slaidburn, Via CLitheroe,
Lancashire BBY 3AG. Tel: 01772 421566

London

Dulwich Picture Gallery - Gallery Road, London SE21 7AD.
Tel: 020 8299 8711

Handel House Museum - 25 Brook Street,
London W1K 4HB. Tel: 020 7495 1685

Pitzhanger Manor House and Gallery - Walpole Park,
Mattock Lane, Ealing, London W5 5EQ. Tel: 020 8567
1227

Sir John Soane's Museum - 13 Lincoln's Inn Fields,
London WC2A 3BP. Tel: 020 7405 2107

Merseyside

Knowsley Hall - Knowsley Park, Prescot, Merseyside
L32 4AG. Tel: 0151 489 4827

HISTORIC HOUSES, CASTLES & GARDENS

Incorporating Museums & Galleries

www.historichouses.co.uk

Middlesex

Syon House - Syon Park, London Road, Brentford, Middlesex TW8 8JF. Tel: 020 8560 0882

Norfolk

Fairhaven Woodland and Water Garden - School Road, South Walsham, Norwich, Norfolk NR13 6EA. Tel: 01603 270449

Walsingham Abbey Grounds - , Walsingham, Norfolk NR22 6BP. Tel: 01328 820259

Northamptonshire

Cottesbrooke Hall and Gardens - Cottesbrooke, Northampton, Northamptonshire NN6 8PF. Tel: 01604 505808

Haddonstone Show Garden - The Forge House, Church Lane, East Haddon, Northamptonshire NN6 8DB. Tel: 01604 770711

Northumberland

Chillingham Castle - Nr Wooler, Northumberland NE66 5NJ. Tel: 01668 215359

Chipchase Castle - Chipchase, Wark on Tyne, Hexham, Northumberland NE48 3NT. Tel: 01434 230203

Seaton Delaval Hall - Seaton Sluice, Whitley Bay, Northumberland NE26 4QR. Tel: 0191 237 1493 / 0786

Nottinghamshire

Newstead Abbey - Ravenshead, Nottinghamshire NG15 8NA. Tel: 01623 455 900

Oxfordshire

Blenheim Palace - Woodstock, Oxfordshire OX20 1PX. Tel: 08700 602080

Kingston Bagpuize House - Kingston Bagpuize, Abingdon, Oxfordshire OX13 5AX. Tel: 01865 820259

Sulgrave Manor - Manor Road, Sulgrave, Banbury, Oxfordshire OX17 2SD. Tel: 01295 760205

Wallingford Castle Gardens - Castle Street, Wallingford, Oxfordshire OX10 0AL. Tel: 01491 835373

Shropshire

Shipton Hall - Shipton, Much Wenlock, Shropshire TF13 6JZ. Tel: 01746 785225

Weston Park - Weston-under-Lizard, Nr Shifnal, Shropshire TF11 8LE. Tel: 01952 852100

Somerset

The American Museum in Britain - Claverton Manor, Bath, Somerset BA2 7BD. Tel: 01225 460503

Cothay Manor & Gardens - Greenham, Wellington, Somerset TA21 0JR. Tel: 01823 672283

Great House Farm - Wells Road, Theale, Wedmore, Somerset BS28 4SJ. Tel: 01934 713133

Number 1 Royal Crescent - 1 Royal Crescent, Bath, Somerset BA1 2LR. Tel: 01225 428126

Staffordshire

The Ancient High House - Greengate Street, Stafford, Staffordshire ST16 2JA. Tel: 01785 619131

Izaak Walton's Cottage - Shallowford, nr. Stafford, Staffordshire ST15 0PA. Tel: 01785 760 278

Stafford Castle - Newport Road, Stafford, Staffordshire ST16 1DJ. Tel: 01785 257 698

Whitmore Hall - Whitmore, Newcastle-under-Lyme, Staffordshire ST5 5HW. Tel: 01782 680478

Suffolk

Kentwell Hall - Long Melford, Sudbury, Suffolk CO10 9BA. Tel: 01787 310207

Newbourne Hall - Newbourne, Nr. Woodbridge, Suffolk IP12 4NP. Tel: 01473 736277

Otley Hall - Hall Lane, Otley, Suffolk IP6 9PA. Tel: 01473 890264

Surrey

Claremont House - Claremont Drive, Esher, Surrey KT10 9LY. Tel: 01372 473623

Guildford House Gallery - 155, High Street, Guildford, Surrey GU1 3AJ. Tel: 01483 444740

Loseley Park - Guildford, Surrey GU3 1HS. Tel: 01483 304440

Painshill Park - Portsmouth Road, Cobham, Surrey KT11 1JE. Tel: 01932 868113

East Sussex

Bentley Wildfowl & Motor Museum - Halland, Nr Lewes, Sussex BN8 5AF. Tel: 01825 840573

Charleston - Firle, Lewes, East Sussex BN8 6LL. Tel: 01323 811626

Firle Place - Firle, Nr Lewes, East Sussex BN8 6LP. Tel: 01273 858307

Garden and Grounds of Herstmonceux Castle - Herstmonceux Castle, Hailsham, East Sussex BN27 1RN. Tel: 01323 833816

Merriments Gardens - Hurst Green, East Sussex TN19 7RA. Tel: 01580 860666

Preston Manor - Preston Drove, Brighton, East Sussex BN1 6SD. Tel: 01273 292770

Royal Pavilion - Brighton, East Sussex BN1 1EE. Tel: 01273 290900

West Sussex

Denmans Garden - Clock House, Denmans Lane, Fontwell, West Sussex BN18 0SU. Tel: 01243 542808

Goodwood House - Goodwood, Chichester, West Sussex PO18 0PX. Tel: 01243 755000

High Beeches Gardens - High Beeches, Handcross, West Sussex RH17 6HQ. Tel: 01444 400589

Leonardslee - Lakes & Gardens - Lower Beeding, Horsham, West Sussex RH13 6PP. Tel: 01403 891212

Uppark - South Harting, Petersfield, West Sussex GU31 5QR. Tel: 01730 825415

West Dean Gardens - West Dean , Chichester, West Sussex PO18 0QZ. Tel: 01243 818210

Worthing Museum & Art Gallery - Chapel Road, Worthing, West Sussex BN11 1HP. Tel: 01903 239999

Warwickshire

Arbury Hall - Nuneaton, Warwickshire CV10 7PT. Tel: 024 7638 2804

The Shakespeare Houses - The Shakespeare Birthplace Trust, The Shakespeare Centre, Henley Street, Stratford-upon-Avon, Warwickshire CV37 6QW. Tel: 01789 201845

West Midlands

Barber Institute of Fine Arts - The University of Birmingham, Edgbaston, Birmingham, West Midlands B15 2TS. Tel: 0121 414 7333

The Birmingham Botanical Gardens and Glasshouses - Westbourne Road, Edgbaston, Birmingham, West Midlands B15 3TR. Tel: 0121 454 1860

Wiltshire

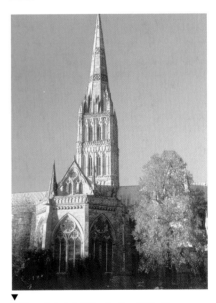

▼
Salisbury Cathedral - Visitor Services, 33 The Close, Salisbury, Wiltshire SP1 2EJ. Tel: 01722 555120

Worcestershire

Harvington Hall - Harvington, Kidderminister, Worcestershire DY10 4LR. Tel: 01562 777846

Little Malvern Court - Nr Malvern, Worcestershire WR14 4JN. Tel: 01684 892988

Spetchley Park Gardens - Spetchley, Worcester, Worcestershire WR5 1RS. Tel: 01453 810303

East Riding of Yorkshire

Burton Agnes Hall & Gardens - Burton Agnes, Driffield, East Yorkshire YO25 4NB. Tel: 01262 490324

HISTORIC HOUSES, CASTLES & GARDENS

Incorporating Museums & Galleries

www.historichouses.co.uk

North Yorkshire

Duncombe Park - Helmsley, York,
North Yorkshire YO62 5EB. Tel: 01439 770213

The Forbidden Corner - Tupgill Park Estate, Coverham, Nr
Middleham, North Yorkshire DL8 4TJ. Tel: 01969 640638

Fountains Abbey & Studley Royal - Ripon,
North Yorkshire HG4 3DY. Tel: 01765 608888

Norton Conyers - Wath, Nr Ripon, North Yorkshire
HG4 5EQ. Tel: 01765 640333

Ripley Castle - Ripley Castle Estate, Harrogate, North
Yorkshire HG3 3AY. Tel: 01423 770152

Skipton Castle - Skipton, North Yorkshire BD23 1AW.
Tel: 01756 792442

West Yorkshire

Bramham Park - Bramham, Wetherby, West Yorkshire
LS23 6ND. Tel: 01937 846000

Harewood House - Harewood, Leeds, West Yorkshire
LS17 9LG. Tel: 0113 218 1010

Ledston Hall - Hall Lane, Ledstone, Castleford,
West Yorkshire WF10 2BB. Tel: 01423 523 423

Northern Ireland

Co Down

Seaforde Gardens - Seaforde, Downpatrick,
Co Down BT30 8PG. Tel: 028 4481 1225

Ireland

Co Cork

Bantry House & Gardens - Bantry, Co Cork.
Tel: 00 353 2 750 047

Co Dublin

Ardgillan Castle - Balbriggan, Co Dublin.
Tel: 00 353 1 849 2212

Co Kildare

The Irish National Stud, Garden & House Museum -
Tully, Kildare Town, Co Kildare. Tel: 00 353 45 521617

Co Offaly

Birr Castle Demesne & Ireland's Historic Science Centre -
Birr, Co Offaly. Tel: 00 353 57 91 20336

Co Waterford

Lismore Castle Gardens - Lismore, Co Waterford.
Tel: 00 353 58 54424

Co Wexford

Kilmokea Country Manor & Gardens - Great Island,
Campile, Co Wexford. Tel: 00 353 51 388109

Co Wicklow

Mount Usher Gardens - Ashford, Co Wicklow.
Tel: +353 404 40205

Scotland

Argyll

Inveraray Castle - Inveraray, Argyll PA32 8XE. Tel: 01499
302203

Ayrshire

Kelburn Castle and Country Centre - South Offices,
Kelburn, Fairlie, Ayrshire KA29 0BE. Tel: 01475 568685

Dumfries

Drumlanrig Castle, Gardens and Country Park -
Thornhill, Dumfries DG3 4AQ. Tel: 01848 330248

Orkney Islands

Balfour Castle - Shapinsay, Orkney Islands KW17 2DY.
Tel: 01856 711282

Peebles

Traquair House - Innerleithen, Peebles EH44 6PW.
Tel: 01896 830323

Perthshire

Scone Palace - Perth, Perthshire PH2 6BD.
Tel: 01738 552300

Scottish Borders

Bowhill House & Country Park - Bowhill, Selkirk,
Scottish Borders TD7 5ET. Tel: 01750 22204

Manderston - Duns, Berwickshire,
Scottish Borders TD11 3PP. Tel: 01361 882636

Strathclyde

Mount Stuart - Isle of Bute, Strathclyde PA20 9LR.
Tel: 01700 503877

West Lothian

Hopetoun House - South Queensferry, Nr Edinburgh
West Lothian EH30 9SL. Tel: 0131 331 2451

Newliston - Kirkliston, West Lothian EH29 9EB.
Tel: 0131 333 3231

Wigtownshire

Ardwell Estate Gardens - Ardwell House, Stranraer DG9
9LY. Tel: 01776 860227

Wales

Conway

Bodnant Garden - Tal-y-Cafn, Nr Colwyn Bay,
Conway LL28 5RE. Tel: 01492 650460

Dyfed

Pembroke Castle - Pembroke, Dyfed SA71 4LA.
Tel: 01646 681510

Flintshire

Golden Grove - Llanasa, Nr. Holywell, Flintshire CH8 9NA.
Tel: 01745 854452

Gwynedd

Plas Brondanw Gardens - Menna Angharad,
Plas Brondanw, Llanfrothen, Gwynedd LL48 6SW.
Tel: 01766 770484

Monmouthshire

Usk Castle - Castle House, Monmouth Road, Usk,
Monmouthshire NP15 1SD.
Tel: 01291 672563

Pembrokeshire

St Davids Cathedral - The Close, St. David's,
Pembrokeshire SA62 6RH. Tel: 01437 720199

France

Château de Chenonceau - Chenonceaux, 37150.
Tel: 00 33 2 47 23 90 07

Château de Thoiry - Thoiry, Yvelines 78770 .
Tel: 00 33 1 34 87 53 65

Treat your hotel business as well as you treat your guests.

Avon Data Systems is a world class provider of hotel management systems. We have been developing hospitality software for over 20 years and have a proven track record in increasing the efficiency of each and every department of the hotel.

Today, our latest generation of software is up and running in hundreds of hotels throughout the UK and across the globe. In independent hotels and hotel groups of every size and combination, it enables owners, managers and staff to take control of business, fast, leaving you more time to spend looking after your guests.

PMS • Conference and Banqueting • EPOS • Real Time Internet Reservations

To find out how to maximise the efficiency of your hotel (and your time) call:

+44 (0)117 910 9166

sales@avondata.co.uk

www.avondata.co.uk

avon data systems
hospitality solutions

Avon Data Systems Ltd,
Unit 2 Vincent Court,
89 Soundwell Road, Staple Hill,
Bristol, BS16 4QR United Kingdom

Condé Nast Johansens are delighted to recommend over 450 properties across Europe and The Mediterranean.

These properties can be found in *Recommended Hotels & Spas - Europe & The Mediterranean*.

Call 0800 269 397 or see the order forms on page 271 to order guides.

Austria

Seeschlössl Velden	Velden	+43 4274 2824

Belgium

Firean Hotel	Antwerp	+32 3 237 02 60
Hostellerie Mardaga	As	+32 89 65 62 65
Hotel Die Swaene	Bruges	+32 50 34 27 98
Romantik Hotel Manoir du Dragon	Knokke~Heist	+32 50 63 05 80
Grand Hotel Damier	Kortrijk	+32 56 22 15 47
Hostellerie Ter Driezen	Turnhout	+32 14 41 87 57

Croatia

Grand Villa Argentina	Dubrovnik	+385 20 44 0555
Villa Lavandula	Trogir	+385 21 798 330

Czech Republic

Alchymist Grand Hotel and Spa	Prague	+420 257 286 011/016
Aria Hotel Prague	Prague	+420 225 334 111
Art Hotel Prague	Prague	+420 233 101 331
Bellagio Hotel Prague	Prague	+420 221 778 999
Golden Well Hotel	Prague	+420 257 011 213
Hotel Hoffmeister & Lily Wellness and Spa	Prague	+420 251 017 111
Nosticova Residence	Prague	+420 257 312 513/516
Romantik Hotel U Raka	Prague	+420 2205 111 00

Estonia

Ammende Villa	Pärnu	+372 44 73 888

France

Hôtel Royal Picardie	Albert	+33 3 22 75 37 00
Château de Pray	Amboise	+33 2 47 57 23 67
Le Choiseul	Amboise	+33 2 47 30 45 45
Le Manoir les Minimes	Amboise	+33 2 47 30 40 40
Bastide du Calalou	Aups	+33 4 94 70 17 91
Château de Vault de Lugny	Avallon	+33 3 86 34 07 86
Château la Chenevière	Bayeux - Port~en~Bessin	+33 2 31 51 25 25
La Chartreuse du Val Saint~Esprit	Bethune - Gosnay	+33 3 21 62 80 00
Hôtel du Palais	Biarritz	+33 5 59 41 64 00
Domaine de Rochevilaine	Billiers	+33 2 97 41 61 61
Château de Cocove	Calais - Recques~sur~Hem	+33 3 21 82 68 29
Château les Bruyères	Cambremer	+33 2 31 32 22 45
Relais Royal	Carcassonne - Mirepoix	+33 5 61 60 19 19
Château de Floure	Carcassonne~Floure	+33 4 68 79 11 29
Château de Challain	Challain~la~Potherie	+33 2 41 92 74 26
Château des Briottières	Champigné - Angers	+33 2 41 42 00 02
Château de L'Yeuse	Châteaubernard	+33 5 45 36 82 60
Le Prieuré	Chênehutte~les~Tuffeaux	+33 2 41 67 90 14
Ermitage de Corton	Chorey~Les~Beaune	+33 3 80 22 05 28
Hôtel Les Têtes	Colmar	+33 3 89 24 43 43

Romantik Hotel le Maréchal	Colmar	+33 3 89 41 60 32
Domaine de la Grange de Condé	Condé Northen	+33 3 87 79 30 50
Le Beau Rivage	Condrieu	+33 4 74 56 82 82
Le Castel	Coutances~Montpinchon	+33 2 33 17 00 45
Manoir de la Poterie, Spa "Les Thermes"	Cricqueboeuf	+33 2 31 88 10 40
Villa Reine Hortense	Dinard	+33 2 99 46 54 31
Château de Divonne	Divonne~les~Bains	+33 4 50 20 00 32
Domaine de Divonne	Divonne~les~Bains	+33 4 50 40 34 34
Le Moulin du Landion	Dolancourt	+ 33 3 25 27 92 17

▼

Château de Remaisnil	**Doullens - Remaisnil**	**+33 3 22 77 07 47**
Château d'Etoges	Etoges~en~Champagne	+33 3 26 59 30 08
Domaine Saint~Clair, Le Donjon	Etretat	+33 2 35 27 08 23
Château Eza	Èze Village	+33 4 93 41 12 24
Château de Fère	Fère~en~Tardenois	+33 3 23 82 21 13
Hostellerie les Bas Rupts Le Chalet Fleuri	Gérardmer - Vosges	+33 3 29 63 09 25
Les Mas des Herbes Blanches	Gordes	+33 4 90 05 79 79
Bastide Saint~Mathieu	Grasse	+33 4 97 01 10 00
Hostellerie St Barnabé	Guebwiller	+33 3 89 62 14 14
Romantik Hotel les Violettes	Jungholtz	+33 3 89 76 91 19
Abbaye de la Bussière	La Bussière~sur~Ouche	+33 3 80 49 02 29
Château de Bonaban	La Gouesnière - Saint~Malo	+33 2 99 58 24 50
Hotel "Résidence de France"	La Rochelle	+33 5 46 28 06 00
Romantik Hotel Relais de la Poste	La Wantzenau	+33 3 88 59 24 80
Domaine le Hameau des Baux	Le Paradou - Les Baux~de~Provence	+33 4 90 54 10 30
Le Bailli de Suffren	Le Rayol - Canadel~sur~Mer	+33 4 98 04 47 00
Oustau de Baumanière	Les Baux~de~Provence	+33 4 90 54 33 07
Chalet Hôtel La Marmotte	Les Gets	+33 4 50 75 80 33
Carlton Hotel	Lille	+33 3 20 13 33 13
Domaine de Beauvois	Luynes, Near Tours	+33 2 47 55 50 11
Château de la Couronne	Marthon	+33 5 45 62 29 96
Domaine des Etangs	Massignac	+33 5 45 61 85 00
Le Fer à Cheval	Megève	+33 4 50 21 30 39
Hôtel de La Bretesche	Missillac	+33 2 51 76 86 96
Manoir de Kertalg	Moëlan~sur~Mer	+33 2 98 39 77 77
Château les Roches	Mont~Saint~Jean	+33 3 80 84 32 71
Château d'Artigny	Montbazon, Near Tours	+33 2 47 34 30 30
Domaine de la Tortinière	Montbazon, Near Tours	+33 2 47 34 35 00
Domaine de Bodeuc	Nivillac - La Roche~Bernard	+33 2 99 90 89 63
Hotel à la Cour d'Alsace	Obernai	+33 3 88 95 07 00
Cazaudehore la Forestière	Paris Region	+33 1 30 61 64 64
Château d'Augerville	Paris Region	+33 2 38 32 12 07
Château d'Esclimont	Paris Region	+33 2 37 31 15 15
Château de Berchères	Paris Region	+33 2 37 82 28 22
Hostellerie du Bas-Breau	Paris Region	+33 1 60 66 40 05
Hôtel de Crillon	Paris	+33 1 44 71 15 00

MINI LISTINGS EUROPE & THE MEDITERRANEAN

Condé Nast Johansens are delighted to recommend over 450 properties across Europe and The Mediterranean.
These properties can be found in *Recommended Hotels & Spas - Europe & The Mediterranean*.
Call 0800 269 397 or see the order forms on page 271 to order guides.

Hôtel de Sers	Paris	+33 1 53 23 75 75
Hôtel du Petit Moulin	Paris	+33 1 42 74 10 10
Hôtel Duc de Saint~Simon	Paris	+33 1 44 39 20 20
Hôtel Duret	Paris	+33 1 45 00 42 60
Hôtel le Lavoisier	Paris	+33 1 53 30 06 06
Hôtel le Saint~Grégoire	Paris	+33 1 45 48 23 23
Hôtel le Tourville	Paris	+33 1 47 05 62 62
Hôtel Opéra Richepanse	Paris	+33 1 42 60 36 00
Hôtel San Régis	Paris	+33 1 44 95 16 16
La Trémoille	Paris	+33 1 56 52 14 00
La Villa Maillot	Paris	+33 1 53 64 52 52
Le Manoir de Gressy	Paris Region	+33 1 60 26 68 00
Le Relais Médicis	Paris	+33 1 43 26 00 60
Le Sainte~Beuve	Paris	+33 1 45 48 20 07
Hotel l'Agapa & Spa	Perros~Guirec	+33 2 96 49 01 10
Hostellerie des Monts de Vaux	Poligny	+33 3 84 37 12 50
Le Spinaker	Port Camargue	+33 4 66 53 36 37
La Ferme d'Augustin	Ramatuelle	+33 4 94 55 97 00
Château le Mas de Montet	Riberac - Dordogne	+33 5 53 90 08 71
Château d'Isenbourg	Rouffach	+33 3 89 78 58 50
Château de Montcaud	Sabran - Bagnols~sur~Cèze	+33 4 66 89 60 60
Château de la Barre	Saint~Calais	+33 2 43 35 00 17
Château la Thillaye	Saint~Christophe~sur~Conde	+33 2 32 56 07 24
Manoir du Vaumadeuc	Saint~Malo - Pleven	+33 2 96 84 46 17
Le Mas d'Artigny	Saint~Paul~de~Vence	+33 4 93 32 84 54
Relais de Saint~Preuil	Saint~Preuil	+33 5 45 80 80 08
La Villa Mauresque	Saint~Raphaël	+33 494 83 02 42
Château des Alpilles	Saint~Rémy~de~Provence	+33 4 90 92 03 33
Domaine des Andéols	Saint~Saturnin~Les~Apt	+33 4 90 75 50 63
Hostellerie des Hauts de Sainte~Maure	Sainte~Maure~de~Touraine	+33 2 47 65 50 65
Domaine du Château de Barive	Sainte~Preuve	+33 3 23 22 15 15
Château de Sanse	Sainte~Radegonde - Saint~Emilion	+33 5 57 56 41 10
Château de Coudrée	Sciez~sur~Léman	+33 4 50 72 62 33
Le Chaufourg~en~Périgord	Sourzac-Dordogne	+33 5 53 81 01 56
Château de L'Ile	Strasbourg - Ostwald	+33 3 88 66 85 00
Romantik Hotel Beaucour-Baumann	Strasbourg	+33 3 88 76 72 00
Romantik Hotel L'Horizon	Thionville	+33 3 82 88 53 65
Ti al Lannec	Trebeurden	+33 2 96 15 01 01
Hôtel Cantemerle	Vence	+33 4 93 58 08 18
Château de Gilly	Vougeot	+33 3 80 62 89 98

Great Britain

The Crab at Chieveley	Berkshire	+44 1635 247550
The French Horn	Berkshire	+44 1189 692 204
Hillbark Hotel	Cheshire	+44 151 625 2400
Soar Mill Cove Hotel	Devon	+44 1548 561566
Ashdown Park Hotel	East Sussex	+44 1342 824988
The Grand Hotel	East Sussex	+44 1323 412345
Rye Lodge	East Sussex	+44 1797 223838
Tylney Hall	Hampshire	+44 1256 764881
The Cranley	London	+44 20 7373 0123
Jumeirah Carlton Tower	London	+44 20 7235 1234
Jumeirah Lowndes Hotel	London	+44 20 7823 1234
The Mayflower Hotel	London	+44 20 7370 0991
The Royal Park	London	+44 20 7479 6600
Twenty Nevern Square	London	+44 20 7565 9555
Phyllis Court Club	Oxfordshire	+44 1491 570 500
Hoar Cross Hall Spa Resort	Staffordshire	+44 1283 575671
Amberley Castle	West Sussex	+44 1798 831 992

Greece

Astir Palace Vouliagmeni	Athens	+30 210 890 2000
Hotel Pentelikon	Athens	+30 2 10 62 30 650
Argentikon	Chios	+30 227 10 33 111
Villa de Loulia	Corfu	+30 266 30 95 394
Athina Luxury Villas	Crete	+30 28210 20960
Elounda Gulf Villas & Suites	Crete	+30 28410 90300
Elounda Peninsula All Suite Hotel	Crete	+30 28410 68012
Pleiades Luxurious Villas	Crete	+30 28410 90450
St Nicolas Bay Hotel	Crete	+30 2841 025041
Imaret	Kavala	+30 2510 620 151-55
Pavezzo Country Retreat	Lefkada	+30 26450 71782
Apanema	Mykonos	+30 22890 28590
Tharroe of Mykonos	Mykonos	+30 22890 27370
Fashion Hotel	Rhodes	+30 22410 70773/4
Melenos Lindos	Rhodes	+30 224 40 32 222
Alexander's Boutique Hotel of Oia	Santorini	+30 22860 71818
Canaves Oia	Santorini	+30 22860 71453/71128

▼

Fanari Villas	**Santorini**	**+30 22860 71007**
Orloff Resort	Spetses, Near Athens	+30 229 807 5444/5

Ireland

Aberdeen Lodge	Dublin	+353 1 283 8155

Italy

Grand Hotel Arciduca	Aeolian Islands - Lipari	+39 090 9812 136
Hotel Signum	Aeolian Islands - Salina	+39 090 9844 222
Hotel Cristallo	Alagna - Monte Rosa	+39 0163 922 822/23
Villa Las Tronas	Alghero	+39 079 981 818
Furore Inn Resort & Spa	Amalfi Coast & Naples	+39 089 830 4711
Le Case Del Borgo - Tuscan Luxury Living	Ambra - Chianti Aretino	+39 055 991 871
Romantik Hotel le Silve di Armenzano	Assisi - Armenzano	+39 075 801 9000
San Crispino Resort & Spa	Assisi - Tordandrea	+39 075 804 3257
Hotel Villa Ca' Sette	Bassano del Grappa	+39 0424 383 350
Grand Hotel Villa Serbelloni	Bellagio - Lake Como	+39 031 950 216
Romantik Hotel Turm	Bolzano - Fiè Allo Sciliar	+39 0471 725014
Posthotel Cavallino Bianco	Bolzano - Nova Levante	+39 0471 613113
Bagni di Bormio Spa Resort	Bormio-Bagni Nuovi - Valtellina	+39 0342 901890
Castello di San Marco	Calatabiano	+39 095 641 181
Albergo Madonnina	Cantello - Varese	+39 0332 417 731
Tombolo Talasso Resort	Castagneto Carducci - Marina	+39 0565 74530

Condé Nast Johansens are delighted to recommend over 450 properties across Europe and The Mediterranean.

These properties can be found in *Recommended Hotels & Spas - Europe & The Mediterranean*.

Call 0800 269 397 or see the order forms on page 271 to order guides.

Castel di Luco	Castel di Luco - Acquasanta Terme	+39 0736 802319
Relais Falisco	Civita Castellana	+39 0761 54 98
Hotel Bes	Clavière	+39 0122 878735
Romantik Hotel Art Hotel Cappella	Colfosco - Corvara	+39 0471 836183
Relais Alla Corte del Sole	Cortona - Petrignano	+39 075 9689008
Villa Marsili	Cortona	+39 0575 605 252
Mont Blanc Hotel Village	Courmayeur - Mont Blanc	+39 0165 864 111
Hotel Villa Ottone	Elba Island - Portoferraio	+39 0565 933 042
Hotel Punta Est	Finale Ligure	+39 019 600611
Monsignor Della Casa Country Resort	Florence - Borgo San Lorenzo	+39 055 840 821
Casa Howard	Florence	+39 066 992 4555
Hotel Lorenzo Il Magnifico	Florence	+39 055 463 0878
Marignolle Relais & Charme	Florence	+39 055 228 6910
Relais Piazza Signoria	Florence	+39 055 3987239
Relais Santa Croce	Florence	+39 055 2342230
Residenza del Moro	Florence	+39 055 290884
Villa Montartino	Florence	+39 055 223520
Hotel Byron	Forte dei Marmi	+39 0584 787 052
Albergo L'Ostelliere	Gavi	+39 0143 607 801
Hotel Jolanda Sport	Gressoney~La~Trinite	+39 0125 366 140
Castello di Petroia	Gubbio	+39 075 92 02 87
I Due Roccoli Relais	Iseo Hills - Lake Iseo	+39 030 9822 977/8
Grand Hotel Gardone Riviera	Lake Garda - Gardone Riviera	+39 0365 20261
Hotel Bellerive	Lake Garda - Salò	+39 0365 520 410
Color Hotel	Lake Garda - Verona - Bardolino	+39 045 621 0857
Ai Capitani Hotel	Lake Garda - Verona - Peschiera del Garda	+39 045 6400782

▼

Locanda San Vigilio	**Lake Garda - Verona - San Vigilio**	**+39 045 725 66 88**
Villa dal Pozzo d'Annone	Lake Maggiore - Belgirate	+39 0322 7255
Hotel Pironi	Lake Maggiore - Cannobio	+39 0323 70624
Hotel Villa Aminta	Lake Maggiore - Stresa	+39 0323 933 818
Park Hotel Brasilia	Lido di Jesolo	+39 0421 380851
Hotel Marzia	Livigno - Valtellina	+39 0342 996 020
Relais Villa Belpoggio Historical House	Loro Ciuffenna - Arezzo	+39 055 9694411
Albergo Pietrasanta - Palazzo Barsanti Bonetti	Lucca - Pietrasanta	+39 0584 793 727
Albergo Villa Marta	Lucca - San Lorenzo a Vaccoli	+39 0583 37 01 01
Relais Villa San Martino	Martina Franca	+39 080 480 5152
Castel Fragsburg	Merano	+39 0473 244071
L'Albereta	Milan - Franciacorta	+39 030 7760 550
Hotel de la Ville	Milan - Monza	+39 039 3942 1
Petit Palais maison de charme	Milan	+39 02 584 891
Palazzo Failla Hotel	Modica	+39 0932 941 059
Abbadia San Giorgio - Historical Residence	Moneglia	+39 0185 491119
Country House Casa Cornacchi	Montebenichi - Chianti Area	+39 055 998229
La Locanda della Chiocciola	Orte	+39 0761 402 734
I Casali di Monticchio	Orvieto - Allerona	+39 0763 62 83 65
La Posta Vecchia Hotel Spa	Palo Laziale - Rome	+39 0699 49501

Palazzo Dalla Rosa Prati	Parma	+39 0521 386 429
Relais Il Borgo	Penango - Asti - Monferrato	+39 0141 921272
L'Antico Forziere	Perugia - Deruta	+39 075 972 4314
Le Torri di Bagnara Medieval Historical Residences	Perugia - Pieve san Quirico	+39 075 579 2001
Alla Posta dei Donini	Perugia - San Martino	+39 075 609 132
Torre di San Martino - Historical Residence	Piacenza - Borgo di Rivalta	+39 0523 972002
Hotel Relais Dell'Orologio	Pisa	+39 050 830 361
Castello di Vicarello	Poggi del Sasso - Maremma	+39 0564 990 718
Grand Hotel in Porto Cervo	Porto Cervo - Costa Smeralda	+39 0789 91533
Il Pellicano Hotel & Spa	Porto Ercole - Argentario	+39 0564 858111
Hotel San Giorgio - Portofino House	Portofino	+39 0185 26991
Locanda Don Serafino	Ragusa Ibla	+39 0932 220 065
Hotel Villa Maria	Ravello	+39 089 857255
Hotel Posta Historical Residence	Reggio Emilia	+39 05 22 43 29 44
Hotel des Nations	Riccione - Adriatic Coast	+39 0541 647878
Pieve di Caminino Historical Residence	Roccatederighi - Grosseto	+39 0564 569 736
Foresteria Duca di Dolle	Rolle di Cison di Valmarino	+39 0438 975 809
Hotel Aventino	Rome	+39 06 5745 231
Hotel dei Borgognoni	Rome	+39 06 6994 1505
Hotel dei Consoli	Rome	+39 0668 892 972
Hotel Fenix	Rome	+39 06 8540 741
Villa Spalletti Trivelli	Rome	+39 06 48907934
Hotel Titano	San Marino Republic	+378 99 10 07
Grand Hotel Diana Majestic	San Remo Coast - Diano Marina	+39 0183 402 727
Grand Hotel Miramare	Santa Margherita - Portofino Coast	+39 0185 287013
Villa del Parco and Spa at Forte Village	Santa Margherita di Pula - Cagliari	+39 070 92171
Hotel Vis à Vis	Sestri Levante	+39 0185 42661
Hotel Borgo CasaBianca	Siena - Asciano	+39 0577 704 362
Borgo La Bagnaia Resort, Spa and Events Venue	Siena - Localita Bagnaia	+39 0577 813000
Relais Dionora	Siena - Montepulciano	+39 0578 717 496
Villa di Poggiano	Siena - Montepulciano	+39 0578 758292
Castel Pietraio	Siena - Monteriggioni - Strove	+39 0577 300020
Relais la Suvera Dimora Storica	Siena - Pievescola	+39 0577 960 300
Grand Hotel Cocumella	Sorrento	+39 081 878 2933
Grand Hotel Atlantis Bay	Taormina Mare	+39 0942 618 011
Grand Hotel Mazzarò Sea Palace	Taormina Mare	+39 0942 612 111
Baia Taormina Hotel - Resort & Spa	Taormina Riviera - Marina d'Agro	+39 0942 756 292
Albergo Al Sole	Treviso - Asolo	+39 0423 951 332
La Preghiera	Umbertide - Calzolaro	+39 075 9302428
Hotel Gardena Grodnerhof	Val Badia	+39 0471 796 315
Albergo Quattro Fontane - Residenza d'Epoca	Venice - Lido	+39 041 526 0227
Ca Maria Adele	Venice	+39 041 52 03 078
Hotel Flora	Venice	+39 041 52 05 844
Hotel Giorgione	Venice	+39 041 522 5810
Hotel Sant' Elena Venezia	Venice	+39 041 27 17 811
Londra Palace	Venice	+39 041 5200533
Novecento Boutique Hotel	Venice	+39 041 24 13 765
Locanda San Verolo	Verona - Costermano	+39 045 720 09 30
Villa Giona	Verona - San Pietro in Cariano	+39 045 685 50 11
Relais la Magioca	Verona - Valpolicella	+39 045 600 0167
Hotel Gabbia d'Oro Historical Residence	Verona	+39 045 8003060
Hotel Plaza e de Russie	Viareggio	+39 0584 44449

Latvia

TB Palace Hotel & Spa	Jurmala	+371 714 7094
Hotel Bergs	Riga	+371 777 09 00

MINI LISTINGS EUROPE & THE MEDITERRANEAN

Condé Nast Johansens are delighted to recommend over 450 properties across Europe and The Mediterranean.
These properties can be found in *Recommended Hotels & Spas - Europe & The Mediterranean*.
Call 0800 269 397 or see the order forms on page 271 to order guides.

Lithuania

Grotthuss Hotel	Vilnius	+370 5 266 0322
The Narutis Hotel	Vilnius	+370 5 2122 894

Luxembourg

Hotel Saint~Nicolas	Remich	+35 226 663

Montenegro

Villa Montenegro	St. Stefan	+381 86 468 802

Poland

Hotel Copernicus		+48 12 424 34 00/1/2

Portugal

Hotel Quinta do Lago	Almancil	+351 289 350 350
Monte da Fornalha	Borba - Estremoz	+351 268 840 314
Casa do Terreiro do Poço	Borba	+351 917 256077
Albatroz Palace, Luxury Suites	Cascais	+351 21 484 73 80
Hotel Cascais Mirage	Cascais	+351 210 060 600
Senhora da Guia	Cascais	+351 214 869 239

▼

Quinta de San José	Ervedosa do Douro	+351 254 420000
Convento do Espinheiro Heritage Hotel & Spa	Évora	+351 266 788 200
Quinta da Bela Vista	Funchal	+351 291 706 400
Quinta Jacintina	Garrão	+351 289 350 090
Villa Esmeralda	Lagos	+351 282 760 430
As Janelas Verdes	Lisbon	+351 21 39 68 143
Heritage Av Liberdade	Lisbon	+351 213 404 040
Hotel Britania	Lisbon	+351 21 31 55 016
Casas do Côro	Marialva - Mêda	+351 91 755 2020
Estalagem São Domingos	Mértola	+351 286 640 000
Monte do Chora Cascas	Montemor~o~Novo	+351 266 899 690
Vintage House	Pinhão	+351 254 730 230
Estalagem da Ponta do Sol	Ponta do Sol	+351 291 970 200
Convento de São Paulo	Redondo	+351 266 989 160
Casa da Torre das Neves	Viana do Castelo	+351 266 197 390
Vidago Palace Hotel & Golf	Vidago	+351 276 990 900

Slovakia

The Château	Salgovce - Piestany	+421 385 395 155

Slovenia

Hotel Golf	Bled	+386 4579 1700

Spain

Tancat de Codorniu	Alcanar	+34 977 737 194
Hospes Amérigo	Alicante	+34 965 14 65 70
Hotel Sidi San Juan & Spa	Alicante	+34 96 516 13 00
Torre la Mina	Alquerias - Castellón	+34 964 57 1746/0180
Hotel La Fuente del Sol	Antequera - La Joya	+34 95 12 39 823
Hacienda el Santiscal	Arcos de La Frontera	+34 956 70 83 13
Hotel Cortijo Faín	Arcos de la Frontera	+34 956 704 131
Hotel Arresi	Armintza	+34 94 68 79 208
Casa Palacio Conde de la Corte	Badajoz - Zafra	+34 924 563 311
Gallery Hotel	Barcelona	+34 934 15 99 11
Grand Hotel Central	Barcelona	+34 93 295 79 00
Hotel Casa Fuster	Barcelona	+34 93 255 30 00
Hotel Claris	Barcelona	+34 93 487 62 62
Hotel Cram	Barcelona	+34 93 216 77 00
Hotel Duquesa de Cardona	Barcelona	+34 93 268 90 90
Hotel Gran Derby	Barcelona	+34 93 445 2544
Hotel Granados 83	Barcelona	+34 93 492 96 70
Hotel Omm	Barcelona	+34 93 445 40 00
Hotel Pulitzer	Barcelona	+34 93 481 67 67
El Convent Begur	Begur	+34 972 62 30 91
Finca Canturias	Belvís de la Jara	+34 925 59 41 08
Gran Hotel Benahavís	Benahavís - Marbella	+34 902 504 862
Hotel Termas Marinas el Palasiet	Benicàssim	+34 964 300 250
Torre del Remei	Bolvir de Cerdanya	+34 972 140 182
Hotel La Cepada	Cangas de Onís	+34 985 84 94 45
Hospes Palacio del Bailío	Cordoba	+34 957 498 993
Hotel Rigat	Costa Brava	+34 972 36 52 00
Hotel Santa Marta	Costa Brava	+34 972 364 904
La Posada del Mar	Dénia	+34 96 643 29 66
Gran Hotel Elba Estepona & Thalasso Spa	Estepona	+34 952 809 200
Hotel Elba Palace Golf	Fuerteventura	+34 928 16 39 22
Kempinski Atlantis Bahía Real	Fuerteventura	+34 928 53 64 44
Hotel Casablanca	Gaucin	+34 952 151 019
Gran Hotel Lopesan Costa Meloneras	Gran Canaria	+34 928 12 81 00
Gran Hotel Lopesan Villa del Conde	Gran Canaria	+34 928 563 200
Casa de los Bates	Granada - Costa Tropical	+34 958 349 495
Barceló la Bobadilla ***** GL	Granada	+34 958 32 18 61
El Ladrón de Agua	Granada	+34 958 21 50 40
Hospes Palacio de los Patos	Granada	+34 958 535 790
Hotel Casa Morisca	Granada	+34 958 221 100
Hotel Palacio de Santa Inés	Granada	+34 958 22 23 62
Palacio de los Navas	Granada	+34 958 21 57 60
Santa Isabel la Real	Granada	+34 958 294 658
Atzaró Agroturismo	Ibiza	+34 971 33 88 38
Can Lluc	Ibiza	+34 971 198 673
Cas Gasi	Ibiza	+34 971 197 700
Hotel Mont Sant	Játiva - Xàtiva	+34 962 27 50 81
Casa Viña de Alcantara	Jerez de la Frontera	+34 956 393 010
Tunel del Hada Hotel & Spa	Jerte - Cáceres	+34 927 470 000

Condé Nast Johansens are delighted to recommend over 450 properties across Europe and The Mediterranean.

These properties can be found in *Recommended Hotels & Spas - Europe & The Mediterranean.*

Call 0800 269 397 or see the order forms on page 271 to order guides.

Gran Hotel Balneario Blancafort	La Garriga	+34 93 860 56 00
Mas Passamaner	La Selva del Camp	+34 977 766 333
Caserío de Mozaga	Lanzarote	+34 928 520 060
Princesa Yaiza Suite Hotel Resort	Lanzarote	+34 928 519 222
Antiguo Convento	Madrid	+34 91 632 22 20
Gran Meliá Fénix	Madrid	+34 91 431 67 00
Hotel Orfila	Madrid	+34 91 702 77 70
Hotel Quinta de los Cedros	Madrid	+34 91 515 2200
Hotel Urban	Madrid	+34 91 787 77 70
Hotel Villa Real	Madrid	+34 914 20 37 67
El Molino de Santillán	Málaga	+34 952 40 09 49
Hotel Molina Lario	Málaga	+34 952 06 002
Blau Porto Petro Beach Resort & Spa	Mallorca	+34 971 648 282
Ca's Xorc	Mallorca	+34 971 63 82 80
Can Simoneta	Mallorca	+34 971 816 110
Hospes Maricel	Mallorca	+34 971 707 744
Hotel Aimia	Mallorca	+34 971 631 200
Hotel Cala Sant Vicenç	Mallorca	+34 971 53 02 50
Hotel Dalt Murada	Mallorca	+34 971 425 300
Hotel Migjorn	Mallorca	+34 971 650 668
Hotel Tres	Mallorca	+34 971 717 333
La Reserva Rotana	Mallorca	+34 971 84 56 85
Palacio Ca Sa Galesa	Mallorca	+34 971 715 400

▼

Read's Hotel & Vespasian Spa	**Mallorca**	**+34 971 14 02 61**
Son Brull Hotel & Spa	Mallorca	+34 971 53 53 53
Valldemossa Hotel & Restaurant	Mallorca	+34 971 61 26 26
Gran Hotel Guadalpin Banús	Marbella	+34 952 89 94 04
Gran Hotel Guadalpin Marbella	Marbella	+34 952 89 94 04
Vasari Resort & Spa	Marbella	+34 952 907 806
Gran Hotel Guadalpin Byblos	Mijas~Costa	+34 952 89 94 04
Hotel Molino del Arco	Ronda	+34 952 114 017
Romantic Villa - Hotel Vistabella	Roses	+34 972 25 62 00
Castillo de Buen Amor	Salamanca - Topas	+34 923 355 002
Hacienda Zorita	Salamanca - Valderón	+34 923 129 400
Hotel Rector	Salamanca	+34 923 21 84 82
Palacio de San Benito	Sevilla - Cazalla de La Sierra	+34 954 88 33 36
Hotel Palacio de Los Granados	Sevilla - Écija	+34 955 905 344
Hotel Cortijo Águila Real	Sevilla - Guillena	+34 955 78 50 06
Cortijo Soto Real	Sevilla - Las Cabezas	+34 955 869 200
Palacio Marqués de la Gomera	Sevilla - Osuna	+34 95 4 81 22 23
Hacienda Benazuza el Bulli Hotel	Sevilla - Sanlúcar la Mayor	+34 955 70 33 44
Casa No 7	Sevilla	+34 954 221 581
Hospes las Casas del Rey de Baeza	Sevilla	+34 954 561 496
Dolce Sitges Hotel	Sitges	+34 938 109 000
San Sebastian Playa Hotel	Sitges	+34 93 894 86 76
Hotel Almenara	Sotogrande	+34 956 58 20 00

Casa Lehmi	Tárbena	+34 96 588 4018
Abama	Tenerife	+34 922 126 000
Gran Hotel Bahía del Duque Resort ***** G.Lujo	Tenerife	+34 922 74 69 00
Hotel Jardín Tropical	Tenerife	+34 922 74 60 00
Hotel las Madrigueras	Tenerife	+34 922 77 78 18
Jardín de la Paz	Tenerife	+34 922 578 818
Hotel el Privilegio de Tena	Tramacastilla de Tena	+34 974 487 206
Palacio de la Rambla	Úbeda	+34 953 75 01 96
La Torre del Visco	Valderrobres	+34 978 76 90 15
Hospes Palau de la Mar	Valencia	+34 96 316 2884
Hotel Sidi Saler & Spa	Valencia	+34 961 61 04 11
Mas de Canicattí	Vilamarxant	+34 96 165 05 34
Palacio de Cutre	Villamayor	+34 985 70 80 72

Switzerland

Villa Sassa - Hotel & Spa	Lugano	+41 91 911 41 11
Park Hotel Weggis	Weggis - Lake Lucerne	+41 41 392 05 05
Alden Hotel Splügenschloss	Zürich	+41 44 289 99 99

The Netherlands

Ambassade Hotel	Amsterdam	+31 20 5550222
Bliss Hotel	Noord Brabant - Breda	+31 076 533 5980
Duin & Kruidberg Country Estate	Santpoort - Amsterdam	+31 23 512 1800
Hotel Restaurant de Nederlanden	Vreeland	+31 294 232 326
Auberge de Campveerse Toren	Zeeland - Veere	+31 0118 501 291

Turkey

The Marmara Antalya	Antalya	+90 242 249 36 00
Divan Bodrum Palmira	Bodrum Peninsula - Mugla	+90 252 377 5601
The Marmara Bodrum	Bodrum	+90 252 313 8130
Degirmen Otel	Çesme - Izmir	+90 232 716 6714
Cappadocia Cave Suites	Göreme - Cappadocia	+90 384 271 2800
Ajia Hotel	Istanbul	+90 216 413 9300
The Marmara Istanbul	Istanbul	+90 212 251 4696
The Marmara Pera	Istanbul	+90 212 251 4646
Sumahan On The Water	Istanbul	+90 216 422 8000
Tuvana Residence	Kaleiçi - Antalya	+90 242 247 60 15
Villa Mahal	Kalkan - Antalya	+90 242 844 32 68

▼

Villa Hotel Tamara	**Kas - Antalya**	**+90 242 836 3273**
Richmond Nua Wellness - Spa	Sapanca - Adapazari	+90 264 582 2100
Sacred House	Ürgüp - Cappadocia	+90 384 341 7102

MINI LISTINGS THE AMERICAS

Condé Nast Johansens are delighted to recommend 310 properties across The Americas, Atlantic, Caribbean and Pacific.

Call 0800 269 397 or see the order forms on page 271 to order guides.

Recommendations in Canada

CANADA - BRITISH COLUMBIA (SALT SPRING ISLAND)

Hastings House Country Estate
160 Upper Ganges Road, Salt Spring Island,
British Columbia V8K 2S2
Tel: +1 250 537 2362
Fax: +1 250 537 5333
Web: www.johansens.com/hastingshouse

CANADA - BRITISH COLUMBIA (TOFINO)

The Wickaninnish Inn
Box 250, Tofino, British Columbia V0R 2Z0
Tel: +1 250 725 3100
Fax: +1 250 725 3110
Web: www.johansens.com/wickaninnish

CANADA - BRITISH COLUMBIA (VANCOUVER)

The Sutton Place Hotel Vancouver
845 Burrard Street, Vancouver, British Columbia V6Z 2K6
Tel: +1 604 682 5511
Fax: +1 604 682 5513
Web: www.johansens.com/suttonplacebc

CANADA - BRITISH COLUMBIA (VANCOUVER)

Wedgewood Hotel & Spa
845 Hornby Street, Vancouver, British Columbia V6Z 1V1
Tel: +1 604 689 7777
Fax: +1 604 608 5348
Web: www.johansens.com/wedgewoodbc

CANADA - BRITISH COLUMBIA (VICTORIA)

Villa Marco Polo Inn
1524 Shasta Place, Victoria, British Columbia V8S 1X9
Tel: +1 250 370 1524
Fax: +1 250 370 1624
Web: www.johansens.com/villamarcopolo

CANADA - NEW BRUNSWICK (ST ANDREWS BY-THE-SEA)

Kingsbrae Arms
219 King Street, St. Andrews By-The-Sea,
New Brunswick E5B 1Y1
Tel: +1 506 529 1897
Fax: +1 506 529 1197
Web: www.johansens.com/kingsbraearms

CANADA - ONTARIO (CAMBRIDGE)

Langdon Hall Country House Hotel & Spa
1 Langdon Drive, Cambridge, Ontario N3H 4R8
Tel: +1 519 740 2100
Fax: +1 519 740 8161
Web: www.johansens.com/langdonhall

CANADA - ONTARIO (NIAGARA-ON-THE-LAKE)

Riverbend Inn & Vineyard
16104 Niagara River Parkway, Niagara-on-the-Lake,
Ontario L0S 1J0
Tel: +1 905 468 8866
Fax: +1 905 468 8829
Web: www.johansens.com/riverbend

CANADA - ONTARIO (TORONTO)

Windsor Arms
18 St. Thomas Street, Toronto, Ontario M5S 3E7
Tel: +1 416 971 9666
Fax: +1 416 921 9121
Web: www.johansens.com/windsorarms

CANADA - QUÉBEC (QUÉBEC CITY)

Auberge Saint-Antoine
8, Rue Saint-Antoine, Québec City, Québec G1K 4C9
Tel: +1 418 692 2211
Fax: +1 418 692 1177
Web: www.johansens.com/saintantoine

CANADA - QUÉBEC (MONT-TREMBLANT)

Hôtel Quintessence
3004 chemin de la chapelle, Mont-Tremblant,
Québec J8E 1E1
Tel: +1 819 425 3400
Fax: +1 819 425 3480
Web: www.johansens.com/quintessence

CANADA - QUÉBEC (LA MALBAIE)

La Pinsonnière
124 Saint-Raphaël, La Malbaie, Québec G5A 1X9
Tel: +1 418 665 4431
Fax: +1 418 665 7156
Web: www.johansens.com/lapinsonniere

CANADA - QUÉBEC (MONTRÉAL)

Hôtel Nelligan
106 rue Saint-Paul Ouest, Montréal, Québec H2Y 1Z3
Tel: +1 514 788 2040
Fax: +1 514 788 2041
Web: www.johansens.com/nelligan

CANADA - QUÉBEC (MONTRÉAL)

Le Place d'Armes Hôtel & Suites
55 rue Saint-Jacques Ouest, Montréal, Québec H2Y 3X2
Tel: +1 514 842 1887
Fax: +1 514 842 6469
Web: www.johansens.com/hotelplacedarmes

Recommendations in Mexico

MEXICO - BAJA CALIFORNIA NORTE (TECATE)

Rancho La Puerta
Tecate, Baja California Norte
Tel: +52 665 654 9155
Fax: +52 665 654 1108
Web: www.johansens.com/rancholapuerta

MEXICO - BAJA CALIFORNIA SUR (CABO SAN LUCAS)

Esperanza
Km. 7 Carretera Transpeninsular, Punta Ballena,
Cabo San Lucas, Baja California Sur 23410
Tel: +52 624 145 6400
Fax: +52 624 145 6499
Web: www.johansens.com/esperanza

MEXICO - BAJA CALIFORNIA SUR (LOS CABOS)

Marquis Los Cabos
Lote 74, Km. 21.5 Carretera Transpeninsular, Fraccionamiento
Cabo Real, Los Cabos, Baja California Sur 23400
Tel: +52 624 144 2000
Fax: +52 624 144 2001
Web: www.johansens.com/marquisloscabos

MEXICO - BAJA CALIFORNIA SUR (SAN JOSE DEL CABO)

Casa Natalia
Blvd. Mijares 4, San Jose Del Cabo, Baja California Sur 23400
Tel: +52 624 14671 00
Fax: +52 624 14251 10
Web: www.johansens.com/casanatalia

MINI LISTINGS THE AMERICAS

Condé Nast Johansens are delighted to recommend 310 properties across The Americas, Atlantic, Caribbean and Pacific.
Call 0800 269 397 or see the order forms on page 271 to order guides.

MEXICO - BAJA CALIFORNIA SUR (SAN JOSE DEL CABO)

One & Only Palmilla
Km 7.5 Carretera Transpeninsular, San Jose Del Cabo,
Baja California Sur 23400
Tel: +52 624 146 7000
Fax: +52 624 146 7001
Web: www.johansens.com/oneandonlypalmilla

MEXICO - COLIMA (COLIMA)

Hacienda de San Antonio
Municipio de Comala, Colima, Colima 28450
Tel: +52 312 314 9554
Fax: +52 312 313 4254
Web: www.johansens.com/sanantonio

MEXICO - DISTRITO FEDERAL (MEXICO CITY)

Casa Vieja
Eugenio Sue 45 (Colonia Polanco),
Mexico Distrito Federal 11560
Tel: +52 55 52 82 0067
Fax: +52 55 52 81 3780
Web: www.johansens.com/casavieja

MEXICO - ESTADO DE MEXICO (MALINALCO)

Casa Limon
Rio Lerma 103, Barrio de Santa María, Malinalco,
Estado de Mexico 524040
Tel: +52 714 147 0256
Fax: +52 714 147 0619
Web: www.johansens.com/casalimon

MEXICO - GUANAJUATO (GUANAJUATO)

Quinta Las Acacias
Paseo de la Presa 168, Guanajuato, Guanajuato 36000
Tel: +52 473 731 1517
Fax: +52 473 731 1862
Web: www.johansens.com/acacias

MEXICO - GUANAJUATO (SAN MIGUEL DE ALLENDE)

Dos Casas
Calle Quebrada 101, San Miguel de Allende,
Guanajuato 37700
Tel: +52 415 154 4073
Fax: +52 415 154 4958
Web: www.johansens.com/doscasas

MEXICO - GUANAJUATO (SAN MIGUEL DE ALLENDE)

La Puertecita Boutique Hotel
Santo Domingo 75 Col. Los Arcos, San Miguel de Allende,
Guanajuato 37740
Tel: +52 415 152 5011
Fax: +52 415 152 5505
Web: www.johansens.com/lapuertecita

MEXICO - GUERRERO (ZIHUATANEJO)

Villa del Sol
Playa La Ropa, P.O. Box 84, Zihuatanejo, Guerrero 40880
Tel: +52 755 555 5500
Fax: +52 755 554 2758
Web: www.johansens.com/villadelsol

MEXICO - JALISCO (PUERTA VALLARTA / COSTA ALEGRE)

Las Alamandas Resort
Carretera Barra de Navidad - Puerto Vallarta km 83.5,
Col. Quemaro, Jalisco 48850
Tel: +52 322 285 5500
Fax: +52 322 285 5027
Web: www.johansens.com/lasalamandas

MEXICO - JALISCO (PUERTO VALLARTA)

Casa Velas
Pelicanos 311, Fracc. Marina Vallarta, Puerto Vallarta,
Jalisco 48354
Tel: +52 322 226 9585
Fax: +52 322 226 6690
Web: www.johansens.com/casavelas

MEXICO - JALISCO (PUERTO VALLARTA)

Hacienda San Angel
Miramar 336, Col. Centro Puerto Vallarta, Jalisco 48300
Tel: +52 322 222 2692
Fax: +52 322 223 1941
Web: www.johansens.com/sanangel

MEXICO - MICHOACÁN (MORELIA)

Hotel Los Juaninos
Morelos Sur 39, Centro, Morelia, Michoacán 58000
Tel: +52 443 312 00 36
Fax: +52 443 312 00 36
Web: www.johansens.com/juaninos

MEXICO - MICHOACÁN (MORELIA)

Hotel Virrey de Mendoza
Av. Madero Pte. 310, Centro Histórico, Morelia,
Michoacán 58000
Tel: +52 44 33 12 06 33
Fax: +52 44 33 12 67 19
Web: www.johansens.com/hotelvirrey

MEXICO - MICHOACÁN (MORELIA)

Villa Montaña Hotel & Spa
Patzimba 201, Vista Bella, Morelia, Michoacán 58090
Tel: +52 443 314 02 31
Fax: +52 443 315 14 23
Web: www.johansens.com/montana

MEXICO - NAYARIT (NUEVO VALLARTA)

Grand Velas All Suites & Spa Resort
Av. Cocoteros 98 Sur, Nuevo Vallarta, Nayarit 63735
Tel: +52 322 226 8000
Fax: +52 322 297 2005
Web: www.johansens.com/grandvelas

MEXICO - OAXACA (OAXACA)

Casa Oaxaca
Calle García Vigil 407, Centro, Oaxaca, Oaxaca 68000
Tel: +52 951 514 4173
Fax: +52 951516 4412
Web: www.johansens.com/oaxaca

MEXICO - OAXACA (OAXACA)

Hacienda Los Laureles - Spa
Hidalgo 21, San Felipe del Agua, Oaxaca, Oaxaca 68020
Tel: +52 951 501 5300
Fax: +52 951 501 5301 or +52 951 520 0890
Web: www.johansens.com/laureles

MEXICO - PUEBLA (CHOLULA)

La Quinta Luna
3 sur 702, San Pedro Cholula, Puebla 72760
Tel: +52 222 247 8915
Fax: +52 222 247 8916
Web: www.johansens.com/quintaluna

MEXICO - QUERÉTARO (QUERÉTARO)

La Casa de la Marquesa
Madero 41, Querétaro, Centro Histórico 7600
Tel: +52 442 212 0092
Fax: +52 442 212 0098
Web: www.johansens.com/marquesa

MEXICO - QUINTANA ROO (PLAYA DEL CARMEN)

Royal Hideaway Playacar
Lote Hotelero No. 6, Mza 6 Fracc., Playacar,
Playa del Carmen, Quintana Roo 77710
Tel: +52 984 873 4500
Fax: +52 984 873 4507
Web: www.johansens.com/royalhidewaway

Condé Nast Johansens are delighted to recommend 310 properties across The Americas, Atlantic, Caribbean and Pacific.
Call 0800 269 397 or see the order forms on page 271 to order guides.

MEXICO - QUINTANA ROO (PUERTO MORELOS)

Ceiba del Mar Spa Resort
Costera Norte Lte. 1, S.M. 10, MZ. 26, Puerto Morelos, Quintana Roo 77580
Tel: +52 998 872 8060
Fax: +52 998 872 8061
Web: www.johansens.com/ceibademar

MEXICO - QUINTANA ROO (TULUM)

Casa Nalum
Sian Ka'an Biosphere Reserve, Quintana Roo
Tel: +52 984 806 4905
Web: www.johansens.com/casanalum

MEXICO - YUCATÁN (MÉRIDA)

Hacienda Xcanatun - Casa de Piedra
Carretera Mérida-Progreso, Km 12, Mérida, Yucatán 97302
Tel: +52 999 941 0273
Fax: +52 999 941 0319
Web: www.johansens.com/xcanatun

Recommendations in U.S.A

U.S.A. - ARIZONA (GREER)

Hidden Meadow Ranch
620 Country Road 1325, Greer, Arizona 85927
Tel: +1 928 333 1000
Fax: +1 928 333 1010
Web: www.johansens.com/hiddenmeadow

U.S.A. - ARIZONA (PARADISE VALLEY / SCOTTSDALE)

The Hermosa Inn
5532 North Palo Cristi Road, Paradise Valley, Arizona 85253
Tel: +1 602 955 8614
Fax: +1 602 955 8299
Web: www.johansens.com/hermosa

U.S.A. - ARIZONA (PARADISE VALLEY / SCOTTSDALE)

Sanctuary on Camelback Mountain
5700 East McDonald Drive, Scottsdale, Arizona 85253
Tel: +1 480 948 2100
Fax: +1 480 483 7314
Web: www.johansens.com/sanctuarycamelback

U.S.A. - ARIZONA (SEDONA)

Amara Creekside Resort
310 North Highway 89A, Sedona, Arizona 86336
Tel: +1 928 282 4828
Fax: +1 928 282 4825
Web: www.johansens.com/amaracreekside

U.S.A. - ARIZONA (SEDONA)

L'Auberge de Sedona
301 L'Auberge Lane, Sedona, Arizona 86336
Tel: +1 928 282 1661
Fax: +1 928 282 2885
Web: www.johansens.com/laubergedesedona

U.S.A. - ARIZONA (SEDONA)

Sedona Rouge Hotel & Spa
2250 West Highway 89A, Sedona, Arizona 86336
Tel: +1 928 203 4111
Fax: +1 928 203 9094
Web: www.johansens.com/sedonarouge

U.S.A. - ARIZONA (TUCSON)

Arizona Inn
2200 East Elm Street, Tucson, Arizona 85719
Tel: +1 520 325 1541
Fax: +1 520 881 5830
Web: www.johansens.com/arizonainn

U.S.A. - ARIZONA (TUCSON)

Tanque Verde Ranch
14301 East Speedway Boulevard, Tucson, Arizona 85748
Tel: +1 520 296 6275
Fax: +1 520 721 9427
Web: www.johansens.com/tanqueverde

U.S.A. - ARIZONA (WICKENBURG)

Rancho de los Caballeros
1551 South Vulture Mine Road, Wickenburg, Arizona 85390
Tel: +1 928 684 5484
Fax: +1 928 684 9565
Web: www.johansens.com/caballeros

U.S.A. - CALIFORNIA (ATASCADERO)

The Carlton Hotel
6005 El Camino Real, Atascadero, California 93422
Tel: +1 805 461 5100
Fax: +1 805 461 5116
Web: www.johansens.com/carltoncalifornia

U.S.A. - CALIFORNIA (BIG SUR)

Post Ranch Inn
Highway 1, P.O. Box 219, Big Sur, California 93920
Tel: +1 831 667 2200
Fax: +1 831 667 2512
Web: www.johansens.com/postranchinn

U.S.A. - CALIFORNIA (BIG SUR)

Ventana Inn and Spa
Highway 1, Big Sur, California 93920
Tel: +1 831 667 2331
Fax: +1 831 667 2419
Web: www.johansens.com/ventana

U.S.A. - CALIFORNIA (CARMEL-BY-THE-SEA)

L'Auberge Carmel
Monte Verde at Seventh, Carmel-by-the-Sea, California 93921
Tel: +1 831 624 8578
Fax: +1 831 626 1018
Web: www.johansens.com/laubergecarmel

U.S.A. - CALIFORNIA (CARMEL-BY-THE-SEA)

Tradewinds Carmel
Mission Street at Third Avenue, Carmel-by-the-Sea, California 93921
Tel: +1 831 624 2776
Fax: +1 831 624 0634
Web: www.johansens.com/tradewinds

U.S.A. - CALIFORNIA (EUREKA)

The Carter House Inns
301 L Street, Eureka, California 95501
Tel: +1 707 444 8062
Fax: +1 707 444 8067
Web: www.johansens.com/carterhouse

U.S.A. - CALIFORNIA (GLEN ELLEN)

The Gaige House
13540 Arnold Drive, Glen Ellen, California 95442
Tel: +1 707 935 0237
Fax: +1 707 935 6411
Web: www.johansens.com/gaige

Condé Nast Johansens are delighted to recommend 310 properties across The Americas, Atlantic, Caribbean and Pacific. Call 0800 269 397 or see the order forms on page 271 to order guides.

U.S.A. - CALIFORNIA (HEALDSBURG)

The Grape Leaf Inn

539 Johnson Street, Healdsburg, California 95448
Tel: +1 707 433 8140
Fax: +1 707 433 3140
Web: www.johansens.com/grapeleaf

U.S.A. - CALIFORNIA (KENWOOD)

The Kenwood Inn and Spa

10400 Sonoma Highway, Kenwood, California 95452
Tel: +1 707 833 1293
Fax: +1 707 833 1247
Web: www.johansens.com/kenwoodinn

U.S.A. - CALIFORNIA (LA JOLLA)

Estancia La Jolla Hotel & Spa

9700 North Torrey Pines Road, La Jolla, California 92037
Tel: +1 858 202 3389
Fax: +1 858 202 3399
Web: www.johansens.com/estancialajolla

U.S.A. - CALIFORNIA (LOS ANGELES)

Hotel Bel-Air

701 Stone Canyon Road, Los Angeles, California 90077
Tel: +1 310 472 1211
Fax: +1 310 909 1611
Web: www.johansens.com/belair

U.S.A. - CALIFORNIA (LOS OLIVOS)

The Fess Parker Wine Country Inn

2860 Grand Avenue, Los Olivos, California 93441
Tel: +1 805 688 7788
Fax: +1 805 688 1942
Web: www.johansens.com/fessparker

U.S.A. - CALIFORNIA (MENDOCINO)

The Stanford Inn By The Sea

Coast Highway One & Comptche-Ukiah Road, Mendocino, California 95460
Tel: +1 707 937 5615
Fax: +1 707 937 0305
Web: www.johansens.com/stanford

U.S.A. - CALIFORNIA (MILL VALLEY)

Mill Valley Inn

165 Throckmorton Avenue, Mill Valley, California 94941
Tel: +1 415 389 6608
Fax: +1 415 389 5051
Web: www.johansens.com/millvalleyinn

U.S.A. - CALIFORNIA (MONTEREY)

Old Monterey Inn

500 Martin Street, Monterey, California 93940
Tel: +1 831 375 8284
Fax: +1 831 375 6730
Web: www.johansens.com/oldmontereyinn

U.S.A. - CALIFORNIA (NAPA VALLEY)

1801 First Inn

1801 First Street, Napa, California 94559
Tel: +1 707 224 3739
Fax: +1 707 224 3932
Web: www.johansens.com/1801inn

U.S.A. - CALIFORNIA (NAPA)

Milliken Creek Inn & Spa

1815 Silverado Trail, Napa, California 94558
Tel: +1 707 255 1197
Fax: +1 707 255 3112
Web: www.johansens.com/milliken

U.S.A. - CALIFORNIA (OAKHURST)

Château du Sureau & Spa

48688 Victoria Lane, Oakhurst, California 93644
Tel: +1 559 683 6860
Fax: +1 559 683 0800
Web: www.johansens.com/chateausureau

U.S.A. - CALIFORNIA (PASO ROBLES)

The Villa Toscana

4230 Buena Vista, Paso Robles, California 93446
Tel: +1 805 238 5600
Fax: +1 805 238 5605
Web: www.johansens.com/villatoscana

U.S.A. - CALIFORNIA (RANCHO SANTA FE)

The Inn at Rancho Santa Fe

5951 Linea del Cielo, Rancho Santa Fe, California 92067
Tel: +1 858 756 1131
Fax: +1 858 759 1604
Web: www.johansens.com/ranchosantafe

U.S.A. - CALIFORNIA (SAN DIEGO)

Tower23 Hotel

723 Felspar, San Diego, California 92109
Tel: +1 858 270 2323
Fax: +1 858 274 2333
Web: www.johansens.com/tower23

U.S.A. - CALIFORNIA (SAN FRANCISCO BAY AREA)

Inn Above Tide

30 El Portal, Sausalito, California 94965
Tel: +1 415 332 9535
Fax: +1 415 332 9535
Web: www.johansens.com/innabovetide

U.S.A. - CALIFORNIA (SAN FRANCISCO)

The Union Street Inn

2229 Union Street, San Francisco, California 94123
Tel: +1 415 346 0424
Fax: +1 415 922 8046
Web: www.johansens.com/unionstreetsf

U.S.A. - CALIFORNIA (SANTA BARBARA)

Harbor View Inn

28 West Cabrillo Boulevard, Santa Barbara, California 93101
Tel: +1 805 963 0780
Fax: +1 805 963 7967
Web: www.johansens.com/harborview

U.S.A. - CALIFORNIA (SANTA YNEZ)

The Santa Ynez Inn

3627 Sagunto Street, Santa Ynez, California 93460-0628
Tel: +1 805 688 5588
Fax: +1 805 686 4294
Web: www.johansens.com/santaynez

U.S.A. - CALIFORNIA (SONOMA)

Ledson Hotel & Harmony Restaurant

480 First Street East, Sonoma, California 95476
Tel: +1 707 996 9779
Fax: +1 707 996 9776
Web: www.johansens.com/ledsonhotel

U.S.A. - CALIFORNIA (ST. HELENA)

Meadowood

900 Meadowood Lane, St. Helena, California 94574
Tel: +1 707 963 3646
Fax: +1 707 963 3532
Web: www.johansens.com/meadowood

MINI LISTINGS THE AMERICAS

Condé Nast Johansens are delighted to recommend 310 properties across The Americas, Atlantic, Caribbean and Pacific.

Call 0800 269 397 or see the order forms on page 271 to order guides.

U.S.A. - COLORADO (BOULDER)

The Bradley Boulder Inn
2040 16th Street, Boulder, Colorado 80302
Tel: +1 303 545 5200
Fax: +1 303 440 6740
Web: www.johansens.com/bradleyboulderinn

U.S.A. - COLORADO (DENVER)

Castle Marne Bed & Breakfast Inn
1572 Race Street, Denver, Colorado 80206
Tel: +1 303 331 0621
Fax: +1 303 331 0623
Web: www.johansens.com/castlemarne

U.S.A. - COLORADO (ESTES PARK)

Taharaa Mountain Lodge
P.O. Box 2586, Estes Park, Colorado 80517
Tel: +1 970 577 0098
Fax: +1 970 577 0819
Web: www.johansens.com/taharaa

U.S.A. - COLORADO (MANITOU SPRINGS)

The Cliff House at Pikes Peak
306 Cañon Avenue, Manitou Springs, Colorado 80829
Tel: +1 719 685 3000
Fax: +1 719 685 3913
Web: www.johansens.com/thecliffhouse

U.S.A. - COLORADO (MONTROSE)

Elk Mountain Resort
97 Elk Walk, Montrose, Colorado 81401
Tel: +1 970 252 4900
Fax: +1 970 252 4913
Web: www.johansens.com/elkmountain

U.S.A. - COLORADO (STEAMBOAT SPRINGS)

Vista Verde Guest Ranch
P.O. Box 770465, Steamboat Springs, Colorado 80477
Tel: +1 970 879 3858
Fax: +1 970 879 6814
Web: www.johansens.com/vistaverderanch

U.S.A. - COLORADO (VAIL)

The Tivoli Lodge at Vail
386 Hanson Ranch Road, Vail, Colorado 81657
Tel: +1 970 476 5615
Fax: +1 970 476 6601
Web: www.johansens.com/tivoli

U.S.A. - COLORADO (VAIL)

Vail Mountain Lodge & Spa
352 East Meadow Drive, Vail, Colorado 81657
Tel: +1 970 476 0700
Fax: +1 970 476 6451
Web: www.johansens.com/vailmountain

U.S.A. - CONNECTICUT (GREENWICH)

Delamar Greenwich Harbor
500 Steamboat Road, Greenwich, Connecticut 06830
Tel: +1 203 661 9800
Fax: +1 203 661 2513
Web: www.johansens.com/delamar

U.S.A. - CONNECTICUT (STONINGTON)

The Inn at Stonington
60 Water Street, Stonington, Connecticut 06378
Tel: +1 860 535 2000
Fax: +1 860 535 8193
Web: www.johansens.com/stonington

U.S.A. - DELAWARE (REHOBOTH BEACH)

The Bellmoor
Six Christian Street, Rehoboth Beach, Delaware 19971
Tel: +1 302 227 5800
Fax: +1 302 227 0323
Web: www.johansens.com/thebellmoor

U.S.A. - DELAWARE (REHOBOTH BEACH)

Boardwalk Plaza Hotel
Olive Avenue & The Boardwalk, Rehoboth Beach,
Delaware 19971
Tel: +1 302 227 7169
Fax: +1 302 227 0561
Web: www.johansens.com/boardwalkplaza

U.S.A. - DELAWARE (WILMINGTON)

Inn at Montchanin Village
Route 100 & Kirk Road, Montchanin, Delaware 19710
Tel: +1 302 888 2133
Fax: +1 302 888 0389
Web: www.johansens.com/montchanin

U.S.A. - DISTRICT OF COLUMBIA (WASHINGTON)

The Hay Adams
Sixteenth & H. Streets N.W., Washington D.C. 20006
Tel: +1 202 638 6600
Fax: +1 202 638 2716
Web: www.johansens.com/hayadams

U.S.A. - FLORIDA (COCONUT GROVE)

Grove Isle Hotel & Spa
Four Grove Isle Drive, Coconut Grove, Florida 33133
Tel: +1 305 858 8300
Fax: +1 305 858 5908
Web: www.johansens.com/groveisle

U.S.A. - FLORIDA (DAYTONA BEACH SHORES)

The Shores Resort & Spa
2637 South Atlantic Avenue, Daytona Beach Shores,
Florida 32118
Tel: +1 386 767 7350
Fax: +1 386 760 3651
Web: www.johansens.com/shoresresort

U.S.A. - FLORIDA (FISHER ISLAND)

Fisher Island Hotel & Resort
One Fisher Island Drive, Fisher Island, Florida 33109
Tel: +1 305 535 6000
Fax: +1 305 535 6003
Web: www.johansens.com/fisherisland

U.S.A. - FLORIDA (JUPITER)

Jupiter Beach Resort & Spa
5 North A1A, Jupiter, Florida 33477-5190
Tel: +1 561 746 2511
Fax: +1 561 744 1741
Web: www.johansens.com/jupiterbeachresort

U.S.A. - FLORIDA (KEY WEST)

Ocean Key Resort
Zero Duval Street, Key West, Florida 33040
Tel: +1 305 296 7701
Fax: +1 305 292 7685
Web: www.johansens.com/oceankey

U.S.A. - FLORIDA (KEY WEST)

Simonton Court Historic Inn & Cottages
320 Simonton Street, Key West, Florida 33040
Tel: +1 305 294 6386
Fax: +1 305 293 8446
Web: www.johansens.com/simontoncourt

Condé Nast Johansens are delighted to recommend 310 properties across The Americas, Atlantic, Caribbean and Pacific.

Call 0800 269 397 or see the order forms on page 271 to order guides.

U.S.A. - FLORIDA (KEY WEST)

Sunset Key Guest Cottages
245 Front Street, Key West, Florida 33040
Tel: +1 305 292 5300
Fax: +1 305 292 5395
Web: www.johansens.com/sunsetkey

U.S.A. - FLORIDA (MARCO ISLAND/NAPLES)

Marco Beach Ocean Resort
480 South Collier Boulevard, Marco Island, Florida 34145
Tel: +1 239 393 1400
Fax: +1 239 393 1401
Web: www.johansens.com/marcobeach

U.S.A. - FLORIDA (MIAMI BEACH)

Hotel Victor
1144 Ocean Drive, Miami Beach, Florida 33139
Tel: +1 305 428 1234
Fax: +1 305 421 6281
Web: www.johansens.com/hotelvictor

U.S.A. - FLORIDA (NAPLES)

LaPlaya Beach & Golf Resort
9891 Gulf Shore Drive, Naples, Florida 34108
Tel: +1 239 597 3123
Fax: +1 239 597 8283
Web: www.johansens.com/laplaya

U.S.A. - FLORIDA (ORLANDO)

Portofino Bay Hotel
5601 Universal Boulevard, Orlando, Florida 32819
Tel: +1 407 503 1000
Fax: +1 407 503 1010
Web: www.johansens.com/portofinobay

U.S.A. - FLORIDA (PONTE VEDRA BEACH)

The Lodge & Club at Ponte Vedra Beach
607 Ponte Vedra Boulevard, Ponte Vedra Beach, Florida 32082
Tel: +1 904 273 9500
Fax: +1 904 273 0210
Web: www.johansens.com/ponteverdrabeach

U.S.A. - FLORIDA (SANTA ROSA BEACH)

WaterColor Inn and Resort
34 Goldenrod Circle, Santa rosa Beach, Florida 32459
Tel: +1 850 534 5000
Fax: +1 850 534 5001
Web: www.johansens.com/watercolor

U.S.A. - FLORIDA (ST. PETE BEACH)

Don CeSar Beach Resort
3400 Gulf Boulevard, St. Pete Beach, Florida 33706
Tel: +1 727 360 1881
Fax: +1 727 367 3609
Web: www.johansens.com/doncesar

U.S.A. - GEORGIA (ADAIRSVILLE)

Barnsley Gardens Resort
597 Barnsley Gardens Road, Adairsville, Georgia 30103
Tel: +1 770 773 7480
Fax: +1 770 877 9155
Web: www.johansens.com/barnsleygardens

U.S.A. - GEORGIA (CUMBERLAND ISLAND)

Greyfield Inn
Cumberland Island, Georgia
Tel: +1 904 261 6408
Fax: +1 904 321 0666
Web: www.johansens.com/greyfieldinn

U.S.A. - GEORGIA (SAVANNAH)

The Ballastone
14 East Oglethorpe Avenue, Savannah, Georgia 31401-3707
Tel: +1 912 236 1484
Fax: +1 912 236 4626
Web: www.johansens.com/ballastone

U.S.A. - GEORGIA (SAVANNAH)

Eliza Thompson House
5 West Jones Street, Savannah, Georgia 31401
Tel: +1 912 236 3620
Fax: +1 912 238 1920
Web: www.johansens.com/elizathompsonhouse

U.S.A. - GEORGIA (SAVANNAH)

The Gastonian
220 East Gaston Street, Savannah, Georgia 31401
Tel: +1 912 232 2869
Fax: +1 912 232 0710
Web: www.johansens.com/gastonian

U.S.A. - HAWAII (BIG ISLAND)

The Palms Cliff House
28-3514 Mamalahoa Highway 19, P.O. Box 189, Honomu, Hawaii 96728-0189
Tel: +1 808 963 6076
Fax: +1 808 963 6316
Web: www.johansens.com/palmscliff

U.S.A. - HAWAII (BIG ISLAND)

Shipman House
131 Ka'iulani Street, Hilo, Hawaii 96720
Tel: +1 808 934 8002
Fax: +1 808 934 8002
Web: www.johansens.com/shipman

U.S.A. - HAWAII (MAUI)

Hotel Hana-Maui and Honua Spa
5031 Hana Highway, Hana, Maui, Hawaii 96713
Tel: +1 808 248 8211
Fax: +1 808 248 7202
Web: www.johansens.com/hanamaui

U.S.A. - IDAHO (KETCHUM)

Knob Hill Inn
960 North Main Street, P.O. Box 800, Ketchum, Idaho 83340
Tel: +1 208 726 8010
Fax: +1 208 726 2712
Web: www.johansens.com/knobhillinn

U.S.A. - KANSAS (LAWRENCE)

The Eldridge Hotel
701 Massachusetts, Lawrence, Kansas 66044
Tel: +1 785 749 5011
Fax: +1 785 749 4512
Web: www.johansens.com/eldridge

U.S.A. - LOUISIANA (NEW ORLEANS)

Hotel Maison de Ville
727 Rue Toulouse, New Orleans, Louisiana 70130
Tel: +1 504 561 5858
Fax: +1 504 528 9939
Web: www.johansens.com/maisondeville

U.S.A. - LOUISIANA (NEW ORLEANS)

The Lafayette Hotel
600 St. Charles Avenue, New Orleans, Louisiana 70130
Tel: +1 504 524 4441
Fax: +1 504 962 5537
Web: www.johansens.com/lafayette

Condé Nast Johansens are delighted to recommend 310 properties across The Americas, Atlantic, Caribbean and Pacific.
Call 0800 269 397 or see the order forms on page 271 to order guides.

U.S.A. - LOUISIANA (NEW ORLEANS)
The St. James Hotel
330 Magazine Street, New Orleans, Louisiana 70130
Tel: +1 504 304 4000
Fax: +1 504 304 4444
Web: www.johansens.com/stjamesno

U.S.A. - MAINE (GREENVILLE)
The Lodge At Moosehead Lake
Lily Bay Road, P.O. Box 1167, Greenville, Maine 04441
Tel: +1 207 695 4400
Fax: +1 207 695 2281
Web: www.johansens.com/lodgeatmooseheadlake

U.S.A. - MAINE (KENNEBUNKPORT)
The White Barn Inn
37 Beach Avenue, Kennebunkport, Maine 04043
Tel: +1 207 967 2321
Fax: +1 207 967 1100
Web: www.johansens.com/whitebarninn

U.S.A. - MAINE (PORTLAND)
Portland Harbor Hotel
468 Fore Street, Portland, Maine 04101
Tel: +1 207 775 9090
Fax: +1 207 775 9990
Web: www.johansens.com/portlandharbor

U.S.A. - MARYLAND (EASTON)
Inn at 202 Dover
202 E. Dover Street, Easton, Maryland 21601
Tel: +1 410 819 8007
Fax: +1 410 819 3368
Web: www.johansens.com/innat202dover

U.S.A. - MARYLAND (FROSTBURG)
Savage River Lodge
1600 Mt. Aetna Road, Frostburg, Maryland 21532
Tel: +1 301 689 3200
Fax: +1 301 689 2746
Web: www.johansens.com/savageriver

U.S.A. - MARYLAND (ST. MICHAELS)
Five Gables Inn & Spa
209 North Talbot Street, St. Michaels, Maryland 21663
Tel: +1 410 745 0100
Fax: +1 410 745 2903
Web: www.johansens.com/fivegables

U.S.A. - MASSACHUSETTS (BOSTON)
The Charles Street Inn
94 Charles Street, Boston, Massachusetts 02114
Tel: +1 617 314 8900
Fax: +1 617 371 0009
Web: www.johansens.com/charlesstreetinn

U.S.A. - MASSACHUSETTS (BOSTON)
Clarendon Square Inn
198 West Brookline Street, Boston, Massachusetts 02118
Tel: +1 617 536 2229
Fax: +1 617 536 2993
Web: www.johansens.com/clarendonsquare

U.S.A. - MASSACHUSETTS (BOSTON)
Hotel Commonwealth
500 Commonwealth Avenue, Boston, Massachusetts 02215
Tel: +1 617 933 5000
Fax: +1 617 266 6888
Web: www.johansens.com/commonwealth

U.S.A. - MASSACHUSETTS (BOSTON)
The Lenox
61 Exeter Street at Boylston, Boston, Massachusetts 02116
Tel: +1 617 536 5300
Fax: +1 617 267 1237
Web: www.johansens.com/lenox

U.S.A. - MASSACHUSETTS (BOSTON)
Nine Zero Hotel
90 Tremont Street, Boston, Massachusetts 02108
Tel: +1 617 772 5800
Fax: +1 617 772 5810
Web: www.johansens.com/ninezero

U.S.A. - MASSACHUSETTS (CAMBRIDGE)
Hotel Marlowe
25 Edwin H. Land Boulevard, Cambridge,
Massachusetts 02141
Tel: +1 617 868 8000
Fax: +1 617 868 8001
Web: www.johansens.com/marlowe

U.S.A. - MASSACHUSETTS (CAPE COD)
The Crowne Pointe Historic Inn & Spa
82 Bradford Street, Provincetown, Cape Cod,
Massachusetts 02657
Tel: +1 508 487 6767
Fax: +1 508 487 5554
Web: www.johansens.com/crownepointe

U.S.A. - MASSACHUSETTS (CAPE COD)
Wequassett Inn Resort and Golf Club
On Pleasant Bay, Chatham, Cape Cod, Massachusetts 02633
Tel: +1 508 432 5400
Fax: +1 508 430 3131
Web: www.johansens.com/wequassett

U.S.A. - MASSACHUSETTS (EDGARTOWN)
The Charlotte Inn
27 South Summer Street, Edgartown, Massachusetts 02539
Tel: +1 508 627 4151
Fax: +1 508 627 4652
Web: www.johansens.com/charlotte

U.S.A. - MASSACHUSETTS (IPSWICH)
The Inn at Castle Hill
280 Argilla Road, Ipswich, Massachusetts 01938
Tel: +1 978 412 2555
Fax: +1 978 412 2556
Web: www.johansens.com/castlehill

U.S.A. - MASSACHUSETTS (LENOX)
Blantyre
16 Blantyre Road, P.O. Box 995, Lenox,
Massachusetts 01240
Tel: +1 413 637 3556
Fax: +1 413 637 4282
Web: www.johansens.com/blantyre

U.S.A. - MASSACHUSETTS (LENOX)
Cranwell Resort, Spa & Golf Club
55 Lee Road, Route 20, Lenox, Massachusetts 01240
Tel: +1 413 637 1364
Fax: +1 413 637 4364
Web: www.johansens.com/cranwell

U.S.A. - MASSACHUSETTS (MARTHA'S VINEYARD)
Winnetu Oceanside Resort
31 Dunes Road, Edgartown, Massachusetts 02539
Tel: +1 978 443 1733
Fax: +1 978 443 0479
Web: www.johansens.com/winnetu

Condé Nast Johansens are delighted to recommend 310 properties across The Americas, Atlantic, Caribbean and Pacific.
Call 0800 269 397 or see the order forms on page 271 to order guides.

U.S.A. - MISSISSIPPI (JACKSON)
Fairview Inn & Restaurant
734 Fairview Street, Jackson, Mississippi 39202
Tel: +1 601 948 3429
Fax: +1 601 948 1203
Web: www.johansens.com/fairviewinn

U.S.A. - MISSISSIPPI (NATCHEZ)
Monmouth Plantation
36 Melrose Avenue, Natchez, Mississippi 39120
Tel: +1 601 442 5852
Fax: +1 601 446 7762
Web: www.johansens.com/monmouthplantation

U.S.A. - MISSISSIPPI (NESBIT)
Bonne Terre Country Inn
4715 Church Road West, Nesbit, Mississippi 38651
Tel: +1 662 781 5100
Fax: +1 662 781 5466
Web: www.johansens.com/bonneterre

U.S.A. - MISSISSIPPI (VICKSBURG)
Anchuca Historic Mansion & Inn
1010 First East Street, Vicksburg, Mississippi 39183
Tel: +1 601 661 0111
Fax: +1 601 631 0501
Web: www.johansens.com/anchuca

U.S.A. - MISSOURI (BRANSON)
Chateau on the Lake
415 North State Highway 265, Branson, Missouri 65616
Tel: +1 417 334 1161
Fax: +1 417 339 5566
Web: www.johansens.com/chateaulake

U.S.A. - MISSOURI (KANSAS CITY)
The Raphael Hotel
325 Ward Parkway, Kansas City, Missouri 64112
Tel: +1 816 756 3800
Fax: +1 816 802 2131
Web: www.johansens.com/raphael

U.S.A. - MISSOURI (RIDGEDALE)
Big Cedar Lodge
612 Devil's Pool Road, Ridgedale, Missouri 65739
Tel: +1 417 335 2777
Fax: +1 417 335 2340
Web: www.johansens.com/bigcedar

U.S.A. - MONTANA (BIG SKY)
The Big EZ Lodge
7000 Beaver Creek Road, Big Sky, Montana 59716
Tel: +1 406 995 7000
Fax: +1 406 995 7007
Web: www.johansens.com/bigez

U.S.A. - MONTANA (DARBY)
Triple Creek Ranch
5551 West Fork Road, Darby, Montana 59829
Tel: +1 406 821 4600
Fax: +1 406 821 4666
Web: www.johansens.com/triplecreek

U.S.A. - NEW HAMPSHIRE (JACKSON VILLAGE)
The Wentworth
Jackson Village, New Hampshire 03846
Tel: +1 603 383 9700
Fax: +1 603 383 4265
Web: www.johansens.com/wentworth

U.S.A. - NEW HAMPSHIRE (PLAINFIELD)
Home Hill
703 River Road, Plainfield, New Hampshire 03781
Tel: +1 603 675 6165
Fax: +1 603 675 5220
Web: www.johansens.com/homehill

U.S.A. - NEW HAMPSHIRE (WHITEFIELD / WHITE MOUNTAINS)
Mountain View, The Grand Resort & Spa
Mountain View Road, Whitefield, New Hampshire 03598
Tel: +1 603 837 2100
Fax: +1 603 837 8884
Web: www.johansens.com/mountainview

U.S.A. - NEW MEXICO (ESPAÑOLA)
Rancho de San Juan
P.O. Box 4140, Highway 285, Española, New Mexico 87533
Tel: +1 505 753 6818
Fax: +1 505 753 6818
Web: www.johansens.com/ranchosanjuan

U.S.A. - NEW MEXICO (SANTA FE)
Inn and Spa at Loretto
211 Old Santa Fe Trail, Santa Fe, New Mexico 87501
Tel: +1 505 988 5531
Fax: +1 505 984 7968
Web: www.johansens.com/innatloretto

U.S.A. - NEW MEXICO (TAOS)
El Monte Sagrado Living Resort & Spa
317 Kit Carson Road, Taos, New Mexico 87571
Tel: +1 505 758 3502
Fax: +1 505 737 2985
Web: www.johansens.com/elmontesagrado

U.S.A. - NEW YORK (BANGALL)
The Inn at Bullis Hall
P.O. Box 630, Bangall (Stanfordville), New York 12506
Tel: +1 845 868 1665
Fax: +1 845 868 1441
Web: www.johansens.com/bullishall

U.S.A. - NEW YORK (BOLTON LANDING)
The Sagamore
110 Sagamore Road, Bolton Landing, New York 12814
Tel: +1 518 644 9400
Fax: +1 518 644 2851
Web: www.johansens.com/sagamore

U.S.A. - NEW YORK (BUFFALO)
Mansion on Delaware
414 Delaware Avenue, Buffalo, New York 14202
Tel: +1 716 886 3300
Fax: +1 716 883 3923
Web: www.johansens.com/mansionondelaware

U.S.A. - NEW YORK (EAST AURORA)
The Roycroft Inn
40 South Grove Street, East Aurora, New York 14052
Tel: +1 716 652 5552
Fax: +1 716 655 5345
Web: www.johansens.com/roycroftinn

U.S.A. - NEW YORK (LAKE PLACID)
Whiteface Lodge
7 Whiteface Inn Lane, Lake Placid, New York 12946
Tel: +1 518 523 0500
Fax: +1 518 523 0559
Web: www.johansens.com/whiteface

MINI LISTINGS THE AMERICAS

Condé Nast Johansens are delighted to recommend 310 properties across The Americas, Atlantic, Caribbean and Pacific.
Call 0800 269 397 or see the order forms on page 271 to order guides.

U.S.A. - NEW YORK (NEW YORK CITY)
Hotel Plaza Athénée
37 East 64th Street, New York, New York 10021
Tel: +1 212 734 9100
Fax: +1 212 772 0958
Web: www.johansens.com/athenee

U.S.A. - NEW YORK (NEW YORK CITY)
The Inn at Irving Place
56 Irving Place, New York, New York 10003
Tel: +1 212 533 4600
Fax: +1 212 533 4611
Web: www.johansens.com/irvingplace

U.S.A. - NEW YORK (TARRYTOWN)
Castle On The Hudson
400 Benedict Avenue, Tarrytown, New York 10591
Tel: +1 914 631 1980
Fax: +1 914 631 4612
Web: www.johansens.com/hudson

U.S.A. - NEW YORK (VERONA)
The Lodge at Turning Stone
5218 Patrick Road, Verona, New York 13478
Tel: +1 315 361 8525
Fax: +1 315 361 8686
Web: www.johansens.com/turningstone

U.S.A. - NEW YORK/LONG ISLAND (EAST HAMPTON)
The Baker House 1650
181 Main Street, East Hampton, New York 11937
Tel: +1 631 324 4081
Fax: +1 631 329 5931
Web: www.johansens.com/bakerhouse

U.S.A. - NEW YORK/LONG ISLAND (EAST HAMPTON)
The Mill House Inn
31 North Main Street, East Hampton, New York 11937
Tel: +1 631 324 9766
Fax: +1 631 324 9793
Web: www.johansens.com/millhouse

U.S.A. - NEW YORK/LONG ISLAND (SOUTHAMPTON)
1708 House
126 Main Street, Southampton, New York 11968
Tel: +1 631 287 1708
Fax: +1 631 287 3593
Web: www.johansens.com/1708house

U.S.A. - NORTH CAROLINA (ASHEVILLE)
Inn on Biltmore Estate
One Antler Hill Road, Asheville, North Carolina 28803
Tel: +1 828 225 1600
Fax: +1 828 225 1629
Web: www.johansens.com/biltmore

U.S.A. - NORTH CAROLINA (BLOWING ROCK)
Gideon Ridge Inn
202 Gideon Ridge Road, Blowing Rock,
North Carolina 28605
Tel: +1 828 295 3644
Fax: +1 828 295 4586
Web: www.johansens.com/gideonridge

U.S.A. - NORTH CAROLINA (CHARLOTTE)
Ballantyne Resort
10000 Ballantyne Commons Parkway, Charlotte,
North Carolina 28277
Tel: +1 704 248 4000
Fax: +1 704 248 4005
Web: www.johansens.com/ballantyneresort

U.S.A. - NORTH CAROLINA (DUCK)
The Sanderling Resort & Spa
1461 Duck Road, Duck, North Carolina 27949
Tel: +1 252 261 4111
Fax: +1 252 261 1638
Web: www.johansens.com/sanderling

U.S.A. - NORTH CAROLINA (HIGHLANDS)
Inn at Half Mile Farm
P.O. Box 2769, 214 Half Mile Drive, Highlands,
North Carolina 28741
Tel: +1 828 526 8170
Fax: +1 828 526 2625
Web: www.johansens.com/halfmilefarm

U.S.A. - NORTH CAROLINA (HIGHLANDS)
Old Edwards Inn and Spa
445 Main Street, Highlands, North Carolina 28741
Tel: +1 828 526 8008
Fax: +1 828 526 8301
Web: www.johansens.com/oldedwards

U.S.A. - NORTH CAROLINA (NEW BERN)
The Aerie Inn
509 Pollock Street, New Bern, North Carolina 28562
Tel: +1 252 636 5553
Fax: +1 252 514 2157
Web: www.johansens.com/aerieinn

U.S.A. - NORTH CAROLINA (PITTSBORO)
The Fearrington House
2000 Fearrington Village Center, Pittsboro,
North Carolina 27312
Tel: +1 919 542 2121
Fax: +1 919 542 4202
Web: www.johansens.com/fearrington

U.S.A. - NORTH CAROLINA (RALEIGH - DURHAM)
The Siena Hotel
1505 E. Franklin Street, Chapel Hill, North Carolina 27514
Tel: +1 919 929 4000
Fax: +1 919 968 8527
Web: www.johansens.com/siena

U.S.A. - NORTH CAROLINA (TRYON)
Pine Crest Inn and Restaurant
85 Pine Crest Lane, Tryon, North Carolina 28782
Tel: +1 828 859 9135
Fax: +1 828 859 9136
Web: www.johansens.com/pinecrestinn

U.S.A. - OHIO (CINCINNATI)
The Cincinnatian Hotel
601 Vine Street, Cincinnati, Ohio 45202-2433
Tel: +1 513 381 3000
Fax: +1 513 651 0256
Web: www.johansens.com/cincinnatian

U.S.A. - OKLAHOMA (OKLAHOMA CITY)
Colcord Hotel
15 North Robinson, Oklahoma City, Oklahoma 73102
Tel: +1 405 601 4300
Fax: +1 405 208 4399
Web: www.johansens.com/colcord

U.S.A. - OKLAHOMA (TULSA)
Hotel Ambassador
1345 South Main Street, Tulsa, Oklahoma 74119
Tel: +1 918 587 8200
Fax: +1 918 587 8208
Web: www.johansens.com/ambassador

MINI LISTINGS THE AMERICAS

Condé Nast Johansens are delighted to recommend 310 properties across The Americas, Atlantic, Caribbean and Pacific.

Call 0800 269 397 or see the order forms on page 271 to order guides.

U.S.A. - OREGON (ASHLAND)

The Winchester Inn & Restaurant

35 South Second Street, Ashland, Oregon 97520
Tel: +1 541 488 1113
Fax: +1 541 488 4604
Web: www.johansens.com/winchester

U.S.A. - OREGON (PORTLAND)

The Benson Hotel

309 Southwest Broadway, Portland, Oregon 97205
Tel: +1 503 228 2000
Fax: +1 503 471 3920
Web: www.johansens.com/benson

U.S.A. - OREGON (PORTLAND)

The Heathman Hotel

1001 S.W. Broadway, Portland, Oregon 97205
Tel: +1 503 241 4100
Fax: +1 503 790 7110
Web: www.johansens.com/heathman

U.S.A. - PENNSYLVANIA (BRADFORD)

Glendorn

1000 Glendorn Drive, Bradford, Pennsylvania 16701
Tel: +1 814 362 6511
Fax: +1 814 368 9923
Web: www.johansens.com/glendorn

U.S.A. - PENNSYLVANIA (FARMINGTON)

Nemacolin Woodlands

1001 LaFayette Drive, Farmington, Pennsylvania 15437
Tel: +1 724 329 8555
Fax: +1 724 329 6947
Web: www.johansens.com/nemacolin

U.S.A. - PENNSYLVANIA (HERSHEY)

The Hotel Hershey & Spa

100 Hotel Road, Hershey, Pennsylvania 17033
Tel: +1 717 533 2171
Fax: +1 717 534 3165
Web: www.johansens.com/hershey

U.S.A. - PENNSYLVANIA (LEOLA)

Leola Village Inn & Suites

38 Deborah Drive, Route 23, Leola, Pennsylvania 17540
Tel: +1 717 656 7002
Fax: +1 717 656 7648
Web: www.johansens.com/leolavillage

U.S.A. - PENNSYLVANIA (PHILADELPHIA)

Rittenhouse 1715, A Boutique Hotel

1715 Rittenhouse Square, Philadelphia, Pennsylvania 19103
Tel: +1 215 546 6500
Fax: +1 215 546 8787
Web: www.johansens.com/rittenhouse

U.S.A. - PENNSYLVANIA (POCONOS)

Skytop Lodge

One Skytop, Skytop, Pennsylvania 18357
Tel: +1 570 595 8905
Fax: +1 570 595 7285
Web: www.johansens.com/skytop

U.S.A. - RHODE ISLAND (NEWPORT)

The Chanler at Cliff Walk

117 Memorial Boulevard, Newport, Rhode Island 02840
Tel: +1 401 847 1300
Fax: +1 401 847 3620
Web: www.johansens.com/chanler

U.S.A. - RHODE ISLAND (PROVIDENCE)

Hotel Providence

311 Westminster Street, Providence, Rhode Island 02903
Tel: +1 401 861 8000
Fax: +1 401 861 8002
Web: www.johansens.com/providence

U.S.A. - SOUTH CAROLINA (BLUFFTON)

The Inn at Palmetto Bluff

476 Mount Pelia Road, Bluffton, South Carolina 29910
Tel: +1 843 706 6500
Fax: +1 843 706 6550
Web: www.johansens.com/palmettobluff

U.S.A. - SOUTH CAROLINA (CHARLESTON)

The Boardwalk Inn at Wild Dunes Resort

5757 Palm Boulevard, Isle of Palms, South Carolina 29451
Tel: +1 843 886 6000
Fax: +1 843 886 2916
Web: www.johansens.com/boardwalk

U.S.A. - SOUTH CAROLINA (CHARLESTON)

Charleston Harbor Resort & Marina

20 Patriots Point Road, Charleston, South Carolina 29464
Tel: +1 843 856 0028
Fax: +1 843 856 8333
Web: www.johansens.com/charlestonharbor

U.S.A. - SOUTH CAROLINA (CHARLESTON)

Woodlands Resort & Inn

125 Parsons Road, Summerville, South Carolina 29483
Tel: +1 843 875 2600
Fax: +1 843 875 2603
Web: www.johansens.com/woodlandssc

U.S.A. - SOUTH CAROLINA (KIAWAH ISLAND)

The Sanctuary at Kiawah Island Golf Resort

One Sanctuary Beach Drive, Kiawah Island,
South Carolina 29455
Tel: +1 843 768 6000
Fax: +1 843 768 5150
Web: www.johansens.com/sanctuary

U.S.A. - SOUTH CAROLINA (PAWLEYS ISLAND)

Litchfield Plantation

Kings River Road, Box 290, Pawleys Island,
South Carolina 29585
Tel: +1 843 237 9121
Fax: +1 843 237 1688
Web: www.johansens.com/litchfieldplantation

U.S.A. - SOUTH CAROLINA (TRAVELERS REST)

La Bastide

10 Road Of Vines, Travelers Rest, South Carolina 29210
Tel: +1 864 836 8463
Fax: +1 864 836 4820
Web: www.johansens.com/labastide

U.S.A. - TENNESSEE (WALLAND)

Blackberry Farm

1471 West Millers Cove Road, Walland,
Great Smoky Mountains, Tennessee 37886
Tel: +1 865 380 2260
Fax: +1 865 681 7753
Web: www.johansens.com/blackberryfarm

U.S.A. - TEXAS (AUSTIN)

The Mansion at Judges' Hill

1900 Rio Grande, Austin, Texas 78705
Tel: +1 512 495 1800
Fax: +1 512 691 4461
Web: www.johansens.com/judgeshill

MINI LISTINGS THE AMERICAS

Condé Nast Johansens are delighted to recommend 310 properties across The Americas, Atlantic, Caribbean and Pacific.
Call 0800 269 397 or see the order forms on page 271 to order guides.

U.S.A. - TEXAS (GRANBURY)
The Inn on Lake Granbury
205 West Doyle Street, Granbury, Texas 76048
Tel: +1 817 573 0046
Fax: +1 817 573 0047
Web: www.johansens.com/lakegranbury

U.S.A. - TEXAS (SAN ANTONIO)
The Havana Riverwalk Inn
1015 Navarro, San Antonio, Texas 78205
Tel: +1 210 222 2008
Fax: +1 210 222 2717
Web: www.johansens.com/havanariverwalkinn

U.S.A. - TEXAS (WAXAHACHIE)
The Chaska House
716 West Main Street, Waxahachie, Texas 75165
Tel: +1 972 937 3390
Fax: +1 972 937 1780
Web: www.johansens.com/chaskahouse

U.S.A. - UTAH (MOAB)
Sorrel River Ranch Resort & Spa
Highway 128 Mile 17, H.C. 64 BOX 4000, Moab, Utah 84532
Tel: +1 435 259 4642
Fax: +1 435 259 3016
Web: www.johansens.com/sorrelriver

U.S.A. - VERMONT (BARNARD)
Twin Farms
P.O. Box 115, Barnard, Vermont 05031
Tel: +1 802 234 9999
Fax: +1 802 234 9990
Web: www.johansens.com/twinfarms

U.S.A. - VERMONT (KILLINGTON)
Mountain Top Inn & Resort
195 Mountain Top Road, Chittenden, Vermont 05737
Tel: +1 802 483 2311
Fax: +1 802 483 6373
Web: www.johansens.com/mountaintopinn

U.S.A. - VERMONT (WARREN)
The Pitcher Inn
275 Main Street, P.O. Box 347, Warren, Vermont 05674
Tel: +1 802 496 6350
Fax: +1 802 496 6354
Web: www.johansens.com/pitcherinn

U.S.A. - VIRGINIA (ABINGDON)
The Martha Washington Inn
150 West Main Street, Abingdon, Virginia 24210
Tel: +1 276 628 3161
Fax: +1 276 628 8885
Web: www.johansens.com/themartha

U.S.A. - VIRGINIA (CHARLOTTESVILLE)
200 South Street Inn
200 South Street, Charlottesville, Virginia 22901
Tel: +1 434 979 0200
Fax: +1 434 979 4403
Web: www.johansens.com/200southstreetinn

U.S.A. - VIRGINIA (GLOUCESTER)
The Inn at Warner Hall
4750 Warner Hall Road, Gloucester, Virginia 23061
Tel: +1 804 695 9565
Fax: +1 804 695 9566
Web: www.johansens.com/warnerhall

U.S.A. - VIRGINIA (IRVINGTON)
Hope and Glory Inn
65 Tavern Road, Irvington, Virginia 22480
Tel: +1 804 438 6053
Fax: +1 804 438 5362
Web: www.johansens.com/hopeandglory

U.S.A. - VIRGINIA (MIDDLEBURG)
The Goodstone Inn & Estate
36205 Snake Hill Road, Middleburg, Virginia 20117
Tel: +1 540 687 4645
Fax: +1 540 687 6115
Web: www.johansens.com/goodstoneinn

U.S.A. - VIRGINIA (STAUNTON)
Frederick House
28 North New Street, Staunton, Virginia 24401
Tel: + 1 540 885 4220
Fax: +1 540 885 5180
Web: www.johansens.com/frederickhouse

U.S.A. - VIRGINIA (WASHINGTON METROPOLITAN AREA)
Morrison House
116 South Alfred Street, Alexandria, Virginia 22314
Tel: +1 703 838 8000
Fax: +1 703 684 6283
Web: www.johansens.com/morrisonhouse

U.S.A. - WASHINGTON (BELLINGHAM)
The Chrysalis Inn and Spa
804 10th Street, Bellingham, Washington 98225
Tel: +1 360 756 1005
Fax: +1 360 647 0342
Web: www.johansens.com/chrysalis

U.S.A. - WASHINGTON (FRIDAY HARBOR)
Friday Harbor House
130 West Street, Friday Harbor, Washington 98250
Tel: +1 360 378 8455
Fax: +1 360 378 8453
Web: www.johansens.com/fridayharbor

U.S.A. - WASHINGTON (LEAVENWORTH)
Run of the River Inn and Refuge
9308 E. Leavenworth Road, Leavenworth, Washington 98826
Tel: +1 509 548 7171
Fax: 1 509 548 7547
Web: www.johansens.com/runoftheriver

U.S.A. - WASHINGTON (SPOKANE)
The Davenport Hotel and Tower
10 South Post Street, Spokane, Washington 99201
Tel: +1 509 455 8888
Fax: +1 509 624 4455
Web: www.johansens.com/davenport

U.S.A. - WASHINGTON (UNION)
Alderbrook Resort & Spa
10 East Alderbrook Drive, Union, Washington 98592
Tel: +1 360 898 2200
Fax: +1 360 898 4610
Web: www.johansens.com/alderbrook

U.S.A. - WASHINGTON (WOODINVILLE)
The Herbfarm
14590 North East 145th Street, Woodinville, Washington 98072
Tel: +1 425 485 5300
Fax: +1 425 424 2925
Web: www.johansens.com/herbfarm

Mini Listings The Americas

Condé Nast Johansens are delighted to recommend 310 properties across The Americas, Atlantic, Caribbean and Pacific.
Call 0800 269 397 or see the order forms on page 271 to order guides.

U.S.A. - WEST VIRGINIA (WHITE SULPHUR SPRINGS)

The Greenbrier
300 West Main Street, White Sulphur Springs,
West Virginia 24986
Tel: +1 304 536 1110
Fax: +1 304 536 7818
Web: www.johansens.com/greenbrier

U.S.A. - WISCONSIN (CHETEK)

Canoe Bay
P.O. Box 28, Chetek, Wisconsin 54728
Tel: +1 715 924 4594
Fax: +1 715 924 2078
Web: www.johansens.com/canoebay

U.S.A. - WISCONSIN (DELAFIELD)

The Delafield Hotel
415 Genesee Street, Delafield, Wisconsin 53018
Tel: +1 262 646 1600
Fax: +1 262 646 1613
Web: www.johansens.com/delafield

U.S.A. - WYOMING (CHEYENNE)

Nagle Warren Mansion
222 East 17Th Street, Cheyenne, Wyoming 82001
Tel: +1 307 637 3333
Fax: +1 307 638 6879
Web: www.johansens.com/naglewarrenmansion

U.S.A. - WYOMING (DUBOIS)

Brooks Lake Lodge
458 Brooks Lake Road, Dubois, Wyoming 82513
Tel: +1 307 455 2121
Fax: +1 307 455 2221
Web: www.johansens.com/brookslake

U.S.A. - WYOMING (GRAND TETON NATIONAL PARK)

Jenny Lake Lodge
Inner Park Loop Road, Grand Teton National Park,
Wyoming 83013
Tel: +1 307 543 3300
Fax: +1 307 543 3358
Web: www.johansens.com/jennylake

U.S.A. - WYOMING (TETON VILLAGE)

Teton Mountain Lodge
3385 W. Village Drive, Teton Village, Wyoming 83025
Tel: +1 307 734 7111
Fax: +1 307 734 7999
Web: www.johansens.com/teton

Recommendations in Central America

COSTA RICA - GUANACASTE (ISLITA)

Hotel Punta Islita
Guanacaste
Tel: +506 231 6122
Fax: +506 231 0715
Web: www.johansens.com/hotelpuntaislita

COSTA RICA - GUANACASTE (PLAYA CONCHAL)

Paradisus Playa Conchal
Bahía Brasilito, Playa Conchal, Santa Cruz, Guanacaste
Tel: +506 654 4123
Fax: +506 654 4181
Web: www.johansens.com/paradisusplayaconchal

COSTA RICA - PUNTARENAS (MANUEL ANTONIO)

Gaia Hotel & Reserve
Km 2.7 Carretera Quepos, Manuel Antonio
Tel: +506 777 9797
Fax: +506 777 9126
Web: www.johansens.com/gaiahr

HONDURAS - ATLÁNTIDA (LA CEIBA)

The Lodge at Pico Bonito
A. P. 710, La Ceiba, Atlántida, C. P. 31101
Tel: +504 440 0388
Fax: +504 440 0468
Web: www.johansens.com/picobonito

Recommendations in South America

ARGENTINA - BUENOS AIRES (CIUDAD DE BUENOS AIRES)

1555 Malabia House
Malabia 1555, C1414DME Buenos Aires
Tel: +54 11 4832 3345
Fax: +54 11 4832 3345
Web: www.johansens.com/malabiahouse

ARGENTINA - BUENOS AIRES (CIUDAD DE BUENOS AIRES)

LoiSuites Recoleta Hotel
Vicente López 1955 – C1128ACC, Ciudad de Buenos Aires
Tel: +54 11 5777 8950
Fax: +54 11 5777 8999
Web: www.johansens.com/loisuites

ARGENTINA - PATAGONIA (ISLA VICTORIA)

Hosteria Isla Victoria
Isla Victoria, Parque Nacional Nahuel Huapi,
C.C. 26 (R8401AKU)
Tel: +54 43 94 96 05
Fax: +54 11 43 94 95 99
Web: www.johansens.com/islavictoria

ARGENTINA - PATAGONIA (VILLA LA ANGOSTURA)

Correntoso Lake & River Hotel
Av. Siète Lagos 4505, Villa La Angostura, Neuquén
Tel: +54 2944 15 619728
Web: www.johansens.com/correntoso

BRAZIL - ALAGOAS (SÃO MIGUEL DOS MILAGRES)

Pousada do Toque
Rua Felisberto de Ataide, Povoado do Toque,
São Miguel dos Milagres, Alagoas
Tel: +55 82 3295 1127
Fax: +55 82 3295 1127
Web: www.johansens.com/pousadadotoque

BRAZIL - BAHIA (ITACARÉ)

Txai Resort
Rod. Ilhéus-Itacaré km 48, Itacaré, Bahia 45530-000
Tel: +55 73 2101 5000
Fax: +55 73 2101 5251
Web: www.johansens.com/txairesort

BRAZIL - BAHIA (PORTO SEGURO FRANCOSO)

Estrela d'Agua
Estrada Arraial d'Ajuda - Trancoso S/No,
Trancoso Porto Seguro, Bahia 45818-000
Tel: +55 73 3668 1030
Fax: +55 73 3668 1030
Web: www.johansens.com/estreladagua

Mini Listings South America

Condé Nast Johansens are delighted to recommend 310 properties across The Americas, Atlantic, Caribbean and Pacific.
Call 0800 269 397 or see the order forms on page 271 to order guides.

BRAZIL - BAHIA (PRAIA DO FORTE)

Praia do Forte Eco Resort & Thalasso Spa
Avenida do Farol, Praia do Forte - Mata de São João, Bahia
Tel: +55 71 36 76 40 00
Fax: +55 71 36 76 11 12
Web: www.johansens.com/praiadoforte

BRAZIL - MINAS GERAIS (TIRADENTES)

Pousada dos Inconfidentes
Rua João Rodrigues Sobrinho 91, 36325-000, Tiradentes, Minas Gerais
Tel: +55 32 3355 2135
Fax: +55 32 3355 2135
Web: www.johansens.com/inconfidentes

BRAZIL - MINAS GERAIS (TIRADENTES)

Solar da Ponte
Praça das Mercês S/N, Tiradentes, Minas Gerais 36325-000
Tel: +55 32 33 55 12 55
Fax: +55 32 33 55 12 01
Web: www.johansens.com/solardaponte

BRAZIL - PERNAMBUCO (PORTO DE GALINHAS)

Nannai Beach Resort
Rodovia PE-09, acesso à Muro Alto, Km 3, Ipojuca, Pernambuco 55590-000
Tel: +55 81 3552 0100
Fax: +55 81 3552 1474
Web: www.johansens.com/nannaibeach

BRAZIL - RIO DE JANEIRO (ANGRA DOS REIS)

Sítio do Lobo
Ponta do Lobo, Ilha Grande, Angra dos Reis, Rio de Janeiro
Tel: +55 21 2227 4138
Fax: +55 21 2267 7841
Web: www.johansens.com/sitiodolobo

BRAZIL - RIO DE JANEIRO (ARMAÇÃO DOS BÚZIOS)

Pérola Búzios
Av. José Bento Ribeiro Dantas, 222, Armação dos Búzios, Rio de Janeiro 28950-000
Tel: +55 22 2620 8507
Fax: +55 22 2623 9015
Web: www.johansens.com/perolabuzios

BRAZIL - RIO DE JANEIRO (BÚZIOS)

Casas Brancas Boutique-Hotel & Spa
Alto do Humaitá 10, Armação dos Búzios, Rio de Janeiro 28950-000
Tel: +55 22 2623 1458
Fax: +55 22 2623 2147
Web: www.johansens.com/casasbrancas

BRAZIL - RIO DE JANEIRO (BÚZIOS)

Glenzhaus Lodge
Rua 1 - Quadra F - Lote 27/28, Armação dos Búzios, Rio de Janeiro 28950-000
Tel: +55 22 2623 2823
Fax: +55 22 2623 5293
Web: www.johansens.com/glenzhaus

BRAZIL - RIO DE JANEIRO (ENGENEIRO PAULO DE FRONTIN)

Vivenda Les 4 Saisons
Rua João Cordeiro da Costa E silva, 5, Caixa Postal 127, Engenheiro Paulo de Frontin, Rio de Janeiro 26650-000
Tel: +55 24 2463 2892
Fax: +55 24 2463 1395
Web: www.johansens.com/4saisons

BRAZIL - RIO DE JANEIRO (PETRÓPOLIS)

Parador Santarém Marina
Estrada Correia da Veiga, 96, Petrópolis, Rio de Janeiro 25745-260
Tel: +55 24 2222 9933
Fax: +55 24 2222 9933
Web: www.johansens.com/paradorsantarem

BRAZIL - RIO DE JANEIRO (PETRÓPOLIS)

Solar do Império
Koeler Avenue, 376- Centro, Petrópolis, Rio de Janeiro
Tel: +55 24 2103 3000
Fax: +55 24 2242 0034
Web: www.johansens.com/solardoimperio

BRAZIL - RIO DE JANEIRO (PETRÓPOLIS)

Tankamana EcoResort
Estrada Júlio Cápua, S/N Vale Do Cuiabá, Itaipava - Petrópolis, Rio De Janeiro 25745-050
Tel: +55 24 2222 9181
Fax: +55 24 2222 9181
Web: www.johansens.com/tankamana

BRAZIL - RIO DE JANEIRO (RIO DE JANEIRO)

Hotel Marina All Suites
Av. Delfim Moreira, 696, Praia do Leblon, Rio de Janeiro 22441-000
Tel: +55 21 2172 1001
Fax: +55 21 2172 1110
Web: www.johansens.com/marinaallsuites

BRAZIL - RIO GRANDE DO SUL (SAO FRANCISCO DE PAULA)

Pousada Do Engenho
Rua Odon Cavalcante, 330, São Francisco de Paula 95400-000, Rio Grande do Sul
Tel: +55 54 3244 1270
Fax: +55 54 3244 1270
Web: www.johansens.com/pousadadoengenho

BRAZIL - RIO GRANDE DO SUL (GRAMADO)

Kurotel
Rua Nacões Unidas 533, P.O. Box 65, Gramado, Rio Grande do Sul 95670-000
Tel: +55 54 3295 9393
Fax: +55 54 3286 1203
Web: www.johansens.com/kurotel

BRAZIL - SANTA CATARINA (GOVERNADOR CELSO RAMOS)

Ponta dos Ganchos
Rua Eupídio Alves do Nascimento, 104, Governador Celso Ramos, Santa Catarina 88190-000
Tel: +55 48 3262 5000
Fax: +55 48 3262 5046
Web: www.johansens.com/pontadosganchos

BRAZIL - SÃO PAULO (CAMPOS DO JORDÃO)

Hotel Frontenac
Av. Dr. Paulo Ribas, 295 Capivari, Campos do Jordão 12460-000
Tel: +55 12 3669 1000
Fax: +55 12 3669 1009
Web: www.johansens.com/frontenac

CHILE - ARAUCANIA (PUCON)

Hotel Antumalal
Carretera Pucon-Villarka Highway at Km 2 from Pucon
Tel: +5645 441 011
Fax: +5645 441 013
Web: www.johansens.com/antumalal

CHILE - COLCHAGUA (SAN FERNANDO)

Hacienda Los Lingues
Km 124.5, Ruta 5 Sur + 5km Al Oriente, 6a Region, Colchagua
Tel: +562 431 0510
Fax: +562 431 0501
Web: www.johansens.com/loslingues

CHILE - PATAGONIA (PUERTO GUADAL)

Hacienda Tres Lagos
Carretera Austral Sur Km 274, Localidad Lago Negro, Puerto Guadal
Tel: + 56 2 333 41 22 and + 56 67 411 323
Fax: + 56 2 334 52 94 and + 56 67 411 323
Web: www.johansens.com/treslagos

Mini Listings Atlantic / Caribbean

Condé Nast Johansens are delighted to recommend 310 properties across The Americas, Atlantic, Caribbean and Pacific.

Call 0800 269 397 or see the order forms on page 271 to order guides.

PERU - LIMA PROVINCIAS (YAUYOS)

Refugios Del Peru - Viñak Reichraming
Santiago de Viñak, Yauyos, Lima
Tel: +51 1 421 6952
Fax: +51 1 421 8476
Web: www.johansens.com/refugiosdelperu

Recommendations in the Caribbean

CARIBBEAN - ANGUILLA (RENDEZVOUS BAY)

CuisinArt Resort & Spa
P.O. Box 2000, Rendezvous Bay, Anguilla
Tel: +1 264 498 2000
Fax: +1 264 498 2010
Web: www.johansens.com/cuisinartresort

Recommendations in the Atlantic

ATLANTIC - BAHAMAS (GRAND BAHAMA ISLAND)

Old Bahama Bay Resort & Yacht Harbour
West End, Grand Bahama Island, Bahamas
Tel: +1 242 350 6500
Fax: +1 242 346 6546
Web: www.johansens.com/oldbahamabay

CARIBBEAN - ANTIGUA (ST. JOHN'S)

Blue Waters
P.O. Box 257, St. John's Antigua
Tel: +44 870 360 1245
Fax: +44 870 360 1246
Web: www.johansens.com/bluewaters

ATLANTIC - BAHAMAS (HARBOUR ISLAND)

Rock House
Bay & Hill Street, Harbour Island, Bahamas
Tel: +1 242 333 2053
Fax: +1 242 333 3173
Web: www.johansens.com/rockhouse

CARIBBEAN - ANTIGUA (ST. JOHN'S)

The Inn at English Harbour
English Harbour, Antigua
Tel: +1 268 460 1014
Fax: +1 268 460 1603
Web: www.johansens.com/innatenglishharbour

ATLANTIC - BERMUDA (HAMILTON)

Rosedon Hotel
P.O. Box Hm 290, Hamilton Hmax, Bermuda
Tel: +1 441 295 1640
Fax: +1 441 295 5904
Web: www.johansens.com/rosedonhotel

CARIBBEAN - ANTIGUA (ST. JOHN'S)

Curtain Bluff
P.O. Box 288, St. John's, Antigua
Tel: +1 268 462 8400
Fax: +1 268 462 8409
Web: www.johansens.com/curtainbluff

ATLANTIC - BERMUDA (HAMILTON)

Waterloo House
P.O. Box H.M. 333, Hamilton H.M. B.X., Bermuda
Tel: +1 441 295 4480
Fax: +1 441 295 2585
Web: www.johansens.com/waterloohouse

CARIBBEAN - ANTIGUA (ST. JOHN'S)

Galley Bay
Five Islands, St. John's, Antigua
Tel: +1 954 481 8787
Fax: +1 954 481 1661
Web: www.johansens.com/galleybay

ATLANTIC - BERMUDA (PAGET)

Horizons and Cottages
33 South Shore Road, Paget, P.G.04, Bermuda
Tel: +1 441 236 0048
Fax: +1 441 236 1981
Web: www.johansens.com/horizonscottages

CARIBBEAN - BARBADOS (CHRIST CHURCH)

Little Arches
Enterprise Beach Road, Christ Church, Barbados
Tel: +1 246 420 4689
Fax: +1 246 418 0207
Web: www.johansens.com/littlearches

ATLANTIC - BERMUDA (SOMERSET)

Cambridge Beaches
Kings Point, Somerset, Bermuda
Tel: +1 441 234 0331
Fax: +1 441 234 3352
Web: www.johansens.com/cambridgebeaches

CARIBBEAN - BARBADOS (ST. JAMES)

Coral Reef Club
St. James, Barbados
Tel: +1 246 422 2372
Fax: +1 246 422 1776
Web: www.johansens.com/coralreefclub

ATLANTIC - BERMUDA (SOUTHAMPTON)

The Reefs
56 South Shore Road, Southampton, Bermuda
Tel: +1 441 238 0222
Fax: +1 441 238 8372
Web: www.johansens.com/thereefs

CARIBBEAN - BARBADOS (ST. JAMES)

Lone Star
Mount Standfast, St. James, Barbados
Tel: +1 246 419 0599
Fax: +1 246 419 0597
Web: www.johansens.com/lonestar

ATLANTIC - BERMUDA (WARWICK)

Surf Side Beach Club
90 South Shore Road, Warwick, Bermuda
Tel: +1 441 236 7100
Fax: +1 441 236 9765
Web: www.johansens.com/surfside

CARIBBEAN - BARBADOS (ST. JAMES)

The Sandpiper
Holetown, St. James, Barbados
Tel: +1 246 422 2251
Fax: +1 246 422 0900
Web: www.johansens.com/sandpiper

MINI LISTINGS CARIBBEAN / PACIFIC

Condé Nast Johansens are delighted to recommend 310 properties across The Americas, Atlantic, Caribbean and Pacific.

Call 0800 269 397 or see the order forms on page 271 to order guides.

CARIBBEAN - BARBADOS (ST. PETER)

Cobblers Cove

Speightstown, St. Peter, Barbados
Tel: +1 246 422 2291
Fax: +1 246 422 1460
Web: www.johansens.com/cobblerscove

CARIBBEAN - BARBADOS (ST. PETER)

Little Good Harbour

Shermans, St. Peter, Barbados
Tel: +1 246 439 3000
Fax: +1 246 439 2020
Web: www.johansens.com/goodharbour

CARIBBEAN - BONAIRE

Harbour Village Beach Club

Kaya Gobernador N. Debrot No. 71, Bonaire,
Netherlands Antilles
Tel: +1 305 567 9509
Fax: +1 305 648 0699
Web: www.johansens.com/harbourvillage

CARIBBEAN - BRITISH VIRGIN ISLANDS (VIRGIN GORDA)

Biras Creek Resort

North Sound, Virgin Gorda, British Virgin Islands
Tel: +1 310 440 4225
Fax: +1 310 440 4220
Web: www.johansens.com/birascreek

CARIBBEAN - CURAÇAO (WILLEMSTAD)

Avila Hotel on the beach

Penstraat 130, Willemstad, Curaçao, Netherlands Antilles
Tel: +599 9 461 4377
Fax: +599 9 461 1493
Web: www.johansens.com/avilabeach

CARIBBEAN - DOMINICAN REPUBLIC (PUERTO PLATA)

Casa Colonial Beach & Spa

P.O. Box 22, Puerto Plata, Dominican Republic
Tel: +1 809 320 3232
Fax: +1 809 320 3131
Web: www.johansens.com/casacolonial

CARIBBEAN - GRENADA (ST. GEORGE'S)

Spice Island Beach Resort

Grand Anse Beach, St. George's, Grenada
Tel: +1 473 444 4423/4258
Fax: +1 473 444 4807
Web: www.johansens.com/spiceisland

CARIBBEAN - JAMAICA (MONTEGO BAY)

Half Moon

Montego Bay, Jamaica
Tel: +1 876 953 2211
Fax: +1 876 953 2731
Web: www.johansens.com/halfmoongolf

CARIBBEAN - JAMAICA (MONTEGO BAY)

Round Hill Hotel and Villas

P.O. Box 64, Montego Bay, Jamaica
Tel: +1 876 956 7050
Fax: +1 876 956 7505
Web: www.johansens.com/roundhill

CARIBBEAN - JAMAICA (MONTEGO BAY)

Tryall Club

P.O. Box 1206, Montego Bay, Jamaica
Tel: +1 800 238 5290
Fax: +1 876 956 5673
Web: www.johansens.com/tryallclub

CARIBBEAN - JAMAICA (ORACABESSA)

Goldeneye

Oracabessa, St. Mary, Jamaica
Tel: +1 876 975 3354
Fax: +1 876 975 3620
Web: www.johansens.com/goldeneye

CARIBBEAN - MARTINIQUE (LE FRANÇOIS)

Cap Est Lagoon Resort & Spa

97240 Le François, Martinique
Tel: +596 596 54 80 80
Fax: +596 596 54 96 00
Web: www.johansens.com/capest

CARIBBEAN - NEVIS (CHARLESTOWN)

Montpelier Plantation Inn

Montpelier Estate, Charlestown, Nevis
Tel: +1 869 469 3462
Fax: +1 869 469 2932
Web: www.johansens.com/montpelierplantation

CARIBBEAN - PUERTO RICO (RINCÓN)

Horned Dorset Primavera

Apartado 1132, Rincón, Puerto Rico 00677
Tel: +1 787 823 4030
Fax: +1 787 823 5580
Web: www.johansens.com/horneddorset

CARIBBEAN - SAINT-BARTHÉLEMY (GRAND CUL DE SAC)

Hotel Guanahani & Spa

Grand Cul de Sac, 97133 Saint-Barthélemy
Tel: +590 590 27 66 60
Fax: +590 590 27 70 70
Web: www.johansens.com/guanahani

CARIBBEAN - SAINT-BARTHÉLEMY (GRAND CUL DE SAC)

Le Toiny

Anse de Toiny 97133, Saint-Barthélemy
Tel: +590 590 27 88 88
Fax: +590 590 27 89 30
Web: www.johansens.com/letoiny

CARIBBEAN - SAINT-BARTHÉLEMY (GUSTAVIA)

Carl Gustaf Hotel

Rue des Normands, Gustavia, 97099 Saint-Barthélemy
Tel: +590 590 29 79 00
Fax: +590 590 27 82 37
Web: www.johansens.com/carlgustaf

CARIBBEAN - ST. LUCIA (SOUFRIÈRE)

Ladera

Soufrière, St. Lucia
Tel: +1 758 459 7323
Fax: +1 758 459 5156
Web: www.johansens.com/ladera

CARIBBEAN - ST. LUCIA (SOUFRIÈRE)

Anse Chastanet

Soufrière, St. Lucia
Tel: +1 758 459 7000
Fax: +1 758 459 7700
Web: www.johansens.com/ansechastanet

CARIBBEAN - ST. LUCIA (SOUFRIÈRE)

Jade Mountain at Anse Chastanet

Soufrière, St. Lucia
Tel: +1 758 459 4000
Fax: +1 758 459 4002
Web: www.johansens.com/jademountain

MINI LISTINGS CARIBBEAN / PACIFIC

Condé Nast Johansens are delighted to recommend 310 properties across The Americas, Atlantic, Caribbean and Pacific. Call 0800 269 397 or see the order forms on page 271 to order guides.

CARIBBEAN - ST. MARTIN (BAIE LONGUE)

La Samanna
P.O. Box 4077, 97064 St. Martin - CEDEX
Tel: +590 590 87 64 00
Fax: +590 590 87 87 86
Web: www.johansens.com/lasamanna

Recommendations in the Pacific

CARIBBEAN - THE GRENADINES (MUSTIQUE)

Firefly
Mustique Island, St. Vincent & The Grenadines
Tel: +1 784 488 8414
Fax: +1 784 488 8514
Web: www.johansens.com/firefly

PACIFIC - FIJI ISLANDS (LABASA)

Nukubati Island
P.O. Box 1928, Labasa, Fiji Islands
Tel: +61 2 93888 196
Fax: +61 2 93888 204
Web: www.johansens.com/nukubati

CARIBBEAN - THE GRENADINES (PALM ISLAND)

Palm Island
St. Vincent & The Grenadines
Tel: +1 954 481 8787
Fax: +1 954 481 1661
Web: www.johansens.com/palmisland

PACIFIC - FIJI ISLANDS (LAUTOKA)

Blue Lagoon Cruises
183 Vitogo Parade, Lautoka, Fiji Islands
Tel: +679 6661 622
Fax: +679 6664 098
Web: www.johansens.com/bluelagooncruises

CARIBBEAN - TURKS & CAICOS (PROVIDENCIALES)

Grace Bay Club
P.O. Box 128, Providenciales, Turks & Caicos Islands
Tel: +1 649 946 5050
Fax: +1 649 946 5758
Web: www.johansens.com/gracebayclub

PACIFIC - FIJI ISLANDS (QAMEA ISLAND)

Qamea Resort & Spa
P.A. Matei, Tavenui, Fiji Islands
Tel: +679 888 0220
Fax: +679 888 0092
Web: www.johansens.com/qamea

CARIBBEAN - TURKS & CAICOS (PROVIDENCIALES)

Parrot Cay
P.O. Box 164, Providenciales, Turks & Caicos Islands
Tel: +1 649 946 7788
Fax: +1 649 946 7789
Web: www.johansens.com/parrotcay

PACIFIC - FIJI ISLANDS (SAVUSAVU)

Jean-Michel Cousteau Fiji Islands Resort
Lesiaceva Point, SavuSavu, Fiji Islands
Tel: +415 788 5794
Web: www.johansens.com/jean-michelcousteau

CARIBBEAN - TURKS & CAICOS (PROVIDENCIALES)

Point Grace
P.O. Box 700, Providenciales, Turks & Caicos Islands
Tel: +1 649 946 5096
Fax: +1 649 946 5097
Web: www.johansens.com/pointgrace

PACIFIC - FIJI ISLANDS (SIGATOKA)

Myola Plantation
P.O. Box 638, Sigatoka, Fiji Islands
Tel: +679 652 1084
Fax: +679 652 0899
Web: www.johansens.com/myola

CARIBBEAN - TURKS & CAICOS (PROVIDENCIALES)

Turks & Caicos Club
P.O. Box 687, West Grace Bay Beach, Providenciales,
Turks & Caicos Islands
Tel: +1 649 946 5800
Fax: +1 649 946 5858
Web: www.johansens.com/turksandcaicos

PACIFIC - FIJI ISLANDS (TOBERUA ISLAND)

Toberua Island Resort
P.O. Box 3332, Nausori, Fiji Islands
Tel: +679 347 2777
Fax: +679 347 2888
Web: www.johansens.com/toberuaisland

CARIBBEAN - TURKS & CAICOS (PROVIDENCIALES)

The Somerset
Princess Drive, Providenciales, Turks & Caicos Islands
Tel: +1 649 946 5900
Fax: +1 649 946 5944
Web: www.johansens.com/somersetgracebay

PACIFIC - FIJI ISLANDS (UGAGA ISLAND)

Royal Davui
P.O. Box 3171, Lami, Fiji Islands
Tel: +679 336 1624
Fax: +679 336 1253
Web: www.johansens.com/royaldavui

PACIFIC - FIJI ISLANDS (YAQETA ISLAND)

Navutu Stars Resort
P.O. Box 1838, Lautoka, Fiji Islands
Tel: +679 664 0553 and +679 664 0554
Fax: +679 666 0807
Web: www.johansens.com/navutustars

The International Mark of Excellence

For further information, current news,
e-club membership, hotel search, gift vouchers,
online bookshop and special offers visit:

www.johansens.com

Annually Inspected for the Independent Traveller

PACIFIC - FIJI ISLANDS (YASAWA ISLAND)

Yasawa Island Resort
P.O. Box 10128, Nadi Airport, Nadi, Fiji Islands
Tel: +679 672 2266
Fax: +679 672 4456
Web: www.johansens.com/yasawaisland

A

▼

Amhuinnsuidhe Castle ....Isle of Harris **208**
Ashwick Country House Hotel ......Dulverton 148
The Austwick Traddock...................Austwick 173
Aylestone Court ....Hereford 88

B

Bae Abermaw ....Barmouth 217
Bailhouse Hotel..................................Lincoln 110
Balcary Bay Hotel ....Auchencairn..............192
Barnsdale Lodge.................................Rutland Water 142
Beechfield House ....Beanacre 162
Beechwood Hotel ....North Walsham 118
The Bell At Skenfrith ....Monmouth 220
Bellplot House Hotel
    & Thomas's Restaurant...............Chard...........................147
Beryl ....Wells 151
Bibury Court ....Bibury 77
The Bridge Hotel ....Helmsdale 195
The Bridge House Hotel ....Beaminster 71
Broadoaks Country House.............Windermere 56
The Broadway Hotel ....Broadway 169
Brook Lane Hotel ....Kenmare 187
Broom Hall Country Hotel ....Thetford 124
Brovey Lair..Ovington 122
Broxton Hall ....Chester 29
Bull & Butcher ....Henley 27
Burford Lodge Hotel
    & Restaurant ....Burford 132

C

Cairn Lodge Hotel ....Auchterarder 204
Cantley House ....Wokingham 24
Castle Venlaw ....Peebles 206
Castleton House Hotel.....................Forfar 190
Chandlers Waterside
    Apartment ....Fowey 32
Charlton Kings Hotel ....Cheltenham 79
Chase Lodge ....Hampton Court 157
The Chequers Inn...............................Froggatt Edge 58
The Christopher Hotel ....Eton 18
Clarice House ....Bury St Edmunds 155
Cockliffe Country House Hotel ....Nottingham 131
Colwall Park ....Malvern 171
Combe House Hotel
    & Restaurant ....Exeter 64
Compton House...................................Axbridge 146
Conrah Country House Hotel ....Aberystwyth...............212
Coopershill House ....Riverstown 188
Cornfields Restaurant & Hotel ......Colmworth 15
Corriegour Lodge Hotel ....Fort Willam 194

The Cottage Inn ....Ascot 17
The County Hotel................................Bath 13
Crosby Lodge
    Country House Hotel ....Carlisle 46
Crouchers Country Hotel
    & Restaurant ....Chichester 160
The Crown At Whitebrook............Whitebrook 221
The Crown Hotel ....Stamford 112
The Crown House ....Great Chesterford 76
Culzean Castle
    - The Eisenhower Apartment ....Ayr 207

D

Dale Head Hall Lakeside Hotel......Keswick 51
Dannah Farm Country House ......Belper............................57
The Dashwood Hotel
    & Restaurant ....Oxford 136
The Devonshire Fell ....Burnsall 175
The Dinton Hermit ....Aylesbury 25
The Dower House Hotel ....Woodhall Spa 113
Duke Of Marlborough
    Country Inn ....Woodstock 140
Dunain Park Hotel ....Inverness 196
Dunsley Hall ....Whitby 179

E

Egerton Grey ....Porthkerry 215
Elderton Lodge Hotel
    & Langtry Restaurant ....North Walsham.........117

F

The Falcon Hotel ....Castle Ashby 126
Fallowfields...Oxford 135
Farthings Country House
    Hotel & Restaurant........................near Taunton 150
Fayrer Garden House Hotel...........Windermere 54
The Feathers ....Woodstock 141
Ferrari's Restaurant & Hotel...........Preston 104

▼

Ford Abbey ....Leominster **91**
Forss House Hotel ....Thurso 202
The Four Seasons Hotel ....Loch Earn....................205

G

The George Inn ....Warminster.................167
The Gin Trap Inn ....Ringstead 123
Glangrwyney Court............................Crickhowell...............223
Glencot House......................................Wells 152
Glewstone Court ....Ross-on-Wye..............94

The Grange at Oborne......................Sherborne 74
The Great Escape
    Holiday Company...........................North Norfolk Coast 116
Great Tangley Manor ....Guildford 156
Greshornish House Hotel ....Isle of Skye 198

H

The Hambrough...................................Ventnor 100
Heddon's Gate Hotel ....Martinhoe 69
Hewitt's - Villa Spaldi ....Lynton 68
Hey Green Country
    House Hotel ....Marsden 180
Highland Cottage ....Tobermory 191
Highland Court Lodge......................St Austell 38
Hipping Hall ....Kirkby Lonsdale 52
Hob Green Hotel,
    Restaurant & Gardens..................Harrogate 177

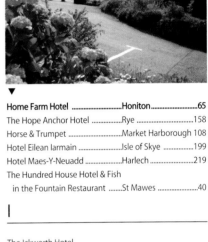

▼

Home Farm Hotel ....Honiton 65
The Hope Anchor Hotel ....Rye 158
Horse & Trumpet ....Market Harborough 108
Hotel Eilean Iarmain ....Isle of Skye 199
Hotel Maes-Y-Neuadd ....Harlech 219
The Hundred House Hotel & Fish
    in the Fountain Restaurant ....St Mawes 40

I

The Ickworth Hotel
    and Apartments ....Bury St Edmunds 154
Idyllic Cottages At Vere Lodge......Fakenham 114
Ilsington Country House Hotel ....Ilsington 66
The Inn at the Elm Tree ....St Brides
                                                        Wentlooge 210
The Inn at Whitewell........................Whitewell 107
The Inn on the Green,
    Restaurant with Rooms ....Maidenhead 19
The Ivy House ....Chalfont-St-Giles.........26

J

The Jersey Arms ....Oxford..........................137

K

Karslake Country House
    & Restaurant ....Winsford 153
The Kings Head Hotel ....Great Bircham 115
The Kings Head Inn
    & Restaurant ....Stow-on-the-Wold ..138
Kingston House ....Staverton 70
Knockomie Hotel ....Forres 203
Koala Cottage ....Godshill 98

INDEX BY PROPERTY

L

L'ortolan Restaurant ....Reading........................22
La Fleur de Lys.................................Shaftesbury..................73

▼

La Sablonnerie................................Sark 183
Lake House Hotel............................Ambleside 43
The Lake Isle Restaurant
   & Townhouse Hotel.....................Uppingham 143
The Lamb at Hindon........................Hindon 166
The Lamb Inn..................................Burford 133
Langar Hall ....Nottingham 130
Langrish House................................Petersfield 86
The Leatherne Bottel
   Riverside Restaurant ....Reading.......................21
The Leathes Head ....Keswick......................50
Linthwaite House Hotel ....Windermere.................55
Little Silver Country Hotel ....Tenterden 103
Lower Barn ....Mevagissey 34
Lower Brook House...........................Moreton-in-marsh.........82
Lydford House.................................Lydford 67
Lypiatt House..................................Cheltenham 78

M

The Malt House................................Chipping Campden....80
The Mill At Gordleton......................Lymington 84
Mill End ....Chagford 62
The Mill House Hotel ....Ashington 159
Mill House Hotel
   with Riverside Restaurant ....Sharnbrook 16
Moccas Court..................................Moccas 92

N

Nent Hall Country House Hotel.....Alston 42
The Neptune Inn & Restaurant .....Old Hunstanton 121
The New French Partridge............Near Northampton ..127
The New Inn ....Coleford 63
The Nurse's Cottage ....Lymington 85
Nuthurst Grange ....Hockley Heath..........161

O

The Old Coastguard Hotel ....Mousehole 35
The Old Manor Hotel ....Bath 164
The Old Rectory ....Norwich 120

P

The Peacock Inn ....Boraston.....................168
The Peat Inn ....St Andrews 193
Pen-Y-Dyffryn Country Hotel ....Oswestry 144
The Pheasant ....Bassenthwaite Lake....44

Plas Dolmelynllyn ....Dolgellau 218
The Plough Hotel,
   Game & Seafood Restaurant ......Clanfield.....................134
The Plough Inn................................Hathersage 60
Porth Tocyn
   Country House Hotel ....Abersoch 216
Primrose Valley Hotel......................Porthminster Beach ..36
The Pump House Apartment ....Billericay -
                                              Great Burstead 75

Q

The Queen's Head Hotel.................Hawkshead 47

R

The Red Lion ....Burnsall......................176
Redcoats Farmhouse Hotel
   and Restaurant ....Hitchin 95
Restaurant Sat Bains
   with Rooms ....Nottingham 129
The Ring O' Roses ....Holcombe 14
Romney Bay House Hotel ....New Romney 102
Rose-In-Vale
   Country House Hotel ....St Agnes 37
The Royal Oak Restaurant ....Maidenhead 20
Ruddyglow Park ....Loch Assynt 201
Rylstone Manor................................Shanklin 99

S

St Clerans Manor House ....Craughwell 186
Seven Ledbury ....Ledbury......................89
Soulton Hall ....Wem 145
The Spread Eagle Hotel...................Thame 139
Springfield House Hotel ....Preston 105

▼

Stanton Manor Hotel
   & Gallery Restaurant ....Chippenham 165
The Steadings
   at The Grouse & Trout ....Inverness 197
Stirrups Country House Hotel ......Windsor 23
Stow House Hotel ....Aysgarth.....................174
The Stower Grange ....Norwich 119
The Swan at Hay..............................Hay-on-Wye 87
Sychnant Pass House ....Conwy........................214
Sysonby Knoll Hotel ....Melton Mowbray 109

T

Tan-Y-Foel Country House..............Betws-Y-Coed 213
Temple Sowerby House Hotel
   and Restaurant ....Penrith........................53

Three Acres Country House ....Dulverton 149
Three Choirs Vineyards Estate ......Newent 83
The Tickell Arms ....Whittlesford 28
Toravaig House................................Isle of Skye 200
Tredethy House ....Wadebridge 41
Tree Tops Country House
   Restaurant & Hotel......................Southport 106
Trehellas House Hotel
   & Restaurant ....Bodmin 30
Trelawne Hotel
   - The Hutches Restaurant ....Falmouth 31
Trevalsa Court Country House
   Hotel & Restaurant......................Mevagissey 33
Ty Mawr Country Hotel ....Brechfa 211

U

Underwood ....Broughton-
                                              in-Furness 45

V

The Verzon ....Ledbury......................90

W

Wallett's Court Hotel & Spa ....Dover..........................101
Waren House Hotel..........................Bamburgh 128
Washingborough Hall ....Lincoln 111

▼

The Wensleydale Heifer ....Wensleydale...............178
West Vale Country House
   & Restaurant ....Hawkshead 48
The Wheatsheaf @ Brigsteer..........Kendal........................49
The White House ....Herm Island 182
The White House and Lion
   & Lamb Bar & Restaurant ....Stansted Airport 96
The White Lion Hotel ....Upton-
                                              upon-Severn 172
Widbrook Grange ....Bath 163
The Wild Duck Inn ....Cirencester 81
Wilton Court Hotel ....Ross-on-Wye...............93
The Wind in the Willows.................Glossop 59
The Windmill at Badby ....Badby 125
Winterbourne Country House ......Bonchurch..................97
Wisteria Lodge & Apartments ......St Austell 39
Wolfscastle Country Hotel
   & Restaurant ....Wolf's castle 222

Y

Yalbury Cottage ....Dorchester..................72
Yeoldon House Hotel......................Bideford 61

England

A

Alston ....Nent Hall Country House Hotel......42
Ambleside ....Lake House Hotel..............................43
Apuldram ....Crouchers Country Hotel...............160
Ascot.............................The Cottage Inn 17
Ashford ....Little Silver Country Hotel 103
Ashington.....................The Mill House Hotel 159
Austwick ....The Austwick Traddock 173
Axbridge ....Compton House 146
Aylesbury ....The Dinton Hermit..........................25
Aysgarth ....Stow House Hotel 174

B

Badby ....The Windmill at Badby 125
Bamburgh ....Waren House Hotel 128
Bassenthwaite Lake ..The Pheasant 44
Bath ....The Old Manor Hotel 164
Bath ....Widbrook Grange 163
Bath ....The County Hotel............................13
Beaminster...................The Bridge House Hotel 71

▼

Beanacre ....Beechfield House 162
Bedford ....Cornfields Restaurant & Hotel 15
Bedford ....Mill House Hotel 16
Belper ....Dannah Farm Country House 57
Bibury ....Bibury Court....................................77
Bideford........................Yeoldon House Hotel......................61
Billericay ....The Pump House Apartment 75
Biscovey ....Highland Court Lodge....................38
Bledington ....The Kings Head Inn 138
Blockley ....Lower Brook House 82
Bodmin ....Trehellas House Hotel 30
Bonchurch ....Winterbourne Country House 97
Boraston ....The Peacock Inn..............................168
Borrowdale ....The Leathes Head 50
Bowness ....Fayrer Garden House Hotel............54
Bowness ....Linthwaite House Hotel 55
Bracknell ....Cantley House 24
Bradford-On-Avon ....Widbrook Grange 163
Brigsteer ....The Wheatsheaf @ Brigsteer 49
Broad Campden ....The Malt House.................................80
Broadway ....The Broadway Hotel 169
Broughton-
   in-Furness ....Underwood.......................................45
Broxton ....Broxton Hall 29
Burford..........................Burford Lodge Hotel 132
Burford..........................The Lamb Inn 133
Burnsall ....The Devonshire Fell 175

Burnsall ....The Red Lion 176
Bury St Edmunds........The Ickworth Hotel
                                    and Apartments 154
Bury St Edmunds ......Clarice House 155

C

Cambridge ....The Crown House 76
Cambridge ....The Tickell Arms.............................28
Carlisle ....Crosby Lodge Country House 46
Castle Ashby ....The Falcon Hotel 126
Chagford.......................Mill End 62
Chalfont-St-Giles ....The Ivy House..................................26
Chard ....Bellplot House Hotel 147
Charlton Kings ....Charlton Kings Hotel 79
Cheddar........................Compton House 146
Cheltenham..................Charlton Kings Hotel 79
Cheltenham..................Lypiatt House 78
Chester..........................Broxton Hall.....................................29
Chichester ....Crouchers Country Hotel...............160
Chippenham ....Stanton Manor Hotel.....................165
Chipping Campden ..The Malt House..................................80
Cirencester ....The Wild Duck Inn..........................81
Clanfield ....The Plough Hotel 134
Coleford........................The New Inn 63
Colmworth....................Cornfields Restaurant & Hotel 15
Colwall ....Colwall Park 171
Cookham Dean ....The Inn on the Green 19
Cotswolds.....................Duke Of Marlborough.....................140

D

Dartmoor ....Ilsington Country House Hotel 66
Daventry ....The Windmill at Badby 125
Dorchester ....Yalbury Cottage 72
Dover ....Wallett's Court Hotel & Spa 101
Drayton ....The Stower Grange 119
Dulverton ....Ashwick Country House Hotel 148
Dulverton ....Three Acres Country House 149

E

Eton...............................The Christopher Hotel....................18
Exeter ....Combe House Hotel........................64
Exmoor
   National Park ....Heddon's Gate Hotel 69
Exmoor
   National Park ....Karslake Country House.................153

F

Fakenham ....Idyllic Cottages At Vere Lodge 114
Falmouth ....Trelawne Hotel................................31
Far Sawrey ....West Vale Country House 48
Ford ....The Dinton Hermit..........................25
Formby ....Tree Tops Country House 106
Fowey............................Chandlers Waterside Apartment...32
Froggatt Edge ....The Chequers Inn............................58

G

Glewstone ....Glewstone Court 94
Glossop ....The Wind in the Willows..................59
Godshill ....Koala Cottage 98
Goring-on-Thames.....The Leatherne Bottel 21
Great Bircham.............The Kings Head Hotel 115
Great Burstead ....The Pump House Apartment 75
Great Chesterford ......The Crown House 76

Guildford.......................Great Tangley Manor......................156

H

Hampton Court ....Chase Lodge 157
Harrogate ....Hob Green Hotel 177
Hatch Beauchamp ....Farthings Country House Hotel ..150
Hathersage ....The Plough Inn 60
Hawkshead ....The Queen's Head Hotel................47
Hawkshead ....West Vale Country House 48
Hay-on-Wye.................Moccas Court 92
Hay-on-Wye.................The Swan at Hay..............................87
Helland Bridge ....Tredethy House 41
Henley ....Bull & Butcher 27
Hereford ....Aylestone Court 88
High Crosby.................Crosby Lodge Country House 46
High Peak ....The Wind in the Willows..................59
Hindon ....The Lamb at Hindon 166
Hitchin ....Redcoats Farmhouse Hotel............95
Hockley Heath ....Nuthurst Grange 161
Holcombe ....The Ring O' Roses 14
Honiton ....Combe House Hotel........................64
Honiton ....Home Farm Hotel 65
Hordle ....The Mill At Gordleton 84
Horton ....The New French Partridge 127

I

▼

Ickworth ....The Ickworth Hotel
                                    and Apartments 154
Ilsington ....Ilsington Country House Hotel 66
Ipsley............................The Old Rectory 170

K

Kendal ....The Wheatsheaf @ Brigsteer...........49
Keswick ....Dale Head Hall Lakeside Hotel.......51
Keswick ....The Leathes Head 50
King's Lynn....................The Kings Head Hotel 115
Kingston Bagpuize ....Fallowfields.....................................135
Kirkby Lonsdale ....Hipping Hall 52
Kirtlington ....The Dashwood Hotel.......................136

L

Lake Thirlmere ....Dale Head Hall Lakeside Hotel.......51
Langar ....Langar Hall 130
Langrish........................Langrish House.................................86
Ledbury ....Seven Ledbury 89
Ledbury ....The Verzon 90

INDEX BY LOCATION

Leominster.................Ford Abbey...91
Lincoln ....Bailhouse Hotel 110
Lincoln ....Washingborough Hall....................111
Littlestone ....Romney Bay House Hotel 102
Longbridge Deverill..The George Inn 167
Longridge...................Ferrari's Restaurant & Hotel 104
Lower
  Bockhampton ....Yalbury Cottage 72
Lydford ....Lydford House.................................67
Lymington ....The Mill At Gordleton 84
Lymington ....The Nurse's Cottage 85
Lynton ....Hewitt's - Villa Spaldi 68

M

Maidenhead ....The Inn on the Green....................19
Maidenhead ....The Royal Oak Restaurant 20
Maidens Green...........Stirrups Country House Hotel 23
Malvern ....Colwall Park...................................171
Malvern ....The White Lion Hotel.....................172

▼
Market Harborough..Horse & Trumpet 108
Markington ....Hob Green Hotel 177
Marsden ....Hey Green Country House 180
Martinhoe..................Heddon's Gate Hotel 69
Mawnan Smith............Trelawne Hotel 31
Medbourne ....Horse & Trumpet 108
Melton Mowbray ......Sysonby Knoll Hotel.......................109
Mevagissey ....Lower Barn 34
Mevagissey ....Trevalsa Court Country House.......33
Middleton Stoney......The Jersey Arms.............................137
Millom ....Underwood 45
Mithian......................Rose-In-Vale Country House.........37
Moccas.......................Moccas Court 92
Moreton-in-marsh ....Lower Brook House.........................82
Mousehole ....The Old Coastguard Hotel 35

N

New Romney ....Romney Bay House Hotel 102
Newent ....Three Choirs Vineyards Estate........83
North Norfolk ....The Gin Trap Inn 123
North Norfolk Coast..The Great Escape
                       Holiday Company 116
North Walsham ....Elderton Lodge Hotel 117
North Walsham ....Beechwood Hotel 118
Northam ....Yeoldon House Hotel.....................61
Northampton ....The New French Partridge 127
Norwich.....................The Old Rectory 120
Norwich.....................The Stower Grange 119
Nottingham................Langar Hall 130
Nottingham................Restaurant Sat Bains
                       with Rooms 129

Nottingham ....Cockliffe Country House Hotel 131

O

Oborne ....The Grange at Oborne 74
Okehampton...............Lydford House.................................67
Old Hunstanton.........The Neptune Inn
                       & Restaurant 121
Oswestry ....Pen-Y-Dyffryn Country Hotel......144
Ovington....................Brovey Lair 122
Oxford ....The Dashwood Hotel......................136
Oxford ....Fallowfields 135
Oxford ....The Jersey Arms.............................137

P

Paley Street ....The Royal Oak Restaurant 20
Penrith ....Temple Sowerby House Hotel........53
Penzance ....The Old Coastguard Hotel.............35
Petersfield ....Langrish House.................................86
Pilling ....Springfield House Hotel................105
Porthminster Beach ..Primrose Valley Hotel.....................36
Preston.......................Ferrari's Restaurant & Hotel 104
Preston.......................Springfield House Hotel.................105

R

Reading ....L'ortolan Restaurant 22
Reading ....The Leatherne Bottel 21
Redditch ....The Old Rectory 170
Ringstead ....The Gin Trap Inn 123
Ross-on-Wye ....Glewstone Court 94
Ross-on-Wye ....Wilton Court Hotel 93
Ruan Highlanes ....The Hundred House Hotel..............40
Rutland Water ....Barnsdale Lodge 142
Rye ....The Hope Anchor Hotel 158

S

Saham Toney ....Broom Hall Country Hotel.............124
St Agnes ....Rose-In-Vale Country House............37
St Austell....................Highland Court Lodge.....................38
St Austell....................Wisteria Lodge & Apartments 39
St Ewe........................Lower Barn 34
St Mawes....................The Hundred House Hotel..............40
Shaftesbury ....La Fleur de Lys 73
Shanklin.....................Rylstone Manor...............................99
Sharnbrook ....Mill House Hotel 16
Sherborne....................The Grange at Oborne 74
Shinfield ....L'ortolan Restaurant 22
Skipton ....The Devonshire Fell 175
Skipton ....The Red Lion 176
Southport ....Tree Tops Country House 106
Stamford ....The Crown Hotel 112
Stansted Airport ....The White House 96
Staverton ....Kingston House 70
Stevenage ....Redcoats Farmhouse Hotel.............95
Stow-on-the-Wold ....The Kings Head Inn 138
Sway ....The Nurse's Cottage 85

T

Takeley.......................The White House 96
Taunton......................Farthings Country House Hotel ..150
Temple Sowerby ....Temple Sowerby House Hotel........53
Tenbury Wells............The Peacock Inn.............................168
Tenterden...................Little Silver Country Hotel 103
Thame ....The Spread Eagle Hotel 139

Thetford ....Broom Hall Country Hotel.............124
Thetford ....Brovey Lair 122
Thorpe Market ....Elderton Lodge Hotel 117
Thorpe St Andrew ....The Old Rectory 120
Totnes ....Kingston House 70
Tregrehan...................Wisteria Lodge & Apartments 39
Troutbeck ....Broadoaks Country House.............56
Trowle ....The Old Manor Hotel 164
Trumpet ....The Verzon 90
Turville ....Bull & Butcher 27

U

Uppingham ....The Lake Isle Restaurant
                       & Townhouse Hotel 143
Upton-
  upon-Severn ....The White Lion Hotel.....................172

V

Ventnor ....The Hambrough 100

W

Wadebridge................Tredethy House 41
Warminster ....The George Inn 167
Washaway ....Trehellas House Hotel 30
Washingborough ....Washingborough Hall.....................111
Wells ....Beryl..151
Wells ....Glencot House 152
Wem ....Soulton Hall 145
Wensleydale ....Stow House Hotel 174
Wensleydale ....The Wensleydale Heifer 178
West Cliffe ....Wallett's Court Hotel & Spa 101
Whitby ....Dunsley Hall 179
Whitewell ....The Inn at Whitewell 107
Whittlesford................The Tickell Arms.............................28
Wilmington ....Home Farm Hotel 65
Windermere ....Broadoaks Country House.............56
Windermere ....Fayrer Garden House Hotel...........54
Windermere ....Linthwaite House Hotel 55
Windsor ....The Christopher Hotel 18
Windsor ....The Cottage Inn 17
Windsor ....Stirrups Country House Hotel 23
Winsford ....Karslake Country House 153
Wokingham................Cantley House 24
Woodhall Spa ....The Dower House Hotel.................113
Woodstock..................Duke Of Marlborough....................140
Woodstock..................The Feathers 141

Y

Yorkshire Dales ....The Austwick Traddock 173

Channel Islands

Herm Island ....The White House............................182
Sark ....La Sablonnerie 183

Ireland

Craughwell..................St Clerans Manor House.................186
Kenmare ....Brook Lane Hotel...........................187
Riverstown ....Coopershill House..........................188

Scotland

Auchencairn ....Balcary Bay Hotel...............................192
Auchterarder................Cairn Lodge Hotel...............................204

▼
Ayr ....Culzean Castle
                - The Eisenhower Apartment 207
By Glamis ....Castleton House Hotel 190
Castle Douglas ....Balcary Bay Hotel...............................192
Dunvegan.................Greshornish House Hotel 198
Edinburgh ....Castle Venlaw 206
Eilean Iarmain............Hotel Eilean Iarmain......................199
Forfar ....Castleton House Hotel...................190
Forres ....Knockomie Hotel..............................203
Fort Willam ....Corriegour Lodge Hotel 194
Helmsdale ....The Bridge Hotel 195
Inverness...................Dunain Park Hotel............................196
Inverness...................The Steadings at
                The Grouse & Trout...................197
Isle of Harris ....Amhuinnsuidhe Castle 208
Isle of Mull ....Highland Cottage 191
Isle of Skye ....Greshornish House Hotel 198
Isle of Skye ....Hotel Eilean Iarmain......................199
Isle of Skye ....Toravaig House 200
Loch Assynt ....Ruddyglow Park.................................201
Loch Earn ....The Four Seasons Hotel 205
lochinver ....Ruddyglow Park.................................201
Peebles ....Castle Venlaw 206
Perthshire ....The Four Seasons Hotel 205
St Andrews................The Peat Inn.......................................193
Sleat ....Toravaig House 200
Thurso ....Forss House Hotel............................202
Tobermory ....Highland Cottage 191

Wales

Abergavenny ....Glangrwyney Court 223
Abersoch...................Porth Tocyn Country House.........216
Aberystwyth ....Conrah Country House Hotel 212
Barmouth ....Bae Abermaw 217
Betws-Y-Coed...........Tan-Y-Foel Country House 213
Brechfa......................Ty Mawr Country Hotel 211
Cardiff.......................Egerton Grey 215
Carmarthen ....Ty Mawr Country Hotel 211
Conwy ....Sychnant Pass House 214
Crickhowell ....Glangrwyney Court 223
Dolgellau ....Plas Dolmelynllyn 218
Harlech......................Hotel Maes-Y-Neuadd.....................219
Haverfordwest ....Wolfscastle Country Hotel.............222
Monmouth.................The Bell At Skenfrith 220

Monmouth.................The Crown At Whitebrook 221
Porthkerry...................Egerton Grey 215
St Brides
  Wentlooge ....The Inn at the Elm Tree 210
Skenfrith ....The Bell At Skenfrith 220
Snowdonia...................Hotel Maes-Y-Neuadd....................219
Sychnant Pass............Sychnant Pass House 214
Whitebrook ....The Crown At Whitebrook 221
Wolf's castle................Wolfscastle Country Hotel............222

≋ Heated indoor swimming pool

England

Underwood ....Cumbria...........................45
Ilsington Country House Hotel ....Devon 66
Kingston House ....Devon 70
Ford Abbey...................................Herefordshire 91

▼
Wallett's Court Hotel & Spa............Kent...................................101
Broom Hall Country Hotel ....Norfolk............................124
Idyllic Cottages At Vere Lodge ....Norfolk............................114
Glencot House ....Somerset.........................152
Clarice House.................................Suffolk 155
The Ickworth Hotel
   and Apartments ....Suffolk 154
Widbrook Grange ....Wiltshire 163

≋ Hotels with outdoor swimming pool

England

Rose-In-Vale Country House ....Cornwall 37
Tredethy House ....Cornwall 41
Trehellas House Hotel ....Cornwall 30
The Pump House Apartment.......Essex 75
Winterbourne Country House......Isle of Wight...................97
Tree Tops Country House ....Lancashire 106
Bailhouse Hotel ....Lincolnshire..................110
Brovey Lair ....Norfolk............................122

The Great Escape
  Holiday Company ....Norfolk............................116
The Old Rectory ....Norfolk............................120
Beryl..Somerset.........................151
Beechfield House...........................Wiltshire 162

Channel Islands

The White House ....Guernsey 182

Wales

Porth Tocyn Country House ....Gwynedd 216

Wales

Sychnant Pass House.......................Conwy 214

SPA Dedicated Spa facilities

England

Lower Barn ....Cornwall 34
Ilsington Country House Hotel ....Devon 66
Wallett's Court Hotel & Spa............Kent..................................101
Clarice House.................................Suffolk 155
The Ickworth Hotel
   and Apartments ....Suffolk 154

✆ Tennis Court on-site

England

Cantley House................................Berkshire 24
Underwood ....Cumbria..........................45
Wallett's Court Hotel & Spa............Kent..................................101
The Great Escape
  Holiday Company ....Norfolk............................116
Idyllic Cottages At Vere Lodge ....Norfolk............................114
Fallowfields ....Oxfordshire 135
The Ickworth Hotel ....Suffolk 154
Great Tangley Manor......................Surrey.............................156
Dunsley Hall..................................North Yorkshire 179
Stow House Hotel ....North Yorkshire 174

Channel Islands

The White House ....Guernsey 182

Ireland

Coopershill House...........................Sligo 188

Scotland

Greshornish House Hotel...............Highland 198

Wales

Porth Tocyn Country House ....Gwynedd 216
Glangrwyney Court ....Powys.............................223

Index by Activity

Shooting on-site

England

Broadoaks Country House ....Cumbria............................56
Ford Abbey...................................Herefordshire 91

Scotland

Amhuinnsuidhe Castle ....Western Isles.............208

Fishing on-site

England

Mill House Hotel...................................Bedfordshire 16
Broadoaks Country House ....Cumbria............................56
Dale Head Hall Lakeside Hotel ....Cumbria............................51
Linthwaite House Hotel ....Cumbria............................55
The Mill At Gordleton ....Hampshire 84
Ford Abbey...................................Herefordshire 91
Moccas Court ....Herefordshire 92
The Inn at Whitewell ....Lancashire 107
Sysonby Knoll Hotel ....Leicestershire 109
Langar Hall ....Nottinghamshire.......130
Soulton Hall ....Shropshire....................145
Glencot House ....Somerset......................152
The Red Lion ....North Yorkshire 176

Ireland

Coopershill House..............................Sligo 188

Scotland

▼

Forss House Hotel ....Highland 202
Hotel Eilean Iarmain.........................Highland 199
Ruddyglow Park................................Highland 201

The Four Seasons Hotel ....Perth & Kinross...........205
Amhuinnsuidhe Castle ....Western Isles.............208

Wales

Plas Dolmelynllyn ....Gwynedd 218
The Crown At Whitebrook ....Monmouthshire 221

Golf course on-site

England

Stanton Manor Hotel.......................Wiltshire 165

Licenced for wedding ceremonies

England

Mill House Hotel...................................Bedfordshire 16
Cantley House......................................Berkshire........................24
The Inn on the Green..........................Berkshire........................19
L'ortolan Restaurant...........................Berkshire........................22
Stirrups Country House Hotel ......Berkshire........................23
Broxton Hall ....Cheshire..........................29
Rose-In-Vale Country House ......Cornwall 37
Broadoaks Country House ....Cumbria............................56
Crosby Lodge Country House ....Cumbria............................46
Fayrer Garden House Hotel ....Cumbria............................54
Hipping Hall ....Cumbria............................52
Lake House Hotel ....Cumbria............................43
Linthwaite House Hotel ....Cumbria............................55
Nent Hall Country House Hotel ..Cumbria............................42
Temple Sowerby House Hotel.....Cumbria............................53
Dannah Farm Country House ......Derbyshire 57
Combe House Hotel...........................Devon..............................64
Hewitt's - Villa Spaldi ....Devon..............................68
Kingston House ....Devon..............................70
Yeoldon House Hotel ....Devon..............................61
The Bridge House Hotel ....Dorset.............................71
The Grange at Oborne ....Dorset.............................74
Bibury Court..Gloucestershire 77
Three Choirs Vineyards Estate ......Gloucestershire 83
Langrish House.....................................Hampshire 86
Aylestone Court ....Herefordshire 88
Ford Abbey...................................Herefordshire 91
The Swan at Hay ....Herefordshire 87
Wilton Court Hotel ....Herefordshire 93
Redcoats Farmhouse Hotel...........Hertfordshire 95
Little Silver Country Hotel ....Kent.................................103
Ferrari's Restaurant & Hotel ....Lancashire 104
The Inn at Whitewell ....Lancashire 107
Springfield House Hotel ....Lancashire 105
Tree Tops Country House ....Lancashire 106
Washingborough Hall.......................Lincolnshire 111
Broom Hall Country Hotel ....Norfolk...........................124
Elderton Lodge Hotel ....Norfolk...........................117
The Kings Head Hotel ....Norfolk...........................115
The Stower Grange............................Norfolk...........................119
The Falcon Hotel ....Northamptonshire 126
The New French Partridge ....Northamptonshire 127
Cockliffe Country House Hotel ....Nottinghamshire........131
Langar Hall ....Nottinghamshire.......130
Burford Lodge Hotel ....Oxfordshire 132
Fallowfields ....Oxfordshire 135
The Spread Eagle Hotel ....Oxfordshire 139
Barnsdale Lodge ....Rutland 142
Soulton Hall ....Shropshire....................145
Compton House ....Somerset......................146
Farthings Country House Hotel ..Somerset......................150
The Ickworth Hotel
    and Apartments ....Suffolk 154
Nuthurst Grange ....Warwickshire 161
Beechfield House...............................Wiltshire 162
Stanton Manor Hotel ....Wiltshire 165
Widbrook Grange ....Wiltshire 163
The Broadway Hotel.........................Worcestershire..........169
The Old Rectory ....Worcestershire..........170
The Devonshire Fell ....North Yorkshire 175
Dunsley Hall.......................................North Yorkshire 179
Hob Green Hotel ....North Yorkshire 177
The Red Lion ....North Yorkshire 176
Hey Green Country House ....West Yorkshire 180

Channel Islands

La Sablonnerie ....Guernsey 183

Ireland

St Clerans Manor House.................Galway 186

Scotland

Castleton House Hotel ....Angus.............................190
Highland Cottage ....Argyll & bute..............191
Corriegour Lodge Hotel ....Highland 194
Forss House Hotel ....Highland 202
Hotel Eilean Iarmain ....Highland 199
Knockomie Hotel..............................Moray............................203
Cairn Lodge Hotel ....Perth & Kinross...........204
The Four Seasons Hotel ....Perth & Kinross...........205
Castle Venlaw ....Scottish Borders 206
Culzean Castle –
    The Eisenhower Apartment ......South Ayrshire 207
Amhuinnsuidhe Castle ....Western Isles.............208

Wales

Sychnant Pass House........................Conwy 214
Egerton Grey ....Glamorgan....................215
Bae Abermaw ....Gwynedd 217
Hotel Maes-Y-Neuadd.....................Gwynedd 219
Plas Dolmelynllyn ....Gwynedd 218
Wolfscastle Country Hotel.............Pembrokeshire............222
Glangrwyney Court ....Powys............................223

Weekly lets

England

The Pump House Apartment........Essex 75
The Great Escape
    Holiday Company ....Norfolk...........................116
Idyllic Cottages At Vere Lodge ....Norfolk...........................114
Great Tangley Manor........................Surrey 156

The great indoors...

...for the great outdoors.

Relax. Take a deep breath. Fill your lungs. There, now you know what it feels like to own a Caravelle. Its calm luxurious interior is set in acres of space. And its surroundings are equally impressive, with levels of safety and build quality that are second to none. Only a test drive will really reveal to you the true nature of a Caravelle, so contact one of our Van Centres to arrange an appointment. OK, you can breathe out now.

www.volkswagen-vans.co.uk/caravelle

NORTH WEST ENGLAND

Hotel location shown in red (hotel) or purple (spa hotel) with page number

SCOTLAND

Northumberland
National Park

Carlisle

46

42

44

53

51

50

Lake District
National Park

Windermere

56 43

47   49

54   48

55

Isle
of
Man

Yorkshire Dales
National Park

178

Douglas

45

52

173

176

175

Barrow-in-
Furness

Fleetwood

105

Blackpool

104 107

Preston

106

Manchester

59

Liverpool

WALES

CENTRAL ENGLAND

Hotel location shown in red (hotel) or purple (spa hotel) with page number

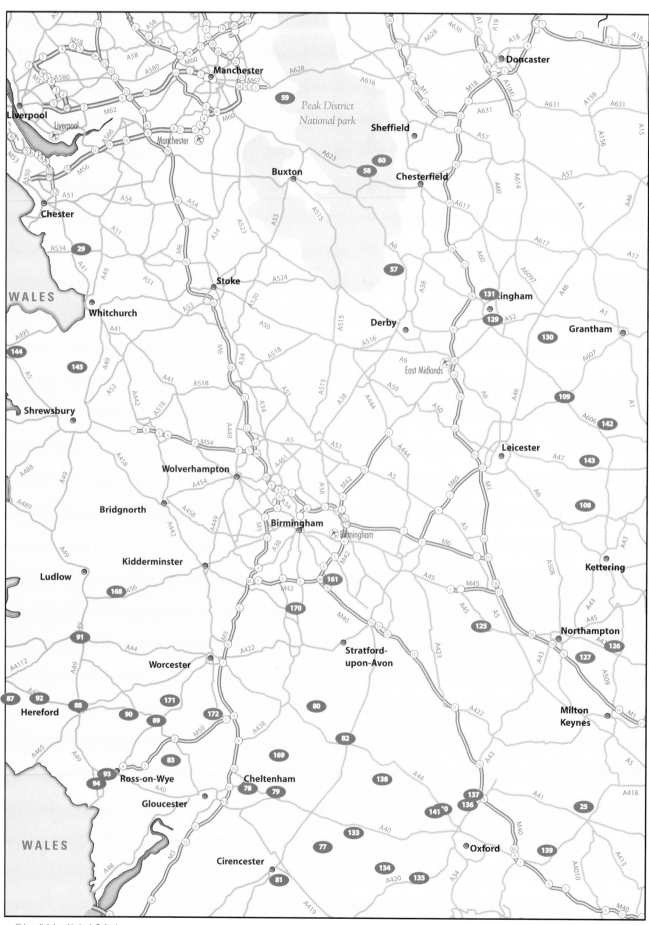

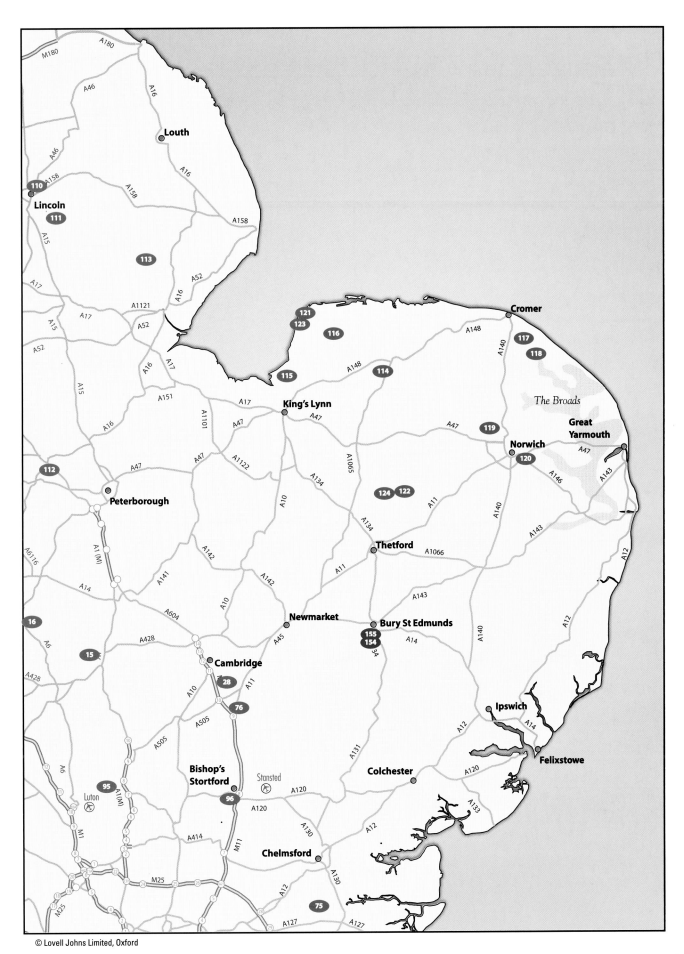

CHANNEL ISLANDS & SOUTH WEST ENGLAND

Hotel location shown in red (hotel) or purple (spa hotel) with page number

THE CHANNEL ISLANDS

GUERNSEY

St Peter Port

182

183 SARK

Guernsey

FRANCE

JERSEY

Jersey

St Helier

WALES

Exmoor National Park

68

69

Barnstaple

61

Bideford

A361

A377

A39

A386

Okehampton

A30

A39

67

62

Launceston

A30

Dartmoor National Park

A388

A386

30 41

A38

Plymouth

Newquay

A392

37

A30

St Austell

38 32

Truro

A390

34 39

33

A39

36

40

St Ives

Penzance

31 Falmouth

35

Helston

ISLES OF SCILLY

SOUTHERN ENGLAND

Hotel location shown in red (hotel) or purple (spa hotel) with page number

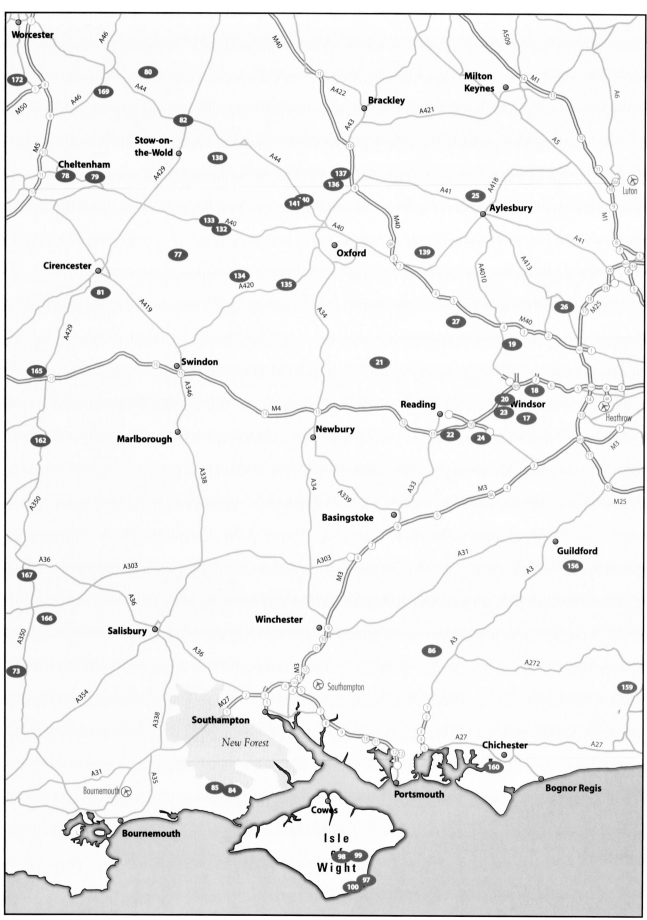

© Lovell Johns Limited, Oxford

IRELAND

Hotel location shown in red (hotel) or purple (spa hotel) with page number

© Lovell Johns Limited,

SCOTLAND

Hotel location shown in red (hotel) or purple (spa hotel) with page number

© Lovell Johns Limited, Oxford

WALES

Hotel location shown in red (hotel) or purple (spa hotel) with page number

GUIDE ORDER FORM

Up to £20 off when you order more than one Guide...

Order 4 Guides get £20 off, 3 Guides get £10 off, 2 Guides £5 off

Hotels & Spas
Great Britain & Ireland
£19.95

QUANTITY	£

Country Houses, Small Hotels
Inns & Restaurants, Great
Britain & Ireland - £16.95

QUANTITY	£

Hotels & Spas
Europe & Mediterranean
£19.95

QUANTITY	£

Hotels, Inns, Resorts & Spas
The Americas, Atlantic,
Caribbean, Pacific - £17.95

QUANTITY	£

Business Venues
(published Feb 2007)
£25.00

QUANTITY	£

Save over £44 when you order the **The International Collection...**

The International Collection
£75.00

QUANTITY	£

a boxed presentation set of the 4 leisure Guides,

PLUS the Business Venues Guide,

PLUS our exclusive silver-plated luggage tag.

A great offer for only £75 (RRP £119.80)

(silver-plated luggage tag RRP £15, presentation box RRP£5)

DISCOUNT - Discount does not apply to The International Collection   2 Guides = £5 off ☐   3 Guides = £10 off ☐   4 Guides = £20 off ☐

PACKING & DELIVERY - All UK Orders add £4.99 (Outside UK add £6 (per Guide) or £25 for The International Collection)   £ _____

GRAND TOTAL - Don't forget to deduct your discount   £ _____

☐ I enclose a cheque payable to Condé Nast Johansens

☐ Please charge my Visa/Mastercard/Amex/Switch/Maestro Card No.:_____

Card Security Code: _____   Exp. Date: _____   Issue No. (Switch/Maestro only): _____   Start Date: _____

The **Card Security Code** is the last 3 digits of the number shown above the signature strip on the reverse side of the credit card.
For Amex, the 4 digit code is printed on the front of the card just above and to the right of your main credit card number.

Name: _____   Signature: _____

Address: _____

Postcode: _____   Tel: _____   E-mail: _____

Please tick if you would like to receive information or offers from The Condé Nast Publications Ltd by telephone☐ or SMS☐ or E-mail☐
Please tick if you would like to receive information or offers from other selected companies by telephone☐ or SMS☐ or E-mail☐
Please tick this box if you prefer not to receive direct mail from The Condé Nast Publications Ltd ☐ and other reputable companies ☐

Mail to Condé Nast Johansens, FREEPOST (CB264), Eastbourne, BN23 6ZW (no stamp required)
or fax your order to 01323 649 350 or register online at www.cnjguides.co.uk quoting the reference below

CALL OUR HOTLINE NOW ON FREEPHONE 0800 269 397
OR ORDER ONLINE AT www.cnjguides.co.uk   ref: K007

GUEST SURVEY REPORT

Evaluate your stay in a Condé Nast Johansens Recommendation

Following your stay in a Condé Nast Johansens Recommendation, please spare a moment to complete this Guest Survey Report. This is an important source of information for Condé Nast Johansens, in order to maintain the highest standards for our Recommendations and to support our team of Inspectors. It is also the prime source of nominations for Condé Nast Johansens Awards for Excellence, which are held annually and include properties from all over the world that represent the finest standards and best value for money in luxury, independent travel.

Your details

Name:

Address:

Postcode:

Telephone:

E-mail:

Hotel details

Name of hotel:

Location:

Date of visit:

Your rating of the hotel

	Excellent	Good	Disappointing	Poor
Bedrooms	O	O	O	O
Public Rooms	O	O	O	O
Food/Restaurant	O	O	O	O
Service	O	O	O	O
Welcome/Friendliness	O	O	O	O
Value For Money	O	O	O	O

Any other comments

If you wish to make additional comments, please write separately to the Publisher, Condé Nast Johansens, 6-8 Old Bond Street, London W1S 4PH

Please tick if you would like to receive information or offers from The Condé Nast Publications Ltd by telephone ☐ or SMS ☐ or E-mail ☐
Please tick if you would like to receive information or offers from other selected companies by telephone ☐ or SMS ☐ or E-mail ☐

**Please fax your completed survey to 0207 152 3566
or go to www.johansens.com (E-Club login) where you can complete the survey online**

GUEST SURVEY REPORT

Evaluate your stay in a Condé Nast Johansens Recommendation

Following your stay in a Condé Nast Johansens Recommendation, please spare a moment to complete this Guest Survey Report. This is an important source of information for Condé Nast Johansens, in order to maintain the highest standards for our Recommendations and to support our team of Inspectors. It is also the prime source of nominations for Condé Nast Johansens Awards for Excellence, which are held annually and include properties from all over the world that represent the finest standards and best value for money in luxury, independent travel.

Your details

Name:

Address:

Postcode:

Telephone:

E-mail:

Hotel details

Name of hotel:

Location:

Date of visit:

Your rating of the hotel

	Excellent	Good	Disappointing	Poor
Bedrooms	O	O	O	O
Public Rooms	O	O	O	O
Food/Restaurant	O	O	O	O
Service	O	O	O	O
Welcome/Friendliness	O	O	O	O
Value For Money	O	O	O	O

Any other comments

If you wish to make additional comments, please write separately to the Publisher, Condé Nast Johansens, 6-8 Old Bond Street, London W1S 4PH

Please tick if you would like to receive information or offers from The Condé Nast Publications Ltd by telephone ☐ or SMS ☐ or E-mail ☐
Please tick if you would like to receive information or offers from other selected companies by telephone ☐ or SMS ☐ or E-mail ☐

**Please fax your completed survey to 0207 152 3566
or go to www.johansens.com (E-Club login) where you can complete the survey online**